# PERPETUATING POWER

# PERPETUATING POWER

*How Mexican Presidents Were Chosen*

JORGE G. CASTAÑEDA

TRANSLATED BY
PADRAIC ARTHUR SMITHIES

THE NEW PRESS

NEW YORK

First published in Mexico as *La herencia* by Aguilar, Altea Taurus, Alfaguara, S.A., 1999
Published in the United States by The New Press, New York, 2000
Distributed by W. W. Norton & Company, Inc., New York

ISBN 1-56584-616-8
CIP data available.

The New Press was established in 1990 as a not-for-profit alternative to the large, commercial
publishing houses currently dominating the book publishing industry. The New Press operates in
the public interest rather than for private gain, and is committed to publishing, in innovative
ways, works of educational, cultural, and community value that are often deemed
insufficiently profitable.

The New Press, 450 West 41st Street, 6th Floor, New York, NY 10036
www.thenewpress.com

Set in Fournier
Book design by Mark Melnick
Printed in the United States of America

9  8  7  6  5  4  3  2  1

*A la memoria*
*de mi padre;*
*gracias a él,*
*es tambien mi herencia.*

*In memory*
*of my father;*
*thanks to him*
*it is my inheritance as well.*

# CONTENTS

# INTRODUCTION

The Mexican political system, whose demise has been frequently and mistakenly forecast over the past two decades, has generated marvel and meticulous scrutiny since its inception in the late 1920s. The mechanisms that emerged between 1910 and 1920, generally identified with the heyday of the Mexican Revolution and partly enshrined in the Constitution of 1917, and subsequently in the twenties and thirties, have proved to be unique, both by Mexican historical standards and in comparison with the rest of Latin America. From American classics such as Frank Tannenbaum's *Mexico: The Struggle for Peace and Bread* (1950) and Robert Scott's *Mexican Government in Transition* (1958), or Frank Brandenberg's *The Making of Modern Mexico* (1964), to the works of Mexican scholars such as Daniel Cossío Villegas and Pablo González Casanova, and more recent, journalistic endeavors such as Alan Riding's *Distant Neighbors*, the mysterious and nearly magical clockwork of a political system that simply refused to fit into traditional taxonomies and Manichean matchups has puzzled and bewitched political scientists, historians, sociologists, and foreign correspondents. Certainly not a full-fledged representative democracy, by any definition of the word, evidently unlike any orthodox tropical dictatorship, and distinct at least since the 1930s from any revolutionary regime in the region or elsewhere, Mexico either required its own terminology—as in Peruvian novelist Mario Vargas Llosa's felicitous phrase "the perfect dictatorship," or Brandenberg's splendid observation that "Mexicans avoid personal dictatorship by retiring their dictators every six years"—or fell prey to the self-serving definitions of the system's beneficiaries: a sui generis democracy.

The wonderment wrought by the system among foreign observers and Mexicans (foes and fans alike) has many origins, but three factors stand out. The first is the obvious contrast with the political instability rightly deemed characteristic of Mexican history and Latin American contemporaneity. The second is the ambivalent nature of the machinery constructed by President Plutarco Elías Calles (1924–1928 and de facto 1928–1934) and his successor, Lázaro Cárdenas (1934–1940), neither democratic nor repressive, benignly authoritarian when possible, selectively and sporadically brutal when necessary, sufficiently mobile and accountable to prevent elite divisions and schisms, corrupt and well-entrenched enough to guarantee unparalleled degrees of continuity and complicity. The system's third seductive trait lay in its uncanny capacity to deliver the goods: during its golden years (1940–1980) it assured Mexico higher rates of economic growth than any other nation in Latin America or most of the rest of what was then called the Third World. These three features are worth examining in some detail, since they provide the context for our subsequent focus on the jewel of the system's crown, the chip in its memory, the DNA in its genetic code, the secret of its success: the presidential succession mechanism.

The first factor is the most notable. From independence in 1821 through its first century of national existence, Mexico proved singularly incapable of transferring power in a peaceful, orderly, and regular—let alone democratic—fashion. Either the country was stricken by palace coups, mediocre and ludicrous dictatorships, foreign invasions, dismemberment or insurrections, as occurred through 1876, or it dealt with power the old-fashioned way: by allowing one individual to keep it more or less indefinitely, as with Porfirio Díaz, who ruled Mexico from 1876 to 1911 with one brief, purely nominal, interruption. This solution proved to be costly, indeed; it led to the Mexican Revolution, which plunged the country into violence, civil war, economic chaos, and political fractionalism from 1911 through 1920. But even the Revolution appeared unable to address the central question of power, as every one of its greatest leaders—Madero, Zapata, Carranza, Villa, Obregón—was assassinated by a rival or enemy.

When the final victor of the Revolution, Sonoran rancher Alvaro Obregón, was murdered in Mexico City in 1928, just after his second election to the presidency—he had governed Mexico from 1920 to 1924—the surviving *caudillos*, and first and foremost among them Calles (frequently accused of Obregón's murder), concluded that the time had come to devise a system that would permanently settle Mexico's problem of transferring power. The adoption of an amendment to the Constitution disallowing presidential reelection, and the 1929 founding of the Institutional Revolutionary Party, or PRI—initially named the National Revolutionary Party (PNR) and subsequently the Party of the Mexican Revolution (PRM)—were the two key formal elements of the scaffolding erected by Calles, who nonetheless retained presidential power, one way or another, from 1924, when he was first elected, through 1936, when Cárdenas banished him to the United States. It was precisely Cárdenas who implemented the third (informal but decisive) component of the system: that Mexican presidents may choose their successors, but cannot themselves remain in power, directly or indirectly. All political disputes among the governing elites were to be dealt with inside the party, where everyone—initially divided into four sectors: the peasantry, the industrial working class, the so-called popular sector of federal employees and middle classes, and the army—was corporatively represented. The sitting president was the "natural-born" leader of the party, and, logically enough, his successor was named within the party, by its "natural-born" leader. The party could hibernate for five years, then suddenly awaken, organize a campaign, "win" an election, fill thousands of jobs, and suddenly disappear once again—until the next time. Every debate, every dissenting voice, if sufficiently modulated and reasonable, every generation, region, and ideology could be fit into the party—no wonder it is the dean of single-party regimes in the world today. From 1934 onward, and through the end of the century, Mexico would experience twelve consecutive, pacific, scheduled transfers of power, a feat unequaled in its history. As John Womack most eloquently put it in a mid-1970s essay, the Revolution's greatest achievement was neither land distribution nor the eventual reappropriation of Mexico's natural resources, but the gradual (between 1920 and 1934) construction of a lasting mechanism for the peaceful, well-choreographed transfer of power. This accomplishment—no mean feat then by Mexican standards—was also remarkable in the larger Latin American context. From the mid-1930s to the early 1980s—when a wave of apparently lasting democratization processes took hold in the region—nations such as Argentina, Brazil, Colombia, Venezuela, and Peru, not to mention Bolivia, the Caribbean, or most of the Central American republics—experienced a succession of coups, civil wars, military regimes, and abortive revolutions that made the hemisphere a synonym for political instability. Even previously stable or democratic countries such as Chile and Uruguay suffered collapses of their republican institutions—on several occasions in the former case, and once, tragically, in the latter, in 1973. This was the period when the Somoza dynasty, Leonidas Trujillo, François "Papa Doc" Duvalier, Marcos Pérez Jiménez, and Colombia's *violencia* became the Latin American political stereotype. It was also the time when events such as Getulio Vargas's suicide in Brazil's Presidential Palace in 1954, the Cuban Revolution in 1959, Che Guevara's death in Bolivia in 1967, Salvador Allende's 1973 suicide in Chile's La Moneda palace, and the tragi-comic Malvinas (or Falklands) War between Argentina and the United Kingdom in 1982 showed how power was contended for, conquered, and lost in Latin America. The first "typical" Mexican handover of power—from Calles to Cárdenas—took place in 1934, just before Sandino's assassination in Nicaragua and the *n*th U.S. intervention in that sad and lonely country. The fourth transfer, from Miguel Alemán to Adolfo Ruiz Cortines—which also witnessed the first true flirtation by an outgoing president with the idea of retaining power—occurred just two years before Alberto Stroessner came to power in Paraguay; he was dethroned barely a decade shy of the end of the century, just after Mexico had lived through the arrival in office of Carlos Salinas de Gortari, the tenth president in a row to reach power in accordance with the rules laid down back in the twenties and thirties.

Also remarkable was the ambivalent nature of the system that sprung up in the 1930s. It clearly was not democratic from any traditional perspective: the first postrevolutionary instances of egregious electoral fraud appeared in 1928, as José Vasconcelos's dissident candidacy for the presidency was drowned in a sea of false ballots, seized ballot boxes, disrupted voting, and so on. The second manipulated election took place in 1940, as Cárdenas organized the tainted victory of his hand-picked successor Manuel Avila Camacho. Rigged local, state, and national elections became the norm in Mexico, with peaks in 1952 and 1988 and valleys in 1958, 1964, and 1976. The fact that the PRI would probably have won most of these contests anyway did not alter the fact that neither power nor legitimacy was contested at the polls; nor did it weaken the widening and accurate conviction that the symbiosis of state and party, of government and electoral machinery, was making the question of whether the PRI could win a "clean" election a moot one. For all intents and purposes, the state's involvement in the election process, and the virtually infinite resources—human and financial—available to PRI candidates at all levels made opposition victories either impossible until the 1980s or heroic since then.

The separation of powers was also fictitious in Mexico, though as in the case of the electoral process, appearances were prudently safeguarded. In Frank Tannenbaum's phrase—and this from an admirer of the regime—"The government of Mexico is the president. There is no other way of expressing it. If the president is not strong enough to be the government, then he is overthrown." As early as the opening years of the 1920s, Congress became little more than a rubber-stamp assembly: the president, through the party and the Ministry of the Interior, chose PRI candidates for the House and Senate. They were assured of winning because they were PRI candidates, and anyone who was not harbored no possibility of winning; thus, their allegiance lay where it had to lie. The same was largely true of the judicial system: the president and the attorney general picked judges, who knew where their interests resided, and whom to obey, whenever questions arose. Still, there *was* a Congress, and there were judges who now and again ruled with the law rather than with the president.

Finally, civil society and the media reflected the same ambivalence. The Church was formally banned from political activities, but was a recognized segment of the elite after the end of the 1927 Cristero war; later in the century, it became a fixture in the education of broad swaths of the Mexican establishment's offspring. Labor unions, from 1936 on, were totally subordinated to the PRI and the government, but they formally negotiated contracts with business and the large state-owned enterprises, and obtained significant benefits for their rank and file on the condition that the latter accept the undisputed hegemony of the appointed bosses, the so-called *charros*, brought to power by a series of labor "coups" in the late thirties and early forties, and chiefly in 1948. The media, first the press and radio, then television from the late fifties onward, were in private hands and nominally free—no *Pravda* or *Granma* in Mexico. In fact, however, they were completely controlled by the state. From the García Valseca newspaper chain—immortalized by Carlos Fuentes's *Artemio Cruz* in 1960—to the three generations of Azcarragas who single-handedly founded and ran Mexico's only television network with a meaningful audience for nearly half a century, the media in Mexico were independently owned, sporadically critical, *and* totally subservient to the state when and where it mattered. As the system progressed in sophistication and criticism and opposition grew, it skillfully jettisoned ballast: editorial columns in *Excelsior*, the country's leading paper in the sixties and early seventies, for example, became increasingly strident in their dissent, until they went too far, causing the publisher to be overthrown in 1976. Radio opened up in the eighties, but its political impact was limited. Television, the only medium to truly unify the country and reach practically every Mexican home, remained heavily controlled and *oficialista* through the late 1990s.

Perhaps the most flagrant and confusing expression of the system's ambivalent character was to be found in its attitude toward repression and the traditional Latin American panoply of state-sponsored excesses: torture, arbitary detention, assassination, "disappearance," and the like. The Mexican sytem, from the thirties through the late nineties, engaged in or countenanced severe and widespread human rights abuses, and rarely respected due process and constitutional rights to protest, dissent, or opposition. The list of repressive incidents is long indeed: the charrazos (labor union coups) in 1948, the breaking of the Nueva Rosita miners' strike and march in 1952, the ferocious repression of the railroad workers' and teachers' strikes in 1958–1959, the assassination of peasant leader Rubén Jaramillo in 1962 (among other anti-Communist persecutions in the sixties), the 1968 Tlatelolco student massacre, the "dirty" counter-insurgency wars of the early seventies and their retinue of disappeared and tortured youth, the Salinas years of harassment, intimidation, and on occasion direct violence against supporters of Cuauhtémoc Cárdenas, the brutal excesses in Chiapas in the nineties. Authoritarian rule in Mexico was no tea party.

However, neither was it similar in brutality, systematicity, scope, and cynicism to its counterparts in Mediterranean or Eastern Europe, or in the rest of Latin America (the comparison with Cuba is the most complex and controversial). Repression was truly a last resort; jailed opposition leaders had a special status in prison—David Siqueiros painted in the penitentiary—and there were always intellectuals or political personalities, starting with former president Lázaro Cárdenas, on whom one could call to spring someone from jail, or get a book published, or allow a dignified exile. Among the intellectuals who held government jobs or received government favors over the years were Fuentes, Octavio Paz, Alfonso Reyes, and several generations of anthropologists, sociologists, political scientists, diplomats, and social commentators. They were not only token opponents brought into the fold, but "voices for the voiceless," go-betweens with the opposition, and figures of great prestige and talent that brought the regime standing and credit abroad. Dissenting labor, peasant, student, and civic leaders could frequently choose between co-optation and repression, or some combination thereof.

So Mexico did not quite fit in the traditional mold; it was not a classical one-party regime under Maurice Duverger's classification, which was probably why he did not include it in his initial, classical classification of political parties; it did not really correspond to Guillermo O'Donnell's much later category of "bureaucratic authoritarianism"; but it certainly did not fulfill the requirements for democracy under the Lipset, Dahl, and Huntington taxonomies of the fifties and sixties. Finally, when the rest of Latin America underwent its so-called transitions to democracy, Mexico again failed to conform: its transition represented an *aggiornamento* of the sitting regime, rather than a break with the past. Hence the unique and paradoxical nature of the debate in Mexico as the century drew to a close: Had the country's transition to democracy taken place, or was it stuck in its tracks? The ambivalence of the Mexican political system was such that Vargas Llosa was able to speak of a dictatorship so perfect that it looked like its opposite.

The third defining feature of the PRI-based regime consisted in its overarching result: four decades of uninterrupted economic growth and the ensuing transformation of the country. The singularity of this feat can be illustrated by two comparisons: some East Asian countries achieved slightly higher rates of growth between the sixties and the late nineties, but they did so either because of their very peculiar character (as in city-states like Singapore and Hong Kong, or Taiwan's exceptional geopolitical situation), or for far shorter periods of time (Indonesia, Malaysia, and Thailand experienced barely two decades of growth). Another of these "tigers," South Korea, has become a paradigm of developmental success. If one prefers a more recent and perhaps more relevant comparison, Chile has been hailed for its economic performance in recent years; yet before the 1998–1999 recession, it had grown at high rates (between 7 and 8 percent yearly) only since 1986—a period of high growth one-third the length of Mexico's.

The causality here is of course a tricky question; one can almost as easily conclude that the explanation for half a century of stability resides in the four decades of 6 percent average yearly expansion of gross domestic product as the contrary: that it was stability that bred growth. The counterfactual examples are not easy to disentangle: Brazil had nearly similar levels of growth, but almost permanent instability (coups, suicides in the government, resignations, and more coups), which would tend to diminish the explanatory power of PRI-based stability; conversely, Chile and Uruguay enjoyed stability similar to Mexico's through the early 1970s, and yet suffered from economic stagnation or mediocre growth at best. But regardless of the exact nature of the causality, it seems difficult to discard a relationship between the two factors, and clearly in Mexico historical precedent and later developments tend to confirm the symbiosis of the two. Mexico grew powerfully when it was stable (i.e., during the reign of Porfirio Díaz and from 1940 to 1980), and has stagnated since 1982, when political and social instability began to show its head; similarly, growth during the Porfiriato and the PRI's golden years bred a degree of stability that disappeared in 1910 and was severely weakened after 1982. The greater importance of the political and social factors can also be demonstrated by events over the past eighteen years, ever since Mexico ceased growing at the continuous, high rates of before: other regimes would have fallen by the wayside, victims of economic backsliding, social frustration, and international censure. The PRI did not.

The magnitude of the change Mexico has undergone during this period is difficult to overestimate. Despite the fact that population growth remained stratospherically high during much of this period—reaching nearly 3.5 percent yearly in the sixties and seventies—and thus per capita expansion was somewhat less than the aggregate figures suggest, the country went from being a small, rural, agricultural, largely illiterate, and extraordinarily unequal nation to an urban, literate, partly industrialized society of, at this writing, one hundred million inhabitants, with a large—by "Third World" standards—middle class, and with some reduction in Mexico's abysmal and ancestral injustice achieved between the late fifties and 1984. Several large cities of a million or more inhabitants have sprung up; the country's infrastructure was improved and maintained; the most remote areas were brought into the communications, transportation, education, and health networks built by the state; and Mexico saw the growth of a governing, business, and intellectual elite that, with the possible exception of Brazil, remains unparalleled in the developing world (including India). In the "modernization" jargon of the late fifties and early sixties, Mexico . . . modernized. This fact was obviously decisive in contributing to the aura of invincibility and success cultivated by the PRI over the years: the proof of the system's virtues and adequacy lay in its prowess in delivering the goods.

Could Mexico have accomplished high growth, substantial stability, and relative absence of bloodshed and violence under different, democratic circumstances? Could it have improved official accountability and rates of popular participation and democratic representation? Achieved a better distribution of income, more significant and rapid reduction of poverty, and greater control over corruption? By definition, these questions are unanswerable, and as we suggested earlier, comparative counterfactuals are inconclusive. Among the large developing nations in the past half century, perhaps only India has fashioned a more democratic, lasting political regime, and in Latin America only Costa Rica, Venezuela, and Colombia (post-1958) come to mind as viable comparisons, but the results in these countries on many fronts—growth, dynastic successions, religious violence, ethnic clashes, corruption, guerrilla wars—are not encouraging. On the other hand, it is also true that the system that seemed to have served Mexico well until 1982, albeit with high costs, ceased performing properly at that time, and the balance has begun to look much less positive over the past twenty years. A cautious, tentative conclusion would probably be that for the four decades spanning the beginning of World War II through the onset of the debt crisis in 1982, Mexico got a good deal out of its Faustian bargain. After 1982, however, it should have shifted gears to move rapidly toward a more democratic political system that would have allowed the many imperfections and accumulated defects of the previous model to be corrected or discarded. But the elites who had benefited from that model over the previous forty years would have none of that, and chose to tinker with and subsequently overhaul the economic design of the country, without substantially affecting the political regime. They chose, belatedly, to follow the advice of such American scholars as Raymond Vernon, whose classic book, *The Dilemma of Mexican Development*

(1963), suggested "Americanizing" the Mexican economy, while retaining the "Mexicanness" of the political system. The result—quite fortunately, from the perspective of those who made the choice—was their permanence in power, at a growing cost to the country in many areas, including, at this writing, the lack of previous, high levels of economic growth.

It is in this context that the "black box" of the Mexican political system must be understood. All we have described, as complex and convoluted as it may appear, can be traced back to one fundamental mechanism, which made all else possible: the presidental succession process. As so many scholars have discovered over the years—without necessarily solving its riddle—the secret of Mexico's success lay in the enigmatic, mysterious, and veiled ritual by which it chose its presidents. As early as 1950, foreign analysts such as Frank Tannenbaum clearly attributed to each president the responsibility for choosing his successor, describing some of the arrangements and procedures involved, but even regarding this period, when this process was supposedly still a simple one, American scholars remained somewhat mystified by it. Thus one William Tucker, in a 1957 publication entitled *The Mexican Government Today*, resignedly concluded of the 1940 succession from Cárdenas to Avila Camacho that, "apparently the final decision was his [Cárdenas's]." Through the sixties and early seventies, scholars mulled various pendulum theories and the alternation in power of the left and right wings of the PRI, or conflicts and compromises between *cardenista* and *alemanista** factions. Later, in the 1980s, American and Mexican academics tried to discover or impose a certain rationality on the process, attempting to conciliate its obviously personal nature with some sort of predictive, theoretical logic. Thus Daniel Cossío Villegas, in his 1975 *La sucessión presidencial* (about the Echeverría to López Portillo succession in 1975–1976), tried to detect elements of participation among key sectors of the Mexican elites. Thus also Steven A. Sanderson, in an important mid-1980s essay, refused to accept what he called "the unsatisfactory alternative," "that the single most important political decision of the sexennium is made capriciously." The fact that the old Porfirian regime had employed a similar system for appointing state governors in the late 1900s and the first decade of the twentieth century did not seem to clarify the mystery.

What *Perpetuating Power* purports to show is how this enigmatic and highly successful mechanism has actually functioned over the last thirty years, as described by the central actors in the sexennial drama. Through four on-the-

*Supporters of the political philosophy of President Miguel Alemán, 1946–1952.

record interviews with Mexico's living ex-presidents (Luis Echeverría, José López Portillo, Miguel de la Madrid, and Carlos Salinas de Gortari) and in six essays dedicated to the presidential successions of 1970, 1976, 1982, 1988, and 1994—based on thirty-odd off-the-record interviews with the "losers" and other key protagonists in the process—this book seeks to explain how Mexican leaders chose their successors. It pays special attention to how the internal dynamics and palace intrigues behind the succession mechanism actually played themselves out, and with what consequences. The answers provided by our sources frequently clash with the previous analyses rapidly reviewed above, describing a process at once much simpler and much more sophisticated than has been generally thought until now. But the reader can judge for him- or herself to what extent the mechanisms portrayed here correspond to traditional views of the Mexican succession procedure.

The interviews and essays herein explain with some detail, both in the abstract and in each specific case, how the succession process worked, but it is worthwhile summarizing some of its features here in order to prepare the reader for the occasionally tortuous workings of the system. Known variously as *el destape* (the unveiling) or *el deda$z$o* (the finger-tap), the Mexican dynastic succession (recalling the Roman Empire's system, whereby the sitting emperor chose his successor and then adopted him as his son)—the procedure that operated fully for the first time in 1940, and whose heyday lasted from 1946 through 1994—followed several basic, easy rules. The incumbent was the PRI president; he picked the party's candidate for regularly scheduled elections, held every six years; the decision was a totally personal one, with no consultation, no vetoes, no ex ante consensus. The president would then build an ex post facto consensus in favor of his designee, who would be elected, inevitably, categorically, and unquestionably. The purpose of Mexican elections, at least until 1994, was not to pick a president among several aspirants, but to ratify and legitimize a decision already made. This is probably why most Mexicans, even when they vote in competitive elections, continue to confess that they cast their vote for so and so "because he is going to win," not because they prefer him to another candidate. The outgoing president, once his choice is made, begins inexorably to lose power, and can neither go back on his choice nor try to influence his successor beyond naming a few of his close aides to Congress or to the incoming cabinet.

The candidate was chosen invariably from among cabinet members, and more specifically, with a couple of exceptions, among ministers of defense (1934, 1940), of the interior (1946, 1952, 1964, 1970, 2000), or of finance and/or the budget (1976, 1982, 1988). The president named his cabinet knowing full well that from it would spring his successor, and that the chief ministers, unless they were constitutionally impaired from running for office, all considered themselves and would be considered candidates for the candidacy. The race was nonetheless a silent, shrouded one, since no one could acknowledge openly (before 1988) that he was contending for the nomination, and as veteran labor leader Fidel Velázquez once declared, "Anyone who moves doesn't come out in the picture." The incumbent, as we shall try to show in the following chapters, was forced to deceive those cabinet members who were not going to be chosen, since they had to be led to believe that they stood a chance. Otherwise, the "unveiling" took place prematurely, in which case the nominee would be destroyed by his rivals and enemies before the time came to begin to hand power over to him. Once the choice was made, it was unappealable, irreversible, and definitive for everyone: the rivals, the president himself, the powers that be, etc. Vetoes were not exercised, because allowing anyone a veto represented a drastic curtailment of the president's power. The displeasure of elite groups—the business community, the Church, the United States, the military, the political class, and (before 1982) the labor movement—was expressed subtly, eliptically, and beforehand, either when someone was about to enter the cabinet, ipso facto becoming a contender, or during his initial months in the cabinet. By the time the short list of finalists was tacitly drawn up, it contained only those who were acceptable to everybody that counted. Whoever had harbored dreams of becoming president, but failed to make it to a first-circle cabinet post by the middle of an administration, simply had no chance.

The system worked because the final word was both definitive and generous—that is, no one could successfully question the president's decision—but at the same time, the losers were at best well rewarded, and at worst simply excluded from power, but never jailed, shot, tortured, or exiled, as had occurred so often before in Mexican history. Those who attempted to dispute the president's choice—such as Juan Andrew Almazán in 1940, Ezequiel Padilla in 1946, Miguel H. Enriquéz Guzmán in 1952, Cuauhtémoc Cárdenas in 1988, and Roberto Madrazo in 2000—were simply overwhelmed by the machinery, before, during, and after the elections themselves. They stood absolutely no chance of winning, because they were not running against another candidate, or even against the party, but against the president and the state, an unbeatable combination in an ancestrally presidential and *dirigiste* country.

In the interviews with the ex-presidents, as well as in the narration of the six successions presented in this book, are innumerable examples of the preordained nature of events, and of the "rules" outlined above. But rather than trying to group these together in a theoretical construct, I have preferred, mostly, to let the reader reach his or her own conclusions about how the regime worked, based on what the former presidents themselves have to say, and on the accounts of the six successions, with some exceptions: certain patterns and recurrences are emphasized in the text, and some conclusions are reached and stated, be they about the nature of the system, its "laws," its costs and benefits, or its future. These more abstract statements are scattered through the six chapters on the successions, as I chose not to tie them together in a single summary.

The interviews were all carried out during 1998 and consequently and intentionally do not touch upon the succession of the year 2000. Nonetheless, a few words are in order regarding the current transfer of power, especially in view of the fact that the *dedazo* has come to an end, and that under President Ernesto Zedillo (1994–2000) Mexico has finally ushered in an era of democratic transfers of power, thus adding the final adjective to the list used before: regular, peaceful, orderly. Much was made of the fact that the PRI organized an open, national primary on November 7, 1999, through which it designated its candidate for the July 2, 2000, presidential elections: former Minister of the Interior Francisco Labastida.

Some tentative conclusions can be reached about the internal PRI process, and whether the classical mechanism has been truly replaced by a new, open, democratic one. There are many views in Mexico—and in the United States, too, of course—on this question, and my own is simply an opinion, as subjective and partisan or objective and scholarly as any other. Despite important changes in the nominating process—from the way in which the PRI tied the president's hands, up to a point, by determining in 1996 that the party's next presidential candidate must previously have held elective office, to the fact of the primary itself, and the presence of "unauthorized" or "unapproved" contenders in it— and more importantly, despite the fact that for the first time the traditional certainty that the PRI candidate would be Mexico's next president was much diminished, on this occasion as on all others, the incumbent once again chose the party's nominee, and that nominee was initially the heavy favorite to win the election. How exactly this occurred is part of another story, but can be suggested briefly here. In my view, notwithstanding the president's repeated denials, there was an "official" candidate—i.e., a Zedillo candidate—in the PRI primary, and consequently a preordained winner (Francisco Labastida). Ernesto Zedillo's recurrent claims of having no favorites, and of not having picked a candidate, were disingenuous. The very fact that one of the contenders was his minister of the interior (the number-one job in the Cabinet), that said contender's campaign manager was the president's preferred protégé and favorite minister (of social affairs, the number-three job in the Cabinet), that the candidate's media person had been the government's virtual minister of propaganda and media affairs, that the entire PRI machinery, the business community, the Church, and even the United States (Labastida had traveled to Washington on an "official visit" months before his resignation from the Cabinet) perceived Labastida to be the president's choice, and finally that Labastida announced his intention to run for the presidency from the Ministry of the Interior, made an explicit statement from Zedillo superfluous. All the more so since, during the primary campaign, Labastida's main rival, Roberto Madrazo, accused him continually and naively of being the "official candidate." He was, and that was why he won.

Despite the president's formal constant proclamations of good faith—which can be taken at face value—every *prista* worth his red, white, and green stripes knew who *el bueno*, that is, the outgoing president's favorite, was, and what had to be done in order for him to win the primary: paint walls, hang posters, offer "goodies" to voters (in an exit poll taken the day of the primary, nearly 5 percent of all voters—almost half a million individuals—acknowledged having been offered some compensation for their vote), bring out the vote one way or another, and, as a last resort, cast votes for those who didn't come out. The political culture of *el aparato* (the machinery) and *la cargada*, or the stampede in favor of the official candidate, is too well known and powerful in Mexico to be neutralized or dismissed by simple, formalistic manifestations of neutrality. Once a stampede begins, nothing need be done to encourage it. No one knows this better in Mexico than the president. There was never any doubt in any political operator's mind as to who the PRI nominee would be, nor that he was carrying the president's colors, so to speak. In town after town across Mexico, in every one of the 300 electoral districts, in each of the thirty-two states of the republic, as the primary campaign got under way, officials began resigning from local public office or from the PRI bureaucracy to join Labastida's team. In so doing, they were complying with the primary rules regarding impartiality, etc., but were also sending a clear signal to lower officials, teachers and local peasant and labor leaders, businessmen and others: the winner, *el bueno*, was Labastida. They were jumping on his bandwagon not because he was leading, but because he had won, even before the contest had begun. The fact that despite the huge resources made available to Madrazo by dubious sources, Labastida heavily outspent him, and could count on far greater human, financial, and logistical resources (from top-flight political operatives to airplanes, unions, state governors, and a sympathetic official media) simply confirmed the generalized aura of his invincibility. There are, of course, many questions pending, not dissimilar to many of those formulated and on occasion answered in this book: Did Ernesto Zedillo explicitly anoint Labastida in private, or simply allow him to resign from the cabinet and contend? Did primary competitors Roberto Madrazo and Manuel Bartlett seriously think they could win, or did they always suspect they could not? Were the final primary results grossly inflated to pad both overall turnout and Labastida's margin of victory, or were they essentially clean by Mexican standards? Was the opposition's weakness and division a purely homegrown liability, or did the government and the PRI unethically and covertly conspire to accentuate these flaws? It is too soon to provide definitive answers to these questions, but the preliminary evidence is not encouraging.

The Mexican succession mechanism as we know it came to an end with opposition candidate Vicente Fox's victory on July 2, 2000. The PRI contender lost by 7 percentage points, and for the first time since the ruling party's creation in 1929, Mexico's new president will not be one of its members. Certainly an era—that of the PRI and the political system it incarnated for more than seventy years—ended on July 2nd. Moreover, Mexico has finally, for the first time in its history, had power contended for, conquered and transferred at the ballot box. Other elections have been relatively clean—1911, 1994—and power has before been passed peacefully between different, often warring factions of the PRI—1946, 1982—but something like this year's events has never occurred in Mexico. If politics in Mexico bears out these preliminary impressions of stability, civility, statesmanship on all sides, and transitional smoothness, more than an era will have concluded: Mexico's age-old *giettatura* and inability to deal with the issue of power will move, finally, to closure.

There are many explanations for Fox's triumph. His charismatic candidacy, his obstinacy and vitality, and his constant efforts to reach out both to the left and the PRI to build a broad coalition all contributed to the resounding opposition victory. But the main explanation must be found in the Mexican electorate's overwhelming desire for change, after many decades of virtual one-party rule and twenty years of economic stagnation. Fox transformed the election from a beauty contest into a referendum on change, challenging Mexicans to vote yes or no, for or against, perpetuating the PRI's power. En masse the people said no, dismissing everything else as a distraction. They stuck to the basics and voted the world's oldest-standing one-party system out of office.

During his campaign, Fox tried—mostly, but not always, with success—to precisely outline how he would effect change in economic and social policy, reestablish law and order and security for people and property, bring about institutional reform and combat inequality and poverty, and eradicate corruption and impunity. Once in office, he will have to strike a perfect, almost impossible balance between the specific, policy-based changes that people want and expect, and the self-evident limits on change that Mexico's domestic and external situation obviously impose. Globalization, economic constraints, a powerful opposition, the logical divisions existing within his coalition, the strains of an excessively long transition period, are all factors that impose strict limitations on the scope of change, on the actual possibilities of improving people's lives and reforming institutions, and on settling scores with Mexico's past. Still, if U.S. economic growth stays strong for the next year or two, and if he avoids major mistakes, he may well be successful in achieving this balance, despite efforts to the contrary both by the PRI and Cuauhtémoc Cárdenas's demoralized PRD.

What is less sure, however, is whether Mexico has outlived its successional demons of the past. The key question is power, and how it is transferred, kept, and ceded. The most delicate issue has always been, as this book shows, how the winners treat the losers, and how the latter react to their defeat. Are the winners both decisive and magnanimous in their victory, and do the losers accept the irreversible, unappealable—though no longer necessarily external—nature of their setback? Does central authority endure under democratic rule, or does the country regress to the dominance of regional caciques and the fragmentation of power, falling prey to the overwhelming centrifugal forces of Mexico's history? Are the new rules of the game equally, if harshly, applied to all contenders, and do they all accept them along with their consequences? More significantly, has Mexico's undoubted economic and social modernization neutralized the effects of its ancestral, abysmal, and maddeningly persistent inequality to the extent that the power contended for is no longer worth killing, maiming, and raping for?

These questions belong properly to a sequel of this book, which can only be written a few years hence as the answers begin to appear in macroeconomic aggregates, election results, the outcome of political struggles across Mexico, and, most importantly, in the meanders of the Mexican soul. For the moment, we can only emphasize the subtitle of the Mexican edition of *Perpetuating Power*, "An Archaeology of Presidential Successions in Mexico." The clockwork machinery we knew and grew up with is now truly a relic, if not a ruin.

In closing this introductory discussion, I would like to express my gratitude, first and foremost, to Mexico's four living ex-presidents—Luis Echeverría, José López Portillo, Miguel de la Madrid, and Carlos Salinas de Gortari—for having granted the interviews included in this book. I also wish to thank Miriam Morales, Javier Barros, and Cassio Luiselli for encouraging me to write the book, and Fausto Zapata, David Ibarra, Bernardo Sepúlveda, and Roberto Mangabeira Unger for their invaluable support in convincing the ex-presidents to participate in this venture. Likewise, thanks are in order to Mariana Campillo for her assistance in research and interview transcription, Padraic Arthur Smithies for his faithful and fluid translation from the Spanish, and to Patricio Navia for his help in research and mainly for his splendid job of editing and abridging the original Spanish version in order to make it accessible to readers not familiar with Mexican politics.

# I

## The Successions

# DÍAZ ORDAZ—ECHEVERRÍA (1970)

L uis Echeverría Álvarez was unveiled as the ruling Institutional Revolutionary Party (PRI) presidential candidate on October 22, 1969, in a manner
fully in keeping with the best Mexican traditions. According to then-PRI President Alfonso Martínez Domínguez, the main PRI leaders were summoned to
President Gustavo Díaz Ordaz's office at Los Pinos. Before they entered the
meeting room, the president revealed his verdict to Martínez Domínguez: the
victor was Ordaz's minister of the interior, Luis Echeverría.

Martínez Domínguez asked his boss insistently if he was sure of his decision.
The president replied with a question: "Why do you ask? It's the most important decision of my life and I've thought it over well." Martínez Domínguez
suggested that the president notify the losing candidates before informing the
others of his decision. At first Díaz Ordaz refused: "We have no reason to
show them any special consideration. Let them find out through the normal
channels; we've done them honor enough by making them government ministers." Martínez Domínguez pressured him further, adducing reasons of tact.
It would be necessary to continue working with them, and it was desirable to
treat them with deference. Díaz Ordaz concluded, "Do it yourself if you want."
So Martínez Domínguez spoke personally with the three losers—Alfonso Corona del Rosal, Emilio Martínez Manatou, and Antonio Ortiz Mena—thereby
guaranteeing their loyalty to the PRI and their acceptance of Luis Echeverría's
candidacy. Thus Luis Echeverría became the seventh presidential candidate in
a row to be designated by the ruling party without incident, controversy, or
setback. The problems would begin later.

Martínez Domínguez has told on several occasions how Díaz Ordaz explained
and justified his decision to designate Luis Echeverría. In 1972, during a dinner
party at his house in Sierra Ventana, in response to a question from one of his

guests, the former president used the simile of a highway robbery to enlighten his friends regarding the rationale for a decision he later regretted. "Let's suppose," he said, "that we're in a car traveling along a mountain road, and suddenly we're held up by bandits. With me in the car is Antonio Ortiz Mena. He hides when they tell us to get out of the vehicle and vanishes from the scene. Emilio Martínez Manatou is also with me, and suggests that the robbers not ask me for money, but make a deal with him. He may be richer and more powerful soon. Alfonso Corona del Rosal, on the other hand, starts negotiating with the criminals and offers them various deals that range from the audacious to the unspeakable. Only Luis Echeverría jumps out of the car, confronts the bandits, and warns them, 'Anything you want with him is with me.'" His conclusion was that, at least at such moments, Echeverría's loyalty greatly exceeded that of his rivals. This was the reason for his choice.

In fact, this anecdote demonstrates something fundamental to the Mexican presidential succession. Carlos Salinas de Gortari has acknowledged, in various moments of candor or clarity, that he prepared Luis Donaldo Colosio well in advance to succeed him in the presidency—that is, Colosio was his candidate by choice rather than by elimination. Gustavo Díaz Ordaz, on the other hand, confessed in his after-dinner conversation that he opted for Luis Echeverría because he lacked alternatives at the critical moment. Díaz Ordaz used a process of elimination. He chose Echeverría because he represented, in Porfirio Muñoz Ledo's fitting words, "the only card left."

Basically, two types of succession have prevailed in Mexico, at least since 1969: successions by choice or decision, and by elimination. Each employs different procedures and has different consequences. Each emanates from a different source. As in any taxonomy in the nonexact sciences, no instance is pure. Each succession has been decided partly by elimination and partly by decision. All have gone through several stages, in which a secondary trait may prevail briefly, but the dominant trait finally leaves its mark on the entire process.

To begin to understand the Mexican presidential succession, it will help to classify the last six successions in these two categories. The successions by elimination favored Luis Echeverría in 1969–1970, Miguel de la Madrid in 1981–1982, and—in what would seem to be the supreme process of elimination—Ernesto Zedillo in 1994. The second category includes the successions by choice or decision that favored José López Portillo in 1975–1976, Carlos Salinas de Gortari in 1987–1988, and Luis Donaldo Colosio, fleetingly, in 1993. In fact, if we go even further back, we find, for example, that, according to Humberto Romero—press secretary under Adolfo Ruiz Cortines (1952–1958) and all-powerful chief of staff to Adolfo López Mateos (1958–1964)—the dichotomy dates from even earlier days. Ruiz Cortines chose López Mateos at the end of his term of office. In contrast, according to Romero, López Mateos had decided on Gustavo Díaz Ordaz from "the day he took office" and never contemplated any other alternative. If we examine the cases presented herein from this perspective, we may elucidate the effects, costs, and damages that each entailed, in accordance with the category it falls under. In summary, for now, we will present the logic that guides our typology. Successions by elimination exacerbate conflicts between incoming and outgoing presidents; successions by choice maximize the deceit practiced by the outgoing president on the losing prospects and stretch resentments between the competitors to the limit.

A theorem—that is, something demonstrable—of the presidential succession in Mexico indicates that the process of shifting political positions and weighing the support or opposition of the real sources of political power occurs before the final threesome or foursome is defined. Inclusion in the presidential cabinet fulfills this function. Only those who already provide satisfactory guarantees of ideological continuity, alliance-building, and the ability to avoid vetoes are appointed to the cabinet and in due course included in the circle of possible successors. In other words, the candidates who reach the semifinal stage have usually already passed all the necessary tests, and therefore the process of choosing from among them does not really respond to any ideological or strategic criteria. All the finalists identify with the outgoing president's economic, social, and strategic policies, or at least represent an equivalent risk of betrayal or adjustment. They all have the same potential for forming alliances between deputies, senators, governors, union leaders, etc., and all have, in fact, already eluded possible elimination by the real sources of power.

If the acting president learned or suspected that Fidel Velázquez, or the business community, or the Catholic Church—or, as López Portillo says in his interview, the United States—was vehemently opposed to any prospective candidate, the individual in question would have been immediately disqualified. Thus, in the endgame, the competition is above all in the political-tactical terrain, focusing on personal differences and on the play of seduction-deceit-reassurance between candidates. Therefore, learned analyses of a candidate's supposed affinity with, or animosity toward, a given political line, or any of the real sources of power, tend to lose touch with reality. In the universe of predetermined candidates, all are partisans of the president, all share his way of thinking, and all have the tacit approval of the main political forces.

Gustavo Díaz Ordaz faithfully observed the axiom put forth by Adolfo Ruiz Cortines. Rafael Moreno Valle—a military doctor from Puebla who became

Díaz Ordaz's closest friend in the final years of his life and was on friendly terms with Ruiz Cortines—recalls how Ruiz Cortines explained the situation: "The president can have neither more nor less than three candidates. If there are only two and he favors one from the start, the jackals tear him to bits and he is very battered by the time he is nominated. Also, if the predestined candidate falls ill or is involved in a scandal, you have to put your hand on someone else, who will either assume he's been chosen as understudy, or believe he made it on his own, and the others will think the president made a mistake. However, the number is never greater than three. The rest are filler to take some of the heat off the real prospect." Curiously enough, thirty years later, Miguel de la Madrid made a similar observation regarding the struggle within the PRI to succeed Ernesto Zedillo. If there are only two candidates, the loser can divide the party. If there are more than three, support is atomized.

As he reached the end of the road to the succession in mid-1969, Díaz Ordaz kept three prospects alive: Minister of the Interior Luis Echeverría, Minister of the Presidency Emilio Martínez Manatou, and Mexico City Mayor Alfonso Corona del Rosal. According to privileged sources, Antonio Ortiz Mena, the financial wizard and architect of the Mexican miracle, never counted among the true finalists. He lacked personal ties to Díaz Ordaz and had competed too aggressively with Díaz Ordaz to succeed Adolfo López Mateos in 1963. Moreover, as Luis Echeverría himself explains in the first interview presented in this book, he had been overzealous in his attempts to gain the support of political and financial circles in the United States.

In successions by elimination, the president tends, almost out of desperation, to continue exploring new alternatives. In the case under consideration, faced with the prospect of choosing between the three disagreeable prospects mentioned above, Díaz Ordaz considered other options. Fernando Gutiérrez Barrios, federal security director and a close colleague of Díaz Ordaz from the López Mateos administration, recalls how Díaz Ordaz flirted with the idea of designating Antonio Rocha Cordero, governor of San Luis Potosí and former attorney general of the republic. He was a natural candidate, with the only impediment being age. He would be fifty-eight years old in 1970.

But Díaz Ordaz dwelt at length on an ideal alternative in Jesús Reyes Heroles, because he satisfied all the imaginable conditions, except for a constitutional requisite. Not yet fifty years old, he would mark an undeniable generation shift, faithful to the theory of generations that Mario Moya Palencia uses to explain José López Portillo's triumph in 1976. He had a political background, but he had acquired the necessary administrative experience in a six-year stint in the Mexican Social Security Institute and another six years heading Petróleos

Mexicanos (PEMEX). His loyalty and personal friendship with Díaz Ordaz had remained, as far as possible, uncorrupted. During the terrible weeks of the 1968 student movement, no one, except perhaps Marcelino García Barragán, the minister of defense, had kept the president's trust as he did. The problem lay in Article 82 of the Constitution. Reyes Heroles's father had been born in Spain, and the law demanded that both parents of the man—or woman, although the issue did not arise at the time—who occupied the presidential chair be Mexican citizens by birth.

Reyes Heroles told his younger son Federico and wrote in his journals— and of course we must be aware of the understandable exaggeration that may prevail in this type of conversation or writing—that Díaz Ordaz sounded him out on at least two occasions about the possibility of making him the PRI's presidential candidate. On one occasion, in the spring of 1969, he was probed during the return flight from a PEMEX trip to the interior. It wasn't the first time the president had attempted to persuade his PEMEX director to embark on such a venture. In his journals—which are in the custody of his family and several passages of which were read to the author by his son Federico—Reyes Heroles relates the events of November 5, 1968, shortly after the Mexico City Olympic Games and the Tlatelolco massacre. "The president asked me what I thought of the constitutional impediment [Article 82] and I said I had defended it in my law school lectures for sixteen years and that it seemed to me to be an appropriate limitation for Mexico. He insisted, 'Then I've lost an ace from my deck?' I replied: 'Two years ago I told doctor Martínez Manatou, and he assured me that it wasn't necessary for me to tell you; that he would inform you . . . Didn't he?' The president answered, 'No. When the matter of the Veracruz governorship came up I heard some rumors that you were the son of a Spaniard.' I confirmed this: 'As I was telling you, that's basically true; my mother is Mexican by birth, and my father Mexican by naturalization.' "

Everything indicates, in fact, that Díaz Ordaz was left without aces. He chose Echeverría by elimination, and because Echeverría had won the race in its final stage. The president probably chose the man who would succeed him in power in the first few months of 1969, although he didn't notify the lucky winner until June—according to Luis Echeverría himself—and the nomination was not officially announced until November 8.

Jorge de la Vega received an early hint of what was to come. In March 1969, he was summoned to the National Palace to discuss the affairs of the PRI's Institute for Political, Economic, and Social Studies (IEPES), which he headed. At the end of the interview, the president told him that thereafter, for inquiries of a political nature, he should see *"don* Luis." He was referring to his minister of the interior. De la Vega comments that the especially cordial tone President Díaz Ordaz used and his suggestion to "hereafter see *don* Luis" constituted, in fact, an unequivocal political clue as to the identity of the PRI presidential candidate. Díaz Ordaz rewarded de la Vega's loyalty with an invaluable "tip," that he could dissimulate or even deny, but that would be conclusive to whoever might want to decipher it. Gutiérrez Barrios, who was, as stated, the Federal Security director at the time, recalls a similar incident. In February of 1969, he suddenly received a call from the president summoning him to Cuernavaca on the following day—a Saturday—in the company of his boss, the minister of the interior. Echeverría and Gutiérrez Barrios went to the president's weekend home, where they were treated to an extended lecture by Díaz Ordaz on the personality of Lyndon Johnson and relations with the United States and foreign policy that was utterly devoid of relevance or urgency, even to Echeverría. On leaving the meeting, Gutiérrez Barrios thought, "The president had wanted to share his reflections on the international situation with the next PRI candidate to get him ready." Gutiérrez Barrios interpreted his own presence as a cryptic sign from the president of his preference for Luis Echeverría.

These incidents illustrate a peculiar characteristic of the mechanism. The chief executive constantly drops hints to the prospective candidates, and in particular to the one destined to win, but the chosen one doesn't necessarily grasp or comprehend them. Echeverría gave me the impression that he had confused this encounter with another that took place months earlier with the same people at the same place—a banal affair, dedicated mainly to the security of Lady Bird Johnson, who was to visit Mexico City to dedicate a statue of Abraham Lincoln. Memories no doubt fade, and in the copious miscellany of signals received, some remain and others fade away over the years. As we will see, however, the pattern repeats itself. Candidates younger than Echeverría in more recent successions also misunderstood, and were misled by, the cryptic and contradictory messages their bosses sent them. It is understandable. Over the years, the acting president gets used to covering his tracks and cultivates circumlocution in the extreme. When he wants to say something clearly, he no longer knows how.

The 1968 student movement played a decisive part in this succession for several reasons, but one in particular stands out, and provides a clue to the essence of the succession, and perhaps also to the events of 1968 themselves. In the whirlwind of hate, passion, and resentment that came to envelop and bewilder Díaz Ordaz, those who proposed negotiation were destined to lose. Whoever abstained from pressing for a negotiated settlement had everything to win. The only one who fully understood this was also the only one who could have succeeded in reaching an agreement with the students, but in doing so would have eliminated himself from the succession race.

Indeed, Echeverría was the ideal official to negotiate with the students. He fit the bill perfectly. He was closer in age to the students than the others. His image as the hardest and most institutional man in the administration would have greatly enhanced the legitimacy of any agreement he might have reached, and he had, in contrast with other real or potential intermediaries, the necessary experience for the task. He didn't do it because he knew that any hint or suspicion of negotiation would doom his candidacy in the eyes of the sole supreme judge. As the succession race got under way, considerations of state began to lose force and personal criteria came to the fore. Something similar occurs in all political systems, but in the absence of checks and balances, autonomous institutions, and restraining barriers, the result can be disastrous for the country in question, and so it was.

The other aspirants were undone by the events of the summer and autumn of 1968. Antonio Ortiz Mena was already sidelined due to health problems, his closeness to the international financial community, and, to a lesser degree, his age—he turned sixty on September 22, 1968. However, Echeverría's other two real rivals were eliminated during the days of lead and horror of the student movement.

Martínez Manatou was Díaz Ordaz's closest friend in the cabinet. Nevertheless, the comments of several witnesses of the presidential race give the impression that the boss showed a certain disdain for his friend. One great defect weakened Dr. Martínez Manatou in Díaz Ordaz's eyes: he wasn't a lawyer, and Díaz Ordaz was, and obsessively so. But the coup de grâce for Emilio Martínez Manatou's potential candidacy no doubt came not from his mistaken choice of profession nor his scant legal expertise, but from his behavior during the final year of the contest. He was, as someone has pointed out, the Manuel Camacho of the day, the man responsible for responding to critics and opponents, who pays a high price for completing his mission successfully.

There is no greater sin in the Mexican presidential succession than forming ties with the chief's enemies, whatever the cause of presidential disfavor may be, whatever indications the president may have given, and whatever the president's relationship with said enemies—of which the interested party may or may not be aware—may be. Martínez Manatou's growing confidence and arrogance irritated Díaz Ordaz. On one occasion, halfway through his term, he commented to his son-in-law, Salim Nasta, "This guy thinks he's already president."

Rafael Moreno Valle, the military doctor who served as Díaz Ordaz's minister of health, also recalls from one of his last conversations with Martínez Manatou at the National Palace before the candidate was announced that Martínez Manatou told him that things were going well. "I'm doing great, I have twenty governors on my side, I have the National Peasant Confederation. Even the president's enemies support me. The president knows it.

Moreno Valle never managed to find out whether or not this behavior did in fact please Díaz Ordaz, although perhaps none of the former president's aides had maintained their friendship with him as Moreno Valle did. Several years after leaving office, Gustavo Díaz Ordaz invited him to accompany him to New Orleans, a carefree and entertaining trip for two old friends. They had never discussed the 1969 succession. During the trip, Moreno Valle finally raised the issue. "Sir," he said, "Emilio told me that he informed you of who supported him, even your enemies. What happened?" Díaz Ordaz replied: "Yes, its true. And then I thought: my enemies should make him president." The remark perfectly matches another, twenty-five years later, that Manuel Camacho attributes to Carlos Salinas: "In politics, Camacho, you made a mistake in allying yourself with my enemies."

If to all this we add the anecdote—possibly false but very well known in circles close to Echeverría, then and now—of the rain of paper clips that pelted the troops beneath the windows of Martínez Manatou's office in August 1968, when the army entered the Mexico City Zócalo, we can understand why, barring the lack of another candidate, the minister of the presidency could not become his successor. The climate of paranoia, isolation, and anti-intellectualism that prevailed in Los Pinos during and after the student movement only exacerbated the president's irritation with Martínez Manatou's arrogance and insensitivity. To Díaz Ordaz, the professors were as guilty as the students were of provoking the crisis.

The other card in his hand was Mexico City Mayor Alfonso Corona del Rosal, "a general among lawyers and a lawyer among generals." He had everything it took to come out ahead, as Echeverría states in his interview, except for the favor of the great elector. He had been a deputy, a senator, governor of his native state of Hidalgo, minister of the national patrimony, and PRI president. Since the 1940s and during his years in the Senate, he had forged a solid friendship with Díaz Ordaz, and as Mexico City mayor before and during the 1968 Olympic Games he was not only in the limelight, but in the most attractive, prominent, and privileged position in the government. He was a natural candidate. Three factors contributed to his downfall. The first—invoked with greater frequency and emphasis—was his age. Corona was born on July 1, 1908. He turned sixty-two only a few months after the 1970 presidential inauguration. If elected president, he would have been over sixty-eight when he left office. A second factor, probably decisive in light of the events of 1968, was his military background. The key here lies in the context rather than in the bare facts of the matter. The events of 1968 had infinite implications for Mexico, among which are that they entailed the reappearance of the armed forces in the public sphere and in the social imagery of the new Mexican middle class. It was certainly not recommendable to press the point. In 1958 and 1959, during the railway workers' and teachers' movements, with the first guerrilla uprisings of the 1960s, and in the sporadic and isolated but ever-present repression of fleeting worker and peasant uprisings, the army was never conspicuous for its absence. But an abyss lay between such interventions and deploying the troops in the vicinity of the central square of Mexico City, the National University (UNAM) campus, the *Casco de Santo Tomas*, and the Square of the Three Cultures (the Plaza de Tlatelolco). The site of the repression, its victims, its motives, and its extent belonged now to another category.

Under the circumstances, the nomination of a military man, however civilian he may have been, looked much less appropriate, whatever the emphasis placed on substituting "*Mi General*" with "*Señor licenciado*," and however prudent and skilled at negotiation the mayor's adepts might swear he was. The mayor himself felt it, and searched, during the weeks leading up to the bloody denouement, for a peaceful solution—not because he preferred it but because it would save him from elimination in the succession race.

As we have mentioned, the last factor was precisely his proclivity for negotiation. Corona del Rosal repeatedly contacted the National Strike Counsel and the Communist Youth Organization. Naturally he didn't hesitate to use force when he considered it indispensable and expeditious, but he understood, at least intuitively, that the use of force would cause him irreparable damage. He didn't oppose the use of force, but made his preference for an alternative solution known. He was too fond of the calm and orderly, suave and subtle solution in the political style that marked his entire life. He was mistaken.

Conversely, one need not possess the talents of a chess master or military strategist to deduce that the hard-line outcome favored the hard-line candidate, Luis Echeverría. With the spread of student agitation and the resulting military response, the minister of the interior killed two birds with one stone. He eliminated his most powerful rival and showed the president his best face: one of loyalty, firmness, and efficiency. Now, thirty years later, clues to something that has been suspected for years are beginning to emerge. To the degree that the student movement favored Echeverría and weakened his two main adversaries, speculation regarding the manipulation, instigation, or exaggeration of the movement by the winning candidate becomes inevitable. From the insistent but flimsy reports of Díaz Ordaz's consternation about the October 2 student massacre, to the contradictory part that certain individuals subsequently associated with Echeverría may have played, and Díaz Ordaz's obstinate insistence on presenting himself as a president deceived by "Echeverría's trickery," the temptation to discern a plot masterminded at the Ministry of the Interior becomes irresistible. (It will not be the last such plot suggested by the facts, the imagination, and guesswork that is presented herein.)

Jesús Reyes Heroles's notes give the argument for a plot masterminded at the Ministry of the Interior a measure of indirect credibility, with the reservation that his relations with Echeverría were terrible and ended years later in public insults. Reyes Heroles's notes—taken down at first on a day-to-day basis and possibly influenced by his scant sympathy for Echeverría, but not, in this case, by a desire to incriminate him—coincide with the thesis of another player who was both near and far at the same time. Rosa Luz Alegría was a young student at the UNAM School of Sciences, with close ties to Marcelino Perelló, one of the movement's most intelligent, adept, and charismatic leaders, whom she frequently accompanied to meetings of the National Strike Counsel. In the early days of August 1968, she began to date Luis Echeverría's eldest son, and a month later they were married. On September 7, the newlyweds left for Paris on government scholarships, according to plans laid well in advance. The minister of the interior was unwavering in his insistence on preventing any contact with the students from contaminating his relations with Díaz Ordaz. He asked Rosa Luz to see that under no circumstances would Perelló appear at the wedding. She was not part of the student leadership, but she knew the leaders. She didn't experience the movement from within Echeverría's family, but she was part of the family nonetheless. She thinks now that her former father-in-law "wanted to seize the moment, and to some extent he succeeded. He blew [the problem] out of proportion and then resolved it with a lot of hype. He encouraged the students, granted permission for the demonstrations, even on the same day [July 26] in the same zone. Then it got out of his hands. However, he ultimately resolved the situation with a turn of the rudder, pulled off the maneuver, and that's what I think won the candidacy for him."

Two weeks later, Reyes Heroles once again detected a strange insistence from Minister of the Interior Echeverría on discovering ties between PEMEX and the student movement. Federico narrates, reading from his father's notes: "At 1:30 PM Echeverría called the PEMEX director: 'Jesús, there's a group of rebels on their way to Petróleos Mexicanos, it would be a good idea that the forces of law and order be there.' I questioned Echeverría for a few minutes to find out what was going on, whether there was any internal conflict, labor dispute, or other type problem that might provide a clue as to why a demonstration would appear at PEMEX headquarters. Five minutes later I got in touch with the minister of the interior and I told him, 'Luis, I've found absolutely nothing in the institution. We've had no report of any kind of movement. The PEMEX security team in the building hasn't reported anything. I don't know if you have any more information.' 'Yes, Jesús. I know there's a group approaching the PEMEX building and that's why I think it would be a good idea if the police were there.' Five minutes later a truck appeared. An individual stood up and began vociferating against the president. Not only were they not oil workers, but some of the slogans they shouted were contrary to the demands of the PEMEX workers who had lost their sons and daughters in a confrontation between the preparatory school and the trade school. It was a provocation to the union itself. A few minutes later the armed forces arrived, not at the request of the PEMEX director, and two groups that had nothing to do with Petróleos Mexicanos were on the verge of violence."

Among the multifarious documents concerning the events of 1968 that have been published or leaked to mark their thirtieth anniversary in 1998, a United States military intelligence report, undated but probably prepared in March 1969, stands out. It discusses the removal of General Mario Ballesteros Prieto, chief national defense administrative officer, and the disgrace that had fallen on Luis Gutiérrez Oropeza, commander of the presidential guards. According to the report, both military men were accused of having contradicted or misinterpreted the orders issued by Defense Minister Marcelino García Barragán. Among the most significant instructions ignored by the aforementioned officers were, according to the report, the order to send a paratrooper battalion to Tlatelolco on October 2—where a massacre of anywhere between 50 and 600 students took place, putting an end to the 1968 Student Movement—merely to "observe what took place and prevent the disturbance from spreading to other parts of the city." The battalion's entry into the Square, which triggered the violent confrontation with the students, "was not part of the military activity mentioned." The informant—whose name is crossed out in the U.S. Defense Department document—clarifies the point: "General García Barragán couldn't tell at the time whether General Ballesteros had misinterpreted his orders, or had deliberately altered them. However, subsequent events convinced General Barragán that Ballesteros and Gutiérrez Oropeza were dealing directly with higher authorities, and had in fact deliberately changed his orders." A final element— difficult to corroborate and decipher—adds to our elaborate interpretation. A plethora of sources—from the president's supposed lover Irma Serrano, to scholar Carlos Monsiváis and the Reyes Heroles family—suggest that Díaz Ordaz took refuge during these days near Guadalajara, according to some recollections, at the home of his Minister of Agriculture Juan Gil Preciado, in the village of Ajijic, on the shore of Lake Chapala, where he would spend some of the last years of his life. Local and Mexico City newspapers omitted the item, and several of the president's close aides questioned by the author were unable to confirm the story, although they do not deny it. The nationwide dailies (*Excelsior* and *El Universal*) reported a meeting of the president with press leaders on the morning of October 2, but without mentioning the location. However, if we grant the validity of Díaz Ordaz's absence from the scene, the following two versions take on full meaning and relevance.

According to Federico Reyes Heroles, his father told him long after the fact that on October 2, 1968, after leaving his wife Gloria and two sons Federico and Jesús in safety at the family's ranch in Hidalgo, he flew to Guadalajara in a Petróleos Mexicanos aircraft. He intended to make known to the president his growing concern over the turn events were taking, and in particular his fear of a tragedy in Tlatelolco, where a student rally had been scheduled. He tried to convince Díaz Ordaz to return to Mexico City and follow events close at hand. Díaz Ordaz listened to his PEMEX director, and limited himself, late in the afternoon, to calming him. He had already talked with the minister of the interior, who had assured him that everything was under control and that there was no need for a tumultuous return by the chief executive that might disturb public opinion.

At the same time, sources close to General Corona del Rosal claim that on the same afternoon, the Mexico City mayor, the defense minister, Minister of the Interior Echeverría, and Mexico City Police Chief General Hernández Cueto met in the Mexico City government offices. There, as 6:00 PM approached, Echeverría began to pressure for orders to be issued to the military battalion posted in the vicinity of the Plaza of the Three Cultures to disperse the demonstration. Corona del Rosal and Defense Minister García Barragán resisted, insisting that only the president, who was out of town, could issue such orders. Echeverría managed to get through to Díaz Ordaz. When he was informed that the president was on the line, he took the call in an adjacent office, explaining that he was the highest authority in the president's absence. He emerged some minutes later, and declared that Díaz Ordaz had authorized clearing the plaza. Only Echeverría knew under what pretenses Díaz Ordaz was called to the phone, and, in turn, why he granted authorization to proceed. It may be true, or the entire story may be part of the black legend worked up over the years against Luis Echeverría, a former president who has inspired more antipathy than he might deserve.

The theory that Díaz Ordaz was cajoled into assenting by his minister of the interior has always rested on relentless logic, and has always come up short against an impeccable logical deduction. The theory is as we have described it. Echeverría magnified the movement. He abstained from negotiating or resolving the matter peacefully. As the Olympic Games approached, the political, military, and psychological pieces of a military solution were put in place. Finally, Echeverría orchestrated the provocation in Tlatelolco as a pretext for armed intervention and the massacre, thereby eliminating all his rivals, decapitating and annulling the student movement, and winning the presidential nomination by elimination. It was a harebrained scheme, born of speculation, silence, and the brutal struggle for power in Mexico, and therefore can't be ignored, although recent research by analysts such as Sergio Aguayo suggests that the story of the deceived president is improbable: "Díaz Ordaz exercised his power to the hilt and wasn't going to let his subordinates deceive him in something so sensitive." It also comes up short against the counterargument concerning the opportunities for the incumbent president to learn the truth of the matter. Several months elapsed between the time the events in question took place and the day Echeverría was notified of his victory—sometime in June 1969—or was formally nominated—October 22, 1969, during which Díaz Ordaz would have been able to discover or be informed of Echeverría's machinations. In particular, the president could count on the friendship, candor, and intuition of General García Barragán and Jesús Reyes Heroles, two sources with sufficient influence and willpower to disqualify Echeverría for having deceived the president. Both had sufficient access to the information and the president's ear—and even, although in a lesser degree, his trust—to react and warn Díaz Ordaz: "You were deceived. Tlatelolco was an ambush. Echeverría is going to betray you. Don't give him power that he will use to destroy you." Nothing of the kind occurred.

In the case of Reyes Heroles, there is only scant evidence that he may have tried to rescue his friend the president from Echeverría's deception. His notes and his recollections of his conversations with his son Federico lack references to any such overtures. García Barragán still represents an enigma. His son, the late Javier García Paniagua, refused to be interviewed, or even to converse on the subject, and if he left any unpublished memoirs or notes, they remain largely unavailable to the public. Some notes of his were published in late 1999, as an appendix to a brief book written by Carlos Monsiváis and Julio Scherer titled *Parte de Guerra*. All this, and above all the subsequent course of events, suggests a deductive hypothesis that is difficult to challenge. There was no deceit, because it would have been impossible to conceal the truth from Díaz Ordaz. He would have found out through one of his two confidants or some other channel, and he would never have given the presidency to the author of a fraud of such magnitude.

Matters grow complicated, however, if we include an additional element, constant in all the successions. The temptation to imagine Echeverría manipulating the 1968 student movement is intimately bound up with a fourth factor, which may have contributed to Corona del Rosal's downfall and Echeverría's victory. The Mexican presidential succession mechanism, individualized and subjective in the extreme, suffers from one central defect, among many others. Everything depends on the president's vision, but for various reasons his vision becomes blurred as the time to make the decision draws near. At the start, as Fernando Gutiérrez Barrios has cogently summarized it, the outgoing president evaluates the prospects, trying to guess how each will behave once in power. But only the president holds power. Power changes people, and the victor is called upon to go from a state of deficient or nonexistent power to one of absolute power in less than one year—a vertiginous transition, with an unpredictable outcome. Furthermore, each candidate strives to present what he believes to be his most attractive strengths and attributes to the president, not his real virtues or vices. As the process proceeds, the solitude of the man who will have the final say increases. He not only sees less, but must also abstain from relying on the opinions of friends, colleagues, and family members to be able to focus his own vision. He believes, and in part knows, that all views are oblique. Though he appeals to broad and varied sources of information, he ends up thinking that no one is speaking the truth, and he is partly correct. Every opinion, every report, is blurred by the reality or suspicion of the informant's political persuasion. Why does a given person bring one or another story, rumor, or criticism? The best chess player or intuitive politician quickly finds his senses of sight, hearing, and even smell insufficient to detect the ambushes and traps that his minions lay for one another. Under these circumstances, a key figure usually emerges, with truthful words and reliable vision, the Lazarus who compensates for the president's increasingly blurred vision, who leads him through the twilight of his presidency, performing his duties with loyalty and with an independent agenda. He or she is a close aide, a member of the president's inner circle, with no personal ambitions for the presidency (at least for the moment) due to age, position, ties to the president, or other unrelated reasons. Without being so naive as to think that the country's foremost politician can rid himself of all suspicion or apprehension toward an aide or family member, it is clear that certain kinds of bonds give rise, over time, to a special kind of trust. The individual in question becomes a kind of false tongue to the "tongue of the balance," to use José López Portillo's well-known expression, the one who apparently "speaks the truth" and whose opinions, interventions, suggestions, and recommendations offer a sense of transparency and honesty that the others lack. The president may know that the individual in question favors one or another of the prospective candidates, but at the same time, he does not think that this preference skews the person's vision or prejudices his participation. He is the classic honest broker, a Dr. Watson with unwavering loyalty, a Richelieu who works, steals, and kills for the crown alone.

A figure of this kind has appeared and shone through in practically every one of the administrations discussed herein, at least in regard to the issue of the succession. The three most notorious cases are José Ramón López Portillo, Emilio Gamboa, and José Córdoba. Miguel de la Madrid, Carlos Salinas, and Ernesto Zedillo respectively owe their presidencies to these three men, not so much because they had their support—although in fact they did—but because their respective "sponsors" contributed, in different ways, to convincing the man who had to be convinced of their talents and attributes.

According to Mario Moya Palencia—Luis Echeverría's close aide and for six years his minister of the interior—the man who acted as a link between Echeverría and Díaz Ordaz was Luis Gutiérrez Oropeza, head of the presidential guards under Díaz Ordaz and director of military industry from 1970 to 1976. Moya Palencia was in a position to know—he was named deputy minister of the interior on July 1, 1969, and he was left in charge of the Ministry of the Interior as of November of the same year, when Echeverría was nominated for the presidency. He already enjoyed a fairly close relationship with Díaz Ordaz, despite their age difference. So much so, according to Moya, that in the final days of the Díaz Ordaz administration, at the end of a luncheon with businessmen who visited him to congratulate him on Echeverría's nomination, Díaz Ordaz was made a gift of two bottles of champagne. One was opened to toast the candidate. As to the second, the president said: "We're not going to drink this other bottle because we have to go to work. Keep it to toast Mario Moya Palencia six years from now."

It may be necessary, in this case, to split the Richelieu figure in two. Another close Díaz Ordaz aide, in whom he trusted implicitly and who to all appearances also cooperated with Echeverría, was another Gutiérrez, Fernando Gutiérrez Barrios. The director of federal security started working with Díaz Ordaz in the early 1950s; his career stretches from the arrest and liberation of Fidel Castro and Che Guevara in Mexico City in 1956, to the organization of the first-ever PRI presidential primary in 1999.

Gutiérrez Barrios could boast of the trust placed in him by both Gustavo

Díaz Ordaz and Luis Echeverría. In November 1969, when Echeverría gave his speech at the Universidad Nicolaíta in Morelia, requesting a minute of silence for the victims of October 2, 1968—a speech that was deeply distressing to the military, especially to the defense minister—the messenger Díaz Ordaz would choose to step into the breach would be none other than Gutiérrez Barrios. As a result, the very next day, candidate Echeverría dedicated his first campaign speech to the armed forces. In early 1970, through the same channel, the two former fellow cabinet members arranged a meeting at General García Barragán's ranch in Jalisco to mend their differences.

The role played within the administration by individuals like those mentioned herein is crucial to the Mexican presidential succession, and the influence of Gutiérrez Oropeza and Gutiérrez Barrios may have been decisive, especially in light of the events of 1968. The hypothetical warning issued by Reyes Heroles or García Barragán to Díaz Ordaz, advising him of a possible conspiracy led by Echeverría to turn events in his own favor, was partially flawed from the outset. Both the defense minister and the director of Petróleos Mexicanos had the defect of being adversaries of Echeverría, and after 1968 the dialogue, at least between Reyes Heroles and Díaz Ordaz, was affected. Federico Reyes Heroles recalls his father confessing to him that the president had isolated himself, that he consulted with no one but the minister of the interior, and that Marcelino García Barragán had the same feeling. If we add to this the devastating physical strain on Díaz Ordaz, who had had an eye operation in early 1969, and was practically blind in one eye for several months thereafter, and his depressed state of mind—his wife was on the verge of insanity and his son on the brink of drug addiction—it is not hard to understand that by this point it appeared all but impossible to row against the current and try to curb Echeverría's increasing control.

But also, if any intervention with Díaz Ordaz to denounce Echeverría's hypothetical plot had materialized, his two sympathizers in the presidential circle—Luis Gutiérrez Oropeza and Fernando Gutiérrez Barrios—would have been able to neutralize it without implicating themselves. It may have been thanks to these two that Luis Echeverría was able to prevent the man who would anoint him shortly thereafter from ever comprehending that if he had been left with no other cards to play, it was because they had been wiped out or marked by Echeverría himself. This is why the idea that Díaz Ordaz would have inevitably learned of an Echeverría-led conspiracy is not entirely satisfactory. If to the president's usual end-of-term blindness we add the possible involvement of Gutiérrez Oropeza and Gutiérrez Barrios, we can confirm that the subterfuge could have existed without Díaz Ordaz catching wind of it.

Conversely, the conspiracy may be entirely the product of the febrile imagination of the author, and many others with him.

As we have maintained, successions by elimination mitigate the suspicion of deceit among the losers, but intensify the feelings of betrayal that haunt the great elector. Naturally this does not mean that the losing candidates celebrate their failure, but their wounds heal quickly. In contrast, in this scenario the conflicts and tensions between successor and predecessor emerge almost immediately after the candidate is nominated, and never cease, even after many years. Luis Echeverría comments in his interview that he detected a slight unease in the president as early as the arrival of the traditional stampede of supporters at the Ministry of the Interior on Avenida Bucareli, when Echeverría's nomination was made public. Resentment and bitterness would never again abandon Gustavo Díaz Ordaz. There were two significant altercations in the course of Echeverría's campaign, one over the aforementioned incident in Morelia, and the other in 1970, for reasons that are not yet clear. Both illustrate the discord inherent in this type of succession and the tremendous frailty of the process.

According to the version that Alfonso Martínez Domínguez has repeated on several occasions—give or take a few details—in November 1969, on the same day Echeverría observed a minute of silence for the victims of the Tlatelolco massacre, Martínez Domínguez, PRI president and by then Echeverría campaign manager, got a call from the defense minister, who stated that they had to "go see the president together and ask him to withdraw Echeverría's candidacy." Martínez answered that if they went together, Díaz Ordaz would react negatively to what he would perceive as joint pressure on him from the party and the armed forces, and that therefore it would be best for them to act separately. He immediately contacted the president's secretary and made an appointment for the same afternoon. In his audience with the president, he expressed García Barragán's concerns. At this point, Díaz Ordaz still defended Echeverría: "Marcelino is a clean, honest person, but we're going to create a plainclothes security team of presidential guards to protect the candidate. You'll decide how many are needed in each city, starting tomorrow in Guanajuato. They'll take care of everything; I'm going to give orders to Gutiérrez Oropeza." And, in fact, special presidential secret service contingents were provided for the rest of Echeverría's campaign, to guarantee his safety. Through Gutiérrez Barrios, Díaz Ordaz convinced García Barragán to desist from his demands, and convinced the candidate to pronounce a eulogistic and respectful speech about the armed forces the next day. Mario Moya Palencia, the deputy minister of the interior who was running the ministry at the time, recalls that Echeverría phoned him around 11:00 that night: "Listen: For my trip to Apatzingán tomorrow, send me a speech praising the armed forces. You know what I think of the army, but the press has reported the fact that I observed a minute of silence as though it meant I agreed with the provocateurs. I had planned to give the speech elsewhere, but I have to do it right away. Please do it." The candidate would give the speech the next day in Guanajuato rather than in Apatzingán. Later, in January, the candidate paid a visit to García Barragán's ranch in Jalisco to make peace, and in principle the matter ended there.

This event's connection with the second conflict remains a mystery in the history of the Mexican presidential succession. As Martínez Domínguez has repeated on several occasions, and according to the first partial confirmation provided by Luis Echeverría in his interview for this book, there was another, more serious, incident in January 1970. On returning from an extended trip through northwest Mexico and Baja California, Echeverría was met at the airport by an out-of-joint Martínez Domínguez: "I have something very serious and urgent to tell you. You've been ignoring the president too much. There's adverse sentiment forming against you. Your trips are too long, and the losing candidates are still here in Mexico City, and they're giving the president negative reports. You have to take steps. Report daily to the president." Echeverría, who hadn't got as far as he had by being naive or foolish, understood that Díaz Ordaz and/or Martínez Domínguez was trying to regain control of the campaign, and chose, obviously, to have none of it. His response to Martínez Domínguez was brief and to the point: "The president knows about everything; there's no need to distract him with trifles. Thanks for your advice. Just the same, let's you and I go to Los Pinos to see him and put an end to these rumors, which I have no doubt are intended to harm us." They were both announced on arriving at Los Pinos, but the president ordered that only Echeverría be shown in to see him. After a few minutes in the waiting room, Martínez Domínguez sent Echeverría a card with an aide, informing him that he would wait at PRI headquarters. According to Martínez Domínguez, he didn't want to listen through the door to Díaz Ordaz heaping imprecation on Echeverría.

Days later, according to Martínez Domínguez's narrative, Martínez Domínguez entered the president's office to be received with a vehement harangue: "What has your damned candidate got to say for himself?" Díaz Ordaz went on, "He's going around saying there's going to be a change. What change? We're going to put a stop to that now. He can go to hell. We're going to make this SOB sick, and he's going to get really sick. He's out of control. He talks about everything. He doesn't know what he's saying. He insists he's going to make changes, but he doesn't say to what end. He doesn't know what he's going to replace the system with. We still have time to repeat the PRI convention. Start getting ready. Stay at home and don't go out for three or four days. Monitor the PRI by telephone." Martínez Domínguez confesses that he never felt it was appropriate to question President Díaz Ordaz about the denouement. He only recalls that he "heard" some time afterward that the incumbent and the heir apparent had reached an agreement. Echeverría apologized and Díaz Ordaz forgave him. Martínez Domínguez himself acknowledges that his version is not entirely disinterested. If the candidate were removed later than February 2, 1970, Díaz Ordaz would be obliged to replace him with someone from outside his cabinet, and the only option available was, precisely, Martínez Domínguez. He was, as he recalls nostalgically, "Díaz Ordaz's only option. He didn't exercise it." Nothing prevents us from assuming that the former PRI president's version of the facts corresponds to reality, but the intentions of the central characters are less evident. Díaz Ordaz may have wanted to send Echeverría a message, to remind him where he came from and to whom he owed his candidacy, and therefore the presidency. Using Martínez Domínguez as his messenger served a twofold purpose. It gave the message solemnity and allowed his friend to collect his debt of gratitude from Echeverría incurred for the favor of brokering the subsequent reconciliation, thereby strengthening Martínez Domínguez in his move, not only to the next cabinet, but to a top-level position.

It is also true that the system may be indebted to Echeverría for the last thirty years of its survival. Without his split with Díaz Ordaz, without his attempts at renewal and opening, without his impetuous desire for change, it is uncertain whether the system would have survived the crisis of 1968. The system's adversaries can reproach Echeverría for his effort and perseverance. Partisans of the system should thank him passionately.

The incidents cited illustrate two recurring themes in the Mexican presidential succession, the presentation of which will allow us to ease into a comfortable, if not elegant, transition to the next succession in 1975–1976. One of the defects of the selection by elimination is the illusion of autonomy or self-sufficiency that it inspires in the chosen candidate. Since he isn't preordained, and feels that he has won "fair and square," since he knows he vanquished his opponents in a real contest, and not one invented *ex profeso* to mislead, the winning candidate tends to claim credit for his victory. If we follow part of Porfirio Muñoz Ledo's theory of the two laws of the Mexican presidential succession—complicity and affiliation (Roman style)—the process of elimination weakens recognition of the father. He may remain convinced of his paternity, but the putative son begins to question it: "No one invented me; I'm the product of a conception, if not immaculate, at least asexual and neutral. My birth obeys my own will." The extreme example of this, no doubt, is Ernesto Zedillo, who has repeatedly affirmed that he owes his presidency to the seventeen million votes he drew at the polls, and not to the Midas touch that put him on the electoral ballot.

A case less nonsensical, but with analogous consequences, involved Miguel de la Madrid. He governed with the apparent conviction that he had triumphed in the succession because his administrative and political expertise was superior to that of his rivals, and therefore that he had nothing to learn or receive from them. The best man won, and the best man doesn't need anyone else.

Predictably, in this situation, the chosen one's feelings of indebtedness or gratitude toward the elector fade faster than in other cases. At the same time, the outgoing president's inevitable disappointment degenerates faster into feelings of betrayal, with no way to banish them later. The split grows. Over time it can assume dimensions and levels of intensity that are intolerable to the system. To this day, Echeverría insists that after December 1, 1970, when Díaz Ordaz passed him the presidential sash, he never again saw or had words with his predecessor, although Fausto Zapata, his former spokesman and friend, assures us that on one occasion in 1972, Echeverría went to the Mexico City airport to meet Díaz Ordaz, who was returning from Europe, accompanied by his wife, in very poor health. Relations between José López Portillo and Miguel de la Madrid are nonexistent a decade after the latter left office, and the palpable animosity between Carlos Salinas and Ernesto Zedillo augurs no good for Mexico in the years ahead.

Beyond these conflicts—which can have calamitous consequences for society—the succession mechanism leads us to reflect on an eternal problem in Mexico's history as an independent nation: the transfer of power. If the great discovery of the Revolution was indeed, following John Womack, the creation of a mechanism that would permit the peaceful and regular transfer of power in the aftermath of a century of alternating between one-man monopolies—from Santa Anna to Porfirio Díaz—and an endless series of coups, pronouncements, and countercoups, the minute dissection of said mechanism demonstrates its incredible fragility, even in its mature period or apogee. To get the outgoing president to hand over power, and the chosen one to accept it without persecuting, shooting, or crucifying his former rivals and, above all, the man who invested in him, would appear to be an achievement of almost Herculean proportions, requiring the precision of a Swiss watch. The resentments, vendettas, illusions, and interests at stake in a heartless zero-sum game all contribute to creating a whirl of ambitions and excesses, which creates an extremely precarious system to control. Díaz Ordaz may never have tried to replace Echeverría, but not for lack of desire. Echeverría may not have overstepped his bounds in his urge to take center stage, renew the system, and break with his predecessor, but only by a hairbreadth. Marcelino García Barragán may not have tried to unseat Echeverría as PRI candidate, but his irritation reached critical levels. And the fact, singular in our narrative and belonging now to our remote past, that the 1969–1970 succession unfolded in a context of economic growth and market stability, leads us to underestimate the tenuous balances that are always prone to disruption. In balancing the pros and cons of the mechanism in use from the 1920s on, in the debit column appears, no doubt, the cost of tragedies such as the repression unleashed against the 1968 student movement and many others. Under assets we find the ability to dominate forces that are extremely difficult to control and channel, almost always under adverse conditions. The lesson for the future is evident. The democratic system Mexico must build for tomorrow has to contain the same passions and interests, and resolve equal or greater amounts of contradiction, confrontation, and bitterness. This is neither a simple matter nor one that can be reduced to issues of electoral formalities, which are a necessary but far from sufficient condition.

# ECHEVERRÍA—LÓPEZ PORTILLO (1976)

The year 1976 occupies a paradoxical position in our overview of successions by elimination or by choice. On the one hand it is a splendid example of an *in pectore*, well-foretold selection of a candidate. On the other hand, however, the dramatic implications of this approach were not immediately evident, and only became so as subsequent events unfolded. Although José López Portillo's nomination on September 22, 1975, and ensuing election to the presidency to a certain degree constituted the least traumatic transfer of power of the four discussed herein, it proved as onerous to Mexico as any of the others. Its singularity lies in the key relevance of personal eccentricities in the succession. The age of the various prospective nominees, their character, the intervention of third parties, all helped clear the way for a preordained successor. This explains why the relationship between López Portillo and Luis Echeverría, despite its stormy and theatrical moments, has stood the test of time better than any other.

By the middle of 1975, three real candidates and two additional options were still in play, although in reality all except the intended winner were used for purely decorative purposes, to dazzle both spectators and the other politicians involved. The three included the eventual victor, one candidate who held an apparently insuperable advantage over the others at the beginning of Echeverría's term of office, and Porfirio Muñoz Ledo—by his own account President Echeverría's second choice. Despite a declaration by the minister of hydraulic resources—deemed close to the president—mentioning seven names, and the commotion this "leak" caused when the media and politicians erroneously assumed that he "had the inside track," the fact is that several of the hopefuls he mentioned never counted. Former presidents tend to abstain from naming the men who they used as "filler," since many continue to be their friends, and may be offended by being exposed as mere instruments of presidential Machiavellianism. Nevertheless, no such scruples prevent them from consciously or unconsciously fulfilling precisely that function. Hugo Cervantes del Río, minister of the presidency throughout Echeverría's term, and Augusto Gómez Villanueva, minister of agricultural reform for nearly the entire six years, clearly played this part for Echeverría. Cervantes stepped into the role toward the end, creating the impression that he was finishing the race strongly. He captured media attention during Echeverría's interminable third world tour in the summer of 1975, and in the final days before López Portillo's nomination, appearing on behalf of the president at events such as the Third World Congress on Education, the meeting of the Rome Club, and others that had nothing to do with his job. Gómez Villanueva fulfilled his mission as straw man for the party's affluent right wing, appearing to be the "leftist" candidate that a magnanimous and resigned Echeverría would reject in his eagerness to appease the Mexican, and in particular the Monterrey, business community.

Another prospective candidate included in the list—and mentioned in the interview by Echeverría with greater emphasis than others—was IMSS (Mexican Institute of Social Security) Director Carlos Gálvez Betancourt, former governor of Michoacán and a colleague of the president's since his early years at the Ministry of the Interior. His case is difficult to decipher. Echeverría felt real affection and respect for Gálvez Betancourt, and presidential power was such that he could perfectly easily have imposed him. At a distance, however, it is difficult to imagine him as president. The minister of public works, a contender mentioned by the presumed presidential spokesman, was included in the list by his friend at Hydraulic Resources out of deference. There was no justification for including him.

Everything indicates that Luis Echeverría's term was divided into two unequal parts, the precise demarcation of which remains vague. During the first year or two of his term, the president seemed to already have a chosen successor, whom no one and nothing could stop, in his young, charismatic, and loyal minister of the interior, Mario Moya Palencia. As Porfirio Muñoz Ledo claims with an evocative sigh, "There never was a prospective candidate more predestined than Mario." Just thirty-seven years old, he was the youngest minister of the interior in modern Mexican history. His ties to Echeverría dated from the Adolfo López Mateos campaign in 1958, and he had followed him rung by rung in his climb to the top of the Mexican political ladder. He had enjoyed excellent relations with the previous regime and was on similarly good terms with the aging Alemán administration, having been Miguel Alemán Jr.'s childhood friend and university companion. There are strong reasons to suppose that Mario Moya was disqualified at some point during the first or second year of his term—Fausto Zapata, Echeverría's press person, gives the date as early 1973—in Echeverría's mind and, by Moya's own account, in his own as well. He nevertheless continued to serve as decoy for the rest of Echeverría's term, to mask the man who from then on would substitute Moya in Luis Echeverría's plans to continue his work: Echeverría's friend from adolescence, the university, and early adulthood, a trial lawyer who had recently entered the public sector, José López Portillo. During the second part of the administration, Echeverría would use all the guile and art learned in more than a quarter-century in Mexican politics to ensure that this inexperienced, middle-aged prospect, with little independent strength, would rise to the PRI candidacy, and ultimately the presidency, without being annihilated by his adversaries. The only way to achieve this goal was through deceit. López Portillo could only hope to win the grand prize of Mexican politics if no one—or nearly no one—suspected that he had a chance.

There are several explanations offered as to why Mario Moya, who fully satisfied the requisites for the candidacy, was not chosen. First we must evaluate Moya's own theory. The theory rests on the axiom—difficult to demonstrate but empirically provable—that since Lázaro Cárdenas, the Mexican presidential succession moves in two-generation stages: each generation gets two presidents, and no president hands power over to a new generation until at least another member of his generation or of a previous one has received the presidency first. Thus Cárdenas handed over the presidency to Ávila Camacho, a member of his own generation—understood as an age difference of approximately seven years or less. Ávila Camacho passed the presidential sash to Alemán, a member of the next generation, who entered office at thirty-nine years of age, and who clearly surrendered the presidency not to a man of his own generation but at least to one from the previous generation—Adolfo Ruiz Cortines. Ruiz Cortines returned to the norm and passed the presidency to a much younger man, Adolfo López Mateos, who in turn chose as his successor Gustavo Díaz Ordaz, a contemporary with whom he had worked for years in the Senate and in the cabinet. Díaz Ordaz once again changed a generation as scheduled, opting for Luis Echeverría, eleven years his junior. Therefore, Echeverría had to have a successor from his own generation, as indeed occurred. José López Portillo was born in 1920, and Echeverría in 1922. According to Moya's theory, if we follow the sequence, López Portillo would have to choose someone from the next generation, as in fact was the case with Miguel de la Madrid. However, de la Madrid was the first to break the rule, ignoring the second member of his own generation and passing the presidency to Carlos Salinas, rejecting Jesús Silva Herzog and Manuel Bartlett Díaz, who were only slightly younger than he.

As a result, the system began to function imperfectly. The mobility encouraged by the two-generation system was curtailed, eliminating a large number of politicians from the lost generation, such as Cuauhtémoc Cárdenas, Porfirio Muñoz Ledo, and others, who became frustrated or embittered or left the party. The theory is not absurd and has in fact remained valid since Miguel de la Madrid. Carlos Salinas fulfilled its requirements on two occasions, first with Luis Donaldo Colosio, and immediately thereafter with Ernesto Zedillo.

There were, however, other reasons to explain Moya's failure to fulfill his ambitions. In the first place—perhaps unintentionally—he accumulated too much power. He was, as Muñoz Ledo has commented, the last of the prospective candidates to seek the PRI nomination by building an independent political power base. Moya marshaled governors, deputies, senators, local PRI leaders, businessmen, the financial sector of the public administration, and intellectuals—in a word, everything he needed to win, except for one vital ingredient: the willingness of the president to accept a successor with independent strength. According to Muñoz Ledo, in the end twenty-eight of the thirty-one governors supported Moya, two supported López Portillo, one supported no one, and no one supported him. The balance was logical. At the Ministry of the Interior, Moya prepared the reports on the states and the gubernatorial candidates. He comments, "The Ministry of the Interior had been doing this for some time, since Echeverría was minister, and I continued the practice. It was something I knew should be done and how to do, because I had been deputy minister under Echeverría. For me, the minister of the interior had an easy option, which was to do the same as his predecessor, because his predecessor was now president. I could not go wrong if I acted as he had." Naturally, Echeverría occasionally reproached him for the way he loaded the dice, but when Moya argued with him, the president consented and allowed him to continue preparing the files on the governorships. This continued until late in Echeverría's term, when Moya's young partisans began to be replaced by older governors, an almost imperceptible adjustment that nevertheless augured the waning of Mario Moya's influence.

There are many facets to the last explanation offered for Moya's defeat, some more important than others but all related to his personal behavior. Further on we will see how, over the years, one of the most noxious effects of the succession mechanism, the elimination of all substance from the politics of power in Mexico, won out. For the time being, we will mention an involuntary consequence of this phenomenon, the homogenization of the political field achieved by the covert, individualized decision-making process in the presidential succession and the filter of the cabinet. This made Mexican politics resemble politics in the United States, by reducing the scope of differences between rivals to the personal terrain. Personal affairs not only became political, they became *the* political issue, replacing the content taken away by the succession procedure. Personal traits became of the essence, and Moya's did not please Echeverría as one might have expected, given Moya's lightheartedness about them. His vulnerability on this front is illustrated by a joke about an Arab caliph that, according to Muñoz Ledo, Moya told repeatedly during Echeverría's presidency. The caliph rose late, ate dates all morning, received his ministers for a while at midday, then had a nap, and in the evening visited his harem or his friends. A foreign visitor once asked, "You rest all day. Who governs?" The answer says it all: "I govern, the others do the work."

Porfirio also vividly remembers a night in June of 1973, soon after his own wedding, which, fittingly enough, had taken place at Moya's house. After several days of uncommon presidential coldness and even hostility toward him, Moya was summoned to Los Pinos, where, after a long wait, Echeverría opened fire point-blank, "I understand age-based, or generational, relationships, but there should never be alliances in a cabinet that can harm the president. Not even between members of the same age group. They can harm a president." He parted with a mysterious and inscrutable remark, the details of which are blurry in Porfirio's memory, but which was clear in its implications: "You know the history of Mexico. A Dostoyevskian family cannot govern Mexico. Good night." In a manner more elegant and complimentary to Moya, a friend and colleague of the then-frontrunner comments with nostalgia, in reference to Moya's wife Marcela Ibañez, "In PRI orthodoxy, Marcela didn't fit in with the traditional pattern of first ladies." Or, in the velvet-gloved formula of another politician close to the events, whose wife was a friend of María Esther Zuno de Echeverría, "The first lady and Marcela were poles apart."

According to versions collected by the author from Luis Echeverría's closest colleagues—all off the record—herein lies the main explanation of Moya's slide in the end of the administration's first or second year. The president was neither a hypocritical puritan nor a diehard workaholic *per se*, but a compulsive politician who intended to hold all the strings in his hand all of the time. It is, in fact, probable that Mexico could only be governed under this system and by this method at the time. On another occasion, Echeverría offered Porfirio an explanation, not at all puritan and eminently political, of his animosity for the dangerous mixture of bohemian lifestyle and Mexican politics. He obliged his aides to work very late because he disliked parties at the houses of his functionaries. "I don't want you to play canasta, poker, or dominos. These provide the context on Saturday nights when cabinet ministers' wives speak out against the president. That's why I keep you here on Saturdays. I don't like parties at the houses of officials; they always end up talking dirt about the president." But Echeverría *was* a control freak, a man obsessed with self-control and absolute domination of his immediate personal surroundings. Marcela Ibañez, twice married to Mario Moya, systematically helped propagate an image diametrically opposed to that of an orderly marriage or household. Moya divorced Marcela for the first time near the end of Echeverría's term. Echeverría's response to learning of the divorce was, "It's about time."

Mario Moya, who admits having organized some parties at his house and being a bohemian—"which neither then nor now have I concealed"—denies any friction between his wife and the first lady, and in general downplays the point, insisting on the previously discussed generation theory. Perhaps, despite his close acquaintance with Echeverría, he underestimated his former boss's controlling obsession and the logic of the succession. To win it was necessary to seduce, and Moya, although a charmingly seductive man in the positive sense of the word, failed to understand that popularity, gregariousness, the accumulation of strengths and alliances, and pure political competition represented the tactic least likely to win the president.

Moya Palencia may have forgotten that personal problems can be crushing in a competition devoid of all content. A marriage that was for all intents and purposes in pieces, but which remained formally intact, like José López Portillo's, was no impediment in aspiring to the presidency. But a restless, jovial, and occasionally indiscreet wife gave the impression of his reigning over a dissipated and unruly household, and cost her husband his chance at power. Porfirio Muñoz Ledo recalls another anecdote that supports Echeverría's confession in his interview regarding the early signs he sent López Portillo and simultaneously demonstrates the president's disappointment with Moya Palencia. Months before the unveiling (or *destape*, meaning the announcement of the chosen successor), during a state visit by Carlos Andrés Pérez, Venezuelan president and Luis Echeverría's kindred spirit, the honored guest unwound at his host's brother's house, singing, playing the piano, swapping jokes with the comedian and actor Cantinflas, and talking politics with Mario Moya. The next morning at the airport, his demeanor reflected the effects of the evening before, and Echeverría, a fine judge of appearances, did not pass up the opportunity to poke fun at his colleague: "I see you were up late, Mr. President." Pérez replied, "Well, Mr. President, the fact of the matter is I was up finding out who's going to be your successor." Echeverría volleyed back: "Don't conduct your inquiries listening to the piano, Mr. President. Just come with me and I'll tell you who it is." Echeverría ordered his presidential guard assistant to summon José López Portillo and Porfirio

Muñoz Ledo, and invited them both to accompany the two presidents on a flight to Chiapas to commemorate the anniversary of the expropriation of the Mexican oil industry. According to Carlos Andrés Pérez, cited by Porfirio Muñoz Ledo, the message was unmistakable. He shouldn't have gone partying with Mario Moya. López Portillo was the chosen one and Muñoz Ledo the backup.

Although López Portillo recalls the incident in his interview, he doesn't remember having given it any great importance at the time. In contrast, Echeverría considers it one of the stellar moments of his smooth and subtle exchange with López Portillo, in light of which his friend was to intuit his destiny. The inferences and innuendo are often so covert, complex, and difficult to discern that they don't always accomplish their intended purpose, even when they satisfy another important requisite: that is, to be simultaneously deniable, plausible, and likely to be remembered years later.

Why was Porfirio not Echeverría's candidate? Partly, based on the evidence provided by Muñoz Ledo himself, because it was impossible for Echeverría to wield theoretical domination over the man who wrote his speeches. But above all, Porfirio lost because López Portillo won. The die was cast the moment Echeverría became disenchanted with Moya Palencia as a possible successor. Unless he committed irreparable errors, from which not even the president could protect him, López Portillo would be the next president. To achieve this, however, it would be necessary for Echeverría to pull off two extremely intricate stunts: to maintain the fiction of Mario Moya's candidacy and to conceal or "cover" López Portillo for the purpose of preparing him for his planned future. Echeverría's deception was masterful. The president brought all his wiles and resources to bear to achieve his objective.

Before we attempt to untangle the conflicting feelings, ambitions, and expectations that led the most strategically minded—others would say calculating—Mexican president in recent history to crown his childhood friend, we would be well advised to examine some details of this dichotomy: deceit and preparation.

The deceit practiced required the complicity—that is to say the inclusion—of its intended object: Moya himself. The minister of the interior resolves the issue elegantly in retrospect, claiming unequivocally that he knew all along that he would not be the candidate: "I never had any illusions. Everything pointed to its being someone from Echeverría's own generation, but there was the possibility that something might come up along the way." And as he played the game, and did well at it, the external part of the deception grew along with his own image. But there was also deception, as the following incident, which summarizes the chain of maneuvers and reactions involved in a presidential succession, demonstrates. Rosa Luz Alegría, then a young Department of Public Education (SEP) functionary, was already separated from the president's eldest son, Luis Vicente Echeverría, but still in residence at Los Pinos, where her mother-in-law had invited her to stay on to ensure the comfort and safety desirable for her newborn son. Among her other tasks, she prepared opinion polls in a decentralized SEP agency on the subject of the presidential candidates. Like many other functionaries, Rosa Luz supported Moya—she was in fact one of Moya's advisers—but her polls were serious and they favored Moya Palencia by a wide margin. He was the best-known candidate, and also the most mentioned in the media and in political circles. In early 1975, the polling team began submitting the results of its work to the president, that is, to Rosa Luz's father-in-law. Echeverría received one of the polls, looked it over, and ordered Rosa Luz, "Take it to Moya," who, she recalls, felt extremely flattered, not by the results so much as by the fact that the president had sent him a poll with his daughter-in-law that favored him so decisively. Despite her marital difficulties, Rosa Luz still maintained close and solid relations with the first family. Her arrival bearing a gift from the president—however poisonous it may have been—was every bit a sign.

Moya Palencia remembers that Echeverría had entrusted him, in his capacity as minister of the interior, with resolving problems between Mexico's two electricians' unions. In September 1971, once Moya had intervened, reconciled the parties in dispute, and resolved the conflict, Echeverría appointed López Portillo general director of the Federal Electricity Commission (CFE). The press reported that the new CFE director had resolved the conflict between the two unions. In fact, everything had been prepared in advance to help him handle the CFE's thorny labor problems. According to Moya, López Portillo's rise began at this point: "President Echeverría had already pardoned him." The pardon Moya refers to had to do with a problem that López Portillo himself mentions in his memoirs. He had been deputy minister of the presidency under Gustavo Díaz Ordaz, and therefore his logical candidate for the succession was Dr. Martínez Manatou. Since he was a longtime friend of Echeverría's, he managed to shake off the inertia of bureaucratic loyalties, but was unable to openly support Echeverría as the then-minister of the interior would have wished. In his memoirs, López Portillo mentions that he had practically no contact with Echeverría during the latter's presidential campaign, and includes an enigmatic remark that the president-elect made when they finally met face-to-face in San Jerónimo, days before he was to take office: "I congratulate you for your loyalty." José López Portillo started Echeverría's term as deputy minister of national patrimony, without the kind of appointment he would have expected from his friend Luis. In 1972, his patience would be rewarded.

Echeverría began to build López Portillo's candidacy step by step from the CFE and above all as of May 29, 1973, with his appointment to head the Ministry of Finance. This does not mean, of course, that everything was preordained. The pupil, however well the master might look after him, could trip up or self-destruct. When the former president explains today—as he explained to Moya on September 25, 1975, during a short conversation at Los Pinos after the unveiling—that the winning candidate was the best informed on economic issues, he is not lying but only bending the truth somewhat. López Portillo was the most familiar with economic issues of the prospective candidates because Echeverría placed him in a position from which to acquire such familiarity. He made López Portillo minister of finance because he planned to make him president; he did not become president because he had been minister of finance. Moreover, if López Portillo did not occupy an alternative post, it was because in the formerly—and once again as of 1992—powerful Ministry of Finance he could reduce the tremendous advantage built up by Mario Moya among businessmen and state governors.

The presidents responsible for the candidates selected *in pectore*—Echeverría, de la Madrid, and Salinas—tend to invoke various reservations or limitations to contradict this thesis. Nothing was for certain; the favorite could stumble. The denials offered are not false, but they omit something: the sitting president could look after the favorite's interests, protecting him, as far as possible, from his own shortcomings, the pitfalls along the way, and the danger of destruction at the hands of his enemies. The front-runner was certainly on the high wire, but equipped with safety net and harness, and aided by coaching from the master acrobat. Under these conditions, an error or slipup, while not impossible, became highly unlikely. Such was the case with López Portillo at two critical junctures in modern Mexican history that unfolded precisely during Luis Echeverría's term: the end of the fixed exchange rate, and the tax reforms that began to put an end to the Mexican state's chronic fiscal shortages. Both issues had implied attractive opportunities for both change and stubborn resistance before López Portillo arrived at the Ministry of Finance. Richard Nixon's decree of the end of the Bretton Woods system and the dollar standard in August 1971 offered a splendid opportunity to adjust the exchange rate for Mexican currency, which had remained frozen since 1954. But Echeverría was not convinced, and the opportunity passed as quickly as it had arisen.

Moreover, his first minister of finance attempted to promote tax reform during the administration's early years, including, among other measures, ending stockholders' anonymity and tax evasion. The business community blocked his efforts. The resulting scarcity of funds, added to a politically motivated increase in public spending, began to exacerbate inflation and the deficit. When Echeverría, partly on sound grounds, rejected any attempt to hinder growth in spending, but at the same time resigned himself to not raising taxes, he obliged himself to choose between several bad options: higher inflation, runaway foreign debt, or a combination of the two. These issues were still debated in the cabinet as late as May 1973. With López Portillo's designation the debates ceased.

Logically, it was absurd to appoint the future presidential candidate to head the Ministry of Finance and then oblige him to devalue the peso or raise taxes. López Portillo himself expresses his situation better than anyone else. He warned his close aides not to even mention the word "devaluation," and told Porfirio Muñoz Ledo in April 1975, in the midst of strong pressure on the peso, "We're not going to devalue anything here, because we've got a lot of balls." In August 1976, when there was no alternative left—despite the balls, there was no money—López Portillo was already president-elect and Mexico's foreign debt had nearly tripled as Echeverría's presidency drew to a close. Political, succession-linked factors paralyzed economic policy, and the paralysis led, inevitably, to crisis.

Otherwise, López Portillo was the kind of minister of finance Echeverría wanted: in short sleeves, leaving the office, granting loans to farmers, and letting "finances be handled from Los Pinos." He held the position because Echeverría concluded that it would provide a suitable platform for launching his bid for the presidency and preparing him for the job. He held the office because Echeverría willed it so, as a function of his political calculations.

With López Portillo, the tacit or implicit claim upheld by all the presidents—that they neither planned nor implemented any strategy to win the nomination, but simply concentrated on doing their jobs—seems to be true. The president, not the candidate, was the strategist. In the words of Rosa Luz Alegría, "Echeverría planned from the start that everyone's attention and commitment would be drawn to and polarized around Mario Moya, in order to then be able to pull a candidate, who was López Portillo, out of his sleeve. From the moment he took him out of the CFE, he started moving him gradually closer [to the presidency]. He thought: 'I'm in the race; I haven't a chance, but I'm in the race.' He had no group and he was doing nothing to try and win [the nomination]; he just tried to do as good a job as possible. He was among the first to be surprised when the president told him; he was truly stunned."

As is common knowledge in Mexico, after being nominated PRI candidate,

José López Portillo began a long and passionate affair with Rosa Luz Alegría. Two months after the nomination, López Portillo took the initiative in approaching her, an advance that would shortly thereafter turn into the "most intense relationship in his life." This detail is significant, not for its prurient interest, but because it gives Rosa Luz Alegría's analysis forcefulness and insight. As we will see, the very fact of this relationship illustrates some of the reasons why Echeverría chose his friend López Portillo early in the game. The flagrant deceit practiced on the rivals and their resulting feelings of betrayal—the possibility for presidential succession by advance designation—did not produce as pernicious an effect as it has on other occasions. This was possible because the main rival, Moya Palencia, while he was certainly deceived, resigned himself, because of his age, his temperament, and his singular capacity for self-persuasion, to the idea that luck was not on his side. Fortunately, López Portillo had no opponent in the 1976 elections, and the minister of the interior's low spirits harmed no one, in contrast with the 1988 fiasco. His attitude contradicts neither the reports of supposed propaganda that was already printed or manufactured to launch his candidacy nor the rumors of a hypothetical coup that Moya or his supporters were on the verge of pulling off when López Portillo was nominated. These things may have occurred without Moya's knowledge or consent, or been part of the play of self-deception and lucidity we have discussed previously. Moya knew he wasn't the one, but he had to act as though he was, to be ready if anything happened.

Porfirio Muñoz Ledo and Augusto Gómez Villanueva—silver medal and red herring respectively—could take comfort in the evident implications for their futures of the president's decision. Both would be called on to fill fundamental positions in the PRI hierarchy on the very day López Portillo was nominated—Porfirio as party president and Gómez Villanueva as general secretary—and both understood that Echeverría clearly had long-term plans for them and himself. Gómez Villanueva would be speaker of the House in the next legislature, and Porfirio would aspire to be minister of the interior during the following administration, thinking, as he says now, that Echeverría attempted a double designation: López Portillo for 1976 and Porfirio for 1982. It would not be the first time a Mexican president had made long-term plans or attempted to dictate his successor's successor. Manuel Camacho has recalled, with a combination of wonder and disbelief, how "Salinas always had Zedillo in mind, if not as his first or second choice, as the one who would come next." The economic debacle of 1976, perhaps more than the famous unwritten rules of the system, would destroy this illusion, but it served its purpose at the time. Neither Muñoz Ledo, Gómez Villanueva, Cervantes del Río, nor Moya Palencia would resent the deception. Porfirio had a flash of hope when on May 1, 1975, Echeverría designated him official speaker at the workers' commemoration ceremonies, and Moya never entirely abandoned his illusions. The advance designation's most damaging consequences would come later, when the first of a series of interminable economic crises broke on August 31, 1976. The main mystery, of course, lies in why Luis Echeverría chose López Portillo perhaps as early as the first or second year of his term, and certainly by 1973. According to the version presented by José Ramón López Portillo in his splendid doctoral thesis presented at Oxford University in 1994, his father "was chosen by Echeverría to be the [PRI] presidential candidate partly because he had the fewest political debts, no secret commitments, and no involvement in political foul play, partly for his personal ability and administrative experience, and partly for his ideological affinity and friendship with Echeverría." In conversation, José Ramón is less elliptical: "López Portillo definitely had no lobby, he only had his team, and it was somewhat loose knit because it included people with different characters, who did not all embrace a single vision for the country. López Portillo did not see himself as completely foreign to the presidential project; he shared dreams from youth with Echeverría. He was not frowned on by the political elite. He was simply alien, he inspired no resistance perhaps because he was unknown [ . . . ] and Echeverría knew him intimately." In other words, López Portillo satisfied all the conditions for any succession, according to José Ramón: "The ideological profile of the outgoing president, the correlation of social, political, and international forces, and the candidate's personality traits." López Portillo fully identified with Echeverría's vision, if not his style. He might differ, as people would believe during the first years of his administration, with Echeverría's stridency, but he shared his basic economic, social, and international stance. No domestic or foreign political force vetoed him, and, thanks to Echeverría's handling, he had in fact gained favor on many sides—with the workers' movement and to a certain extent with the business community, which saw him as an improbable lesser evil compared with options such as Porfirio, or especially Gómez Villanueva.

Rosa Luz Alegría adds a central element, the idea that, she claims, had formed in Echeverría's mind of how the outgoing president would get along with his chosen successor once he had been enthroned: "López Portillo would take care of the glamour, all the paraphernalia and ceremonies, and Echeverría would continue to pull the internal political strings. Not because Echeverría thought to manipulate him, but because he knew him and knew he would not be up to the task." The project may have been crazy, but it was certainly plausible. Echeverría would live on metaphorically through hypothetical minister of the interior Porfirio Muñoz Ledo. López Portillo would handle the economy and foreign affairs, in addition to fulfilling ceremonial functions.

When he finally unveiled his candidate, Echeverría, like all presidents, managed the process with extreme care, once more demonstrating his formidable political expertise and calculating nature. He sent Muñoz Ledo and Moya Palencia off to hear the news that morning at a public event at the International Workers' House.

The day the PRI was to announce its candidate, the first to arrive were the president's brothers, followed by the leaders. PRI president Jesús Reyes Heroles did not arrive until the afternoon. In the morning he had presided over a PRI event, during which Echeverría sought to highlight his subordinate status with inopportune telephone messages. The president received Muñoz Ledo in the afternoon, after seeing Reyes Heroles. He announced to him that the PRI had chosen López Portillo as its candidate, and that he was a patriot. He then informed him that the PRI required a revolution in its internal structure, led by someone who would bear the standard of the Mexican Revolution and coordinate the campaign with skill and finesse, a task that Reyes Heroles—in Echeverría's opinion a great intellectual but a rather unpractical man—was unsuited for. The ideal person to fulfill all these missions, to be the standard bearer for the Revolution alongside the patriotic President López Portillo was precisely Muñoz Ledo. The incoming PRI president saw a strategic and ambitious intent on Echeverría's part in this maneuver, intended to go beyond his immediate concerns: "an ideological balance, a certain political duality, the ultimate objective of which was a double unveiling: 1976 and 1982." Reyes Heroles saw a more modest, but equally nefarious purpose, and he mentioned his feelings to López Portillo as they were leaving Los Pinos that afternoon: "You're a corseted prince, *Pepe*." One can imagine López Portillo thinking, "The important thing is to be the prince. I'll worry about the corset later." It would take him more than two years.

One of the first conflicts in the campaign, immediately after Muñoz Ledo's and Gómez Villanueva's designation in the PRI, confirmed many of Echeverría's reasons for appointing López Portillo. It implicated, precisely, Rosa Luz Alegría, who was still in residence at Los Pinos and who very quickly, despite having supported Mario Moya, took it upon herself to carve out an advantageous niche in the newly minted candidate's campaign. She sought out López Portillo, whom she had met socially a few years before at the Norwegian Embassy. The candidate, no doubt aware of Rosa Luz's closeness to his friend Luis, referred her to the campaign manager's office. Simultaneously, Rosa Luz, an ambitious woman by this point in time fully versed in the Florentine workings of palace politics, elicited her father-in-law's intervention to be allowed to participate in the campaign. Echeverría asked the recently appointed PRI president to find a place for his daughter-in-law in the campaign. Porfirio paid the president's request little mind, understanding that it was modest and had not been put forth with excessive insistence. Moreover, his real obligation may have been to obey but not comply: "My instructions were for her to have a limited involvement." Rosa Luz, in turn, very quickly got the same impression. According to her, "Echeverría gave Porfirio instructions to keep me out. I began to be blocked. Echeverría didn't want me around." What was the reason for Echeverría's reluctance, which Muñoz Ledo has subsequently confirmed? Rosa Luz replies, "I think it was for personal reasons. He knew López Portillo to be a flirt, and knew I was separated from his son, that I had no commitments. Also, he didn't like women getting mixed up in what he felt was not their business." Alegría overcame these hurdles, sought out López Portillo again during a campaign trip to Puebla, and put the problem to him directly. The candidate promised to arrange a solution, and from then on Rosa Luz began to be included in campaign meetings and trips. Echeverría, according to his former daughter-in-law, was irritated but suppressed his anger. She, however, guessed that the blockade against her erected by Muñoz Ledo came from higher up. In Echeverría's version, things were as follows: "I spoke with Muñoz Ledo and I said, 'We've got to renew our female contingent. I'm sending you Vicente's ex-wife Rosa Luz.' And Muñoz Ledo did not like the idea; let him tell you: 'No, I don't want any contact with her here. People aren't going to like the fact that she's married to an influential man.' He didn't allow her on the first campaign trip. On the second, López Portillo's bus was waiting outside PRI headquarters, and when he got on, Rosa Luz was already aboard."

Luis Echeverría probably feared that if his daughter-in-law got too close to his friend, it would develop into more than a professional relationship. He knew them both extremely well, and was and still is a man of great psychological sensitivity. He "immediately" learned of the affair Rosa Luz and López Portillo embarked on during the campaign. The candidate's security and logistics were managed entirely by the Presidential Guards, controlled in its every detail by Luis Echeverría. The news that his fears had been confirmed must have made him furious—although in a passage from his interview omitted from this book, Echeverría downplays the issue, saying only "that's their business; its a sentimental and physical thing, his and her affair. What do I care?" Still, he must have been furious; how could his friend push his shamelessness and frivolity so far as to seduce the separated but not-yet-divorced wife of his own son? Nevertheless, Echeverría very quickly verified the essence of this soap opera (i.e., that López Portillo had proven true to himself and corroborated many of his mentor's intuitions and intentions). In Rosa Luz's eyes, "the candidate's approach to me proved to the president (my father-in-law) that his friend was the way he was: vivacious, bohemian, proud, gallant, reckless—in a word, not at all political. He filled the part prepared for him."

With this episode, López Portillo revealed a strange bent in his character. He was willing to risk his candidacy, or in any event his relationship with the president, for a woman. That there was a measure of defiance and affirmation of autonomy on López Portillo's part is likely. He was not unaware that his friend Echeverría was a dyed-in-the-wool politician who would ultimately adopt a political rather than personal attitude toward his friend's and his daughter-in-law's escapades. But the message could not have been clearer to Echeverría. López Portillo was not as interested in politics as he was in other things. Personal issues aside, Echeverría had chosen well, from start to finish. Tensions of this kind, and many others that emerged during the interregnum between the election and López Portillo's inauguration, and even during his administration, characterized this succession.

Once again it borders on incredible that despite so much friction, conflict, and misunderstanding, presidential power changed hands peacefully; or rather, the system's power appears astonishing in light of so many contradictions and opportunities for disruption. In the transition or interregnum Echeverría complicated matters for López Portillo in several ways, with deputies' and senators' seats to be decided, campaign team members, compromising end-of-term decisions, countless impossible-to-refuse invitations to events or project inaugurations—the Military Academy, the Colegio de México, the Chicoasén dam, and others. We will mention here only two emblematic incidents: one before López Portillo's inauguration, which was the selection of General Hermenegildo Cuenca Díaz, who had been Echeverría's defense minister, as PRI candidate for governor of Baja California; and an incident after the transfer of power, which was Echeverría's telephone calls to cabinet members and to the president himself from then–minister of education Porfirio Muñoz Ledos's office, that led to the banishment of the *Echeverrista* faction in the new López Portillo administration.

Rosa Luz Alegría does not think Cuenca's being imposed on López Portillo by Echeverría, against Mexican tradition, was excessively bothersome to the new president. As it turned out, he died during the campaign and was replaced by Robert "Bob" Delamadrid (a candidate to López Portillo's liking), and in any case she may well be right. When they are soon to be inaugurated president themselves, Mexican presidents-elect tend to be very tolerant of the verbal excesses and whims of their predecessors, in the knowledge that it is a luxury they can easily afford. Furthermore, López Portillo in particular seems sincere in his constant declarations of candor and magnanimity toward Luis Echeverría. He thought then, and remains convinced to this day, that his dear friend, a consummate politician, would never ignore or neglect the rules of the Mexican system to the point of daring to try to maintain his grip on power after leaving office.

After his memorable inauguration address on December 1, 1976, in which he in one fell swoop righted a dramatic political and economic situation, López Portillo was obliged to act on the basis of his own impressions of political appearances and perhaps realities—above all when Luis Echeverría encouraged rampant speculation about his ambitions, and the new minister of the interior, Jesús Reyes Heroles, faithfully informed López Portillo of the restless former president's every move, act, or insinuation. By May 1977, the uncomfortable friend's abuses would overstep the bounds of the system's unwritten rules. His abuse of the presidential telephone network, constant visits to various government ministers, and endless after-dinner harping at the nonstop meetings of political elites that he was holding at his San Jerónimo residence, enabled Reyes Heroles to convince the new president to challenge Echeverría. Reyes Heroles held a key position. He quickly placed himself at the forefront in the attack on Echeverría, using powers that may have been intended for someone else. Muñoz Ledo speculates now that he was passed over as minister of the interior in 1976 precisely because of his ties to Echeverría and the pressure Echeverría placed on the incoming president in different areas. He is correct in his analysis, but his appointment to the Ministry of the Interior was simply not plausible. It was inconsistent with tradition for a former prospect for the candidacy, PRI president, and top aide to the outgoing president to hold the most powerful position in the incoming cabinet.

For an entire year, Echeverría was conspicuously active. One day in May 1977, Porfirio, who had been appointed instead minister of education, got a call on the presidential network. It was Luis Echeverría calling from the minister of foreign affairs' office in Tlatelolco. The campaign against *Echeverrista* congressional leader Augusto Gómez Villanueva was gaining strength. Echeverría asked to visit his former aide at his offices. Resigned, Porfirio agreed to grant his request. Over an hour later Echeverría arrived and, after exchanging pleasantries, sat down to talk politics with Muñoz Ledo. He lamented the rumors against Gómez Villanueva that were appearing in the press, and in general expressed a certain unease over a hint of hostility toward himself that was beginning to be heard from López Portillo officials, in particular Reyes Heroles.

Porfirio remained calm until Echeverría suddenly asked him to put him in touch with López Portillo on the presidential network. Desperate, Muñoz Ledo acceded, knowing that his long struggle to maintain a relative balance between his former boss and his new one had failed. López Portillo usually answered his calls on the presidential network personally. He did so on this occasion, and Porfirio had no other option but to put Echeverría on the line. Echeverría complained bitterly about the campaign against his people in general, and against Gómez Villanueva in particular. López Portillo listened and answered him sparingly.

Some days later, according to Muñoz Ledo, Jesús Reyes Heroles would take the recording of the conversation from the presidential network to his meeting with López Portillo as a sign of the intolerable turn Echeverría's behavior had taken. López Portillo accepted his minister of the interior's reasoning, and agreed when Reyes Heroles suggested assigning Gómez Villanueva to an embassy, leaving his job as Chamber of Deputies leader to a true López Portillo supporter. A few days later, during a weekend when López Portillo was away on a trip to South America, Reyes Heroles summoned Gómez Villanueva to his office and asked him to submit his resignation. He forced him, with threats and accusations of corruption, to accept an embassy, whichever he might like. Near the end of 1977, Muñoz Ledo was coerced into quitting his job as minister of education after having failed to shake off the campaign against him. He had tried to persuade López Portillo of his loyalties but received in reply to his arguments the invocation of reasons of state and an enigmatic remark, typical of López Portillo: "You have my complete confidence as long as you don't lose it." By the following Christmas he had lost it. The personal gulf between the two administrations widened, culminating with Echeverría's appointment as ambassador, first to the UNESCO in Paris and later to Australia. The Monterrey right and the business community in general would accurately grasp, in their resentful and interested appreciation of a crucial episode in this series, that the split between the teams from the two administrations and the relative distancing that the two chief executives would negotiate would not be reflected in a divergence of substance. The two administrations would be as similar as two drops of water in many of their ambitions, objectives, and interests, and together would represent the last gasp of the economic and social project developed by the glorious years of the revolutionary governments. The split between groups, teams, and individuals permitted the underlying continuity of substance. Changes in personnel and style masked and helped postpone real economic, social, and political renewal in Mexico. López Portillo may well have assembled the strongest and most accomplished cabinet in modern Mexican history. At different times, his appointees in the Ministries of the Interior, Foreign Affairs, Finance, Planning and Budget, and Education, and in the Mexico City government and Petróleos Mexicanos, put a stamp on these agencies that they had never had before and have not had again since. But López Portillo's eagerness for renewal was exhausted in the succession. José Ramón López Portillo has elegantly summed the matter up: "The complicity between the presidents consists of their agreement that the rules of the system, and therefore its reproduction, will be guaranteed, and the outgoing president will not violate those rules because he depends on them and sooner or later he's going to have to confront them. Therefore, it has been difficult for the presidents to implement reforms sufficiently radical to break the grip of authoritarianism, corporativism, presidentialism, and the intimate rules of the state. Their hands are virtually tied. However much [they] attempt[ed] to link economic liberalization with political liberalization, it could not be done."

Successions by choice or decision offer undeniable advantages over successions by elimination. The feeling of deceit remains, but it is transferred to the losers, who can be more easily controlled, co-opted, soothed, or neutralized than the incumbent. However, the preordained succession also has its difficulties, above all that of cushioning and easing the transition and turning the tables of deception on the outgoing president. In successions by elimination, the successor always ends up cajoling or blinding his predecessor with his virtues, loyalty, or complicity. In successions by choice, it is the incumbent's responsibility to deceive: to convince the successor that he will let him govern, that he chose him because he is intelligent, strong, and charismatic, and that the friction between them is only the product of misunderstanding or back-stabbing conspiracy.

If in the past the bull was "caped backwards," as Mario Moya says, it was also necessary to read situations backwards. Echeverría perceived with delight and terror Díaz Ordaz's anxiety on finding himself with no cards to play and obliged to exercise a sole option that was not to his liking. Only Echeverría knew how he had maneuvered to place himself and Díaz Ordaz at this juncture. Not in vain did he insist repeatedly in his interview for this book that Díaz Ordaz did not even designate him deputy minister of the interior, but rather that he was appointed directly by outgoing president López Mateos (1958–1964) and that Díaz Ordaz himself had made this clear to him. "I would never," Echeverría might have concluded, "expose myself to such a dilemma. Better to choose in advance in full exercise of my faculties than despair at the end and be obliged to choose blindly in a state of resignation and resentment." But the individual selected must possess certain characteristics. Among other qualities, he must wear his weaknesses on his sleeve and be easily checked or diminished using the political instruments available to the president. Since by definition no politician is devoid of psychological and intuitive sensitivity, they tend not to err in detecting weaknesses and in their drive to weaken the successor's strongest points. The successor, on the other hand, is no newcomer to political intrigue. He cultivates the traits that endear him to and dazzle his boss, and conceals those that might put him off or provoke his ire. But the undesirable traits constitute his very nature, while the favorable ones are *contra natura*, and therefore the former are accentuated and the latter obscured, and the successor ends up being exactly what his predecessor wanted him to be: a president of continuity, rules respected, commitments fulfilled. This, to all appearances, is the story of these two friends, whose affection for one another has remained intact since the 1930s, but whose seamless continuity had an exorbitant cost for Mexico.

# LÓPEZ PORTILLO—DE LA MADRID (1982)

Perhaps because José López Portillo gradually became aware of the cost of placing a childhood friend in Los Pinos, he didn't attempt it. Another possible and more likely explanation is that those of the candidates who were also friends of his lost out along the way, and he ended up taking the same path as Gustavo Díaz Ordaz, designating a candidate through a process of elimination. Another parallel with Díaz Ordaz lies in the feeling of deception that permeated the process. Miguel de la Madrid was chosen for the PRI candidacy in 1981 for several reasons, but chief among them was his ability to understand that birds of ill omen never win, and that only the bearers of good news will stay in the race. José López Portillo's designation of a successor emerges as the process of elimination par excellence. The trend continued through 1994, when Ernesto Zedillo reached the presidency, apparently benefiting from the same advantage—he was the only available successor.

López Portillo's term started with three runners in the race: two who were likely to go the distance, and one with little chance of success. Economists Carlos Tello and Julio Rodolfo Moctezuma were López Portillo's lead cards and Pedro Ojeda Paullada was the choice of friendship, affection, and loyalty. As López Portillo himself has confessed, if he had been able to place Tello in the Ministry of Finance early in the term, thereby obliging him to come to terms with business and in particular with the Mexican banking system, his statist, nationalist, and populist urges would have cooled. On the other hand, had Moctezuma been faced with the responsibility of federal expenditures in the recently created Ministry of Planning and Budget (SPP), the inevitable confrontation with the dramatic Mexican realities of scarcity, poverty, and inequality would have tempered his financial orthodoxy. With Tello moving toward the center and Moctezuma toward the left, the two prospective candidates would have remedied their respective weaknesses and allowed López Portillo to organize an orderly succession, especially in view of the disqualification—once again due to constitutional impediments—of the two most powerful members of his cabinet, Jesús Reyes Heroles at the Ministry of the Interior and Carlos Hank González in the Mexico City government.

However, equilibrium was lost from the start and things came out backwards. López Portillo was obliged to place the financially conservative Moctezuma at the treasury, and Tello, a partisan of vigorous public spending, at SPP, the agency responsible for allocating public funds. The confrontation between Tello and Moctezuma over the 1978 budget would ultimately precipitate matters. López Portillo's entire plan came apart within the first year of his administration, when Carlos Tello presented his resignation and López Portillo in turn felt obliged to request the resignation of Julio Rodolfo Moctezuma to preserve his beloved balance. He was left, as he himself acknowledges, without his two best prospects. A third possible candidate was eliminated when Ricardo García Sainz, Tello's substitute at SPP, failed in his attempt to design a national development plan that would supposedly bring order to the administration and the country's economic planning. By late 1980, six candidates were still in the running, of which only three were truly viable. The six were: Pedro Ojeda, an eligible prospect from the outset, but whose personal, political, and professional shortcomings conflicted with López Portillo's ideals of Mexican grandeur and administrative expertise; Jorge de la Vega Domínguez, whose move from the Chiapas governorship to the Ministry of Commerce introduced him to the economic sector of the cabinet, which gradually became the nerve center of the government and allowed him to exercise his ample and versatile political skills and personal connections; David Ibarra, who held the most powerful credentials of the six when he substituted for Moctezuma at the Ministry of Finance, but who never managed to achieve the proper personal relationship with the president; Jorge Díaz Serrano, whose old friendship with López Portillo and apparently magical success in increasing PEMEX production were a great advantage; Miguel de la Madrid, the third man to head the SPP under López Portillo, who succeeded where his predecessors had failed, winning acceptance of a plan that was acceptable to the other agencies involved; and finally Javier García Paniagua, a strange character whose prodigious rise during the López Portillo administration amazed both friends and foes alike, culminating with his designation as PRI president, the next-to-last rung of the ladder leading to the presidency.

One by one, all were stricken from the list, and in the end López Portillo was left with only one or possibly two options, depending on whose version one wants to believe. As in the case of Díaz Ordaz, the key to understanding the dilemma that the president faced lies in thinking through the logic of his situation, imagining his process of elimination or successive approximation. Pedro Ojeda Paullada, López Portillo's *compadre*, had overcome years of alcoholism, but according to several of his closest aides, López Portillo (partly because of warnings from Jorge Serrano Díaz, another friend and former alcoholic) was convinced that alcoholism is incurable, or at least that relapse was highly likely under the pressures of the presidency. Secondly—and this may have been the main objection—Ojeda was far more skilled in politics than in administration. He did not appear to be sufficiently steeped in the administration's compulsion for planning, and he lacked command of the administrative, economic, and financial issues that had rapidly overwhelmed the López Portillo administration. He failed to form alliances in the cabinet that would have favored his cause, and in a decisive debate demonstrated a certain timidity and inconsistency that may have worked against him. The discussion over Mexico's entry into the General Agreement on Trade and Tariffs (GATT) took up a large part of the time and energies of the cabinet in early 1980. In the end, López Portillo asked each minister to vote, and Ojeda vacillated, checked to see which way the wind was blowing, and acted with a measure of opportunism, spoiling the procedure chosen by the president.

López Portillo knew which aides changed their postures to please him, and he distrusted their convictions, sincerity, and resolve. The example of Ojeda Paullada illustrates this, and something similar happened with Jorge de la Vega Domínguez. Although his agency had been responsible for the GATT negotiations, and therefore he was officially in favor of Mexico's entry, de la Vega ceded the initiative in internal debates to his deputy minister of foreign trade. López Portillo objected to de la Vega's lack of definition. According to José Ramón López Portillo's doctoral dissertation, he "never put his heart into the drive for entry in GATT. He didn't fight enough for the project. He let his deputy do his fighting for him, because he didn't know how the president felt on the issue. He thought, 'If I make an effort to get into GATT and he doesn't want to, I'll lose my chance.' " When writing his dissertation at Oxford University, José Ramón López Portillo had access to his father and de la Madrid's personal papers and documents. For that reason, the information revealed in his academic work is particularly relevant here.

De la Vega couldn't read López Portillo's mind for a simple reason: the president didn't make up his mind until a few days before the decision was announced. According to one of his closest aides, López Portillo concluded that de la Vega was too careful and would "blame everything on his predecessor if things went badly for him." This did in fact occur, but the author of the blasphemy against López Portillo was not de la Vega but rather the man he did choose, Miguel de la Madrid.

A combination of factors also explains the elimination of David Ibarra (on a date that is difficult to specify). The minister of finance allowed two of his character traits, which proved intolerable to López Portillo, to flourish, and they were his political undoing. In the first place, his evident intellectual capacity could be seen as an insensitive or irreverent arrogance distasteful or frankly odious to a man like López Portillo, simultaneously boastful of his own intellectual and cultural accomplishments and conscious of his deficient knowledge of economics. Worse yet, Ibarra exposed López Portillo's favorites, casting light on their technical or rhetorical ineptitude, and the strategy backfired. Not an old friend of López Portillo's, Ibarra may have underestimated the importance of pride in the president's personality. And having entered politics late in life, like López Portillo himself, he may have lacked the savvy and flair needed to navigate waters as shark-infested and treacherous as those of the economic cabinet, the newspaper columns, and the presidential succession in general. David Ibarra's incompatibility with the president played a crucial part in his demise, even though he satisfied most of the requisites mentioned by López Portillo to succeed him.

The former minister of finance has a different explanation of his disqualification. He claims that two factors contributed to his failure: palace intrigue and personal considerations, and his tendency to predict impending doom. The first reason offered by Ibarra is the less substantial but perhaps decisive one. "López Portillo chose Miguel de la Madrid because he thought he knew about economics, because it guaranteed his son's political career, because he would protect [his minister of tourism and lover] Rosa Luz [Alegría], José Andrés de Oteyza and his sister Margarita, and because the family also supported him."

Ibarra's explanation is sketchy, but it reflects certain truths. The fact is that at least two of the three individuals mentioned—José Ramón and Oteyza—did in fact support de la Madrid. Rosa Luz may have been more cautious. At least she admits less, limiting herself to saying "I also thought he was the least objectionable, but the fact is that I had no candidate." As it turned out, she served as deputy minister of evaluation under de la Madrid. It was logical for López Portillo to assume that the good professional relationship between the two would provide grounds for a similarly close collaboration in the future. The simplistic objection that a Mexican president could not have made a decision with such far-reaching implications for the country based on such frivolous and narrow criteria overlooks the previously discussed mechanism of the inner circle and this president's misplaced faith in maintaining a balance.

The second explanation suggested by Ibarra is more complete and brings us closer to the heart of the 1982 succession. His character, transparency, and sense of economic responsibility led the minister of finance to predict the overheating of the Mexican economy as early as mid-1980. Furthermore, paralyzing divisions in the economic cabinet prevented sound decision making. For Ibarra, the only solution was to appoint a kind of economy czar. López Portillo heeded this conclusion, but ignored its premise. He dismissed Ibarra's analysis as stemming from a personal desire to take command of the country's economic policy, making himself indispensable, and therefore the best candidate for the presidency.

López Portillo's suspicions did have some basis in fact. This was how the game was played, and the situation was an inevitable result of his having separated public spending from federal revenues by creating the SPP in 1977. But Ibarra's diagnosis remained valid. In late 1981, López Portillo wrote in his diary, "We will end 1981 with a deficit of 715 billion pesos. I couldn't believe it. Smiling, Ibarra answered, 'What about it? I told you so.' " The infinite arrogance that overcame López Portillo in his years of success, as fleeting as they were dazzling, contributed to his incredulity, making him blind to the signs of his failure, and preventing him from exercising his considerable analytical, psychological, and historical faculties.

As we will see, and as López Portillo acknowledges in his interview—although only partially and with considerable reluctance—the confusion and errors were not unwarranted. Ibarra was a minority of one in the cabinet, against the optimism and enthusiasm of his rivals, Miguel de la Madrid, Jorge de la Vega, and Javier García Paniagua, and against the self-serving analysis of men who should have supported him, such as José Andrés de Oteyza, the young and influential minister of national patrimony who enjoyed López Portillo's favor and the advantage of being constitutionally ineligible for the presidency; Rafael Izquierdo, presidential adviser; Gustavo Romero Kolbeck, governor of the Central Bank, who like Oteyza shared more ideological affinity with Ibarra than de la Madrid but preferred to stand by his personal ally; and José Ramón López Portillo, who maintained an ambiguous position throughout the entire process. With all of them against him, the prophet of doom was sure to fail. In Ibarra's opinion, López Portillo rejected him precisely for this pessimism, for warning him of the inflationary tendencies that were gradually accumulating in the overheated Mexican economy and the pressure on public and external finances that, in turn, encouraged inflation. Ibarra had been against the maximalist goals of achieving annual growth rates of over 10 percent that José Andrés de Oteyza had proposed. The Ministry of Finance, in Ibarra's words, "preferred to set a goal closer to 6 percent." From late 1980 on, tensions began to strain public finances, and Ibarra, instead of downplaying the storm clouds on the horizon, scowled and made melodramatic remarks. This attitude was in part a political tactic to influence the succession. It consisted of making dire predictions of disaster, which could only be confronted and overcome with the transfer of power to the physician who had diagnosed the malady, that is, Minister of Finance Ibarra himself, who would have to be given a presidential mandate to coordinate Mexico's economic policy. López Portillo, as his son says, "interpreted this tendency as reflecting [Ibarra's] ambition to be president" and rejected him. Statistics in 1980 tended to confirm, but not fully prove, Ibarra's skepticism. The fiscal deficit reached 7.5 percent of the gross national product, twice the amount predicted. It totaled seven billion dollars instead of the three billion expected—not cause for panic but certainly a danger sign.

In the middle of 1981, the by then traditional end-of-term economic crisis hit, precipitated by a worldwide interest-rate hike and a fall in oil prices, which, although it amounted to a drop of less than 10 percent from existing prices, was perceived in Mexico as disastrous. Jorge Díaz Serrano tried to lower Mexican prices to avoid losing markets, but proceeded without consulting the economic cabinet, an oversight that cost him his job as PEMEX director and possibly the presidency. It was at this point that Miguel de la Madrid won the grand prize.

The reasons for Díaz Serrano's departure remain enigmatic and mysterious. Two of the president's most trusted aides, Rosa Luz Alegría and José Antonio Ugarte, formally insist that until the debacle described above, the candidacy was his. In the final analysis, the debate regarding Jorge Díaz Serrano's chances is irrelevant, since he was forced to resign in June 1981 either for having acted unilaterally without consulting with the economic cabinet, or because López Portillo changed his mind about the prospects of PEMEX's president. The fact of the matter is that Díaz Serrano fell, above all, for bureaucratic rather than policy-related reasons. Events would prove him correct on the oil pricing issue, although, as David Ibarra laments, he spent too much money on such projects as a new PEMEX headquarters, a mammoth gas pipeline from the underdeveloped south to the industrial north, and the development of the Chicontepec oil fields, and he failed to generate savings. It was because of this and the excessive amounts spent by PEMEX on its director's personal campaign that Ibarra took part in his purge from the economic cabinet. The fact of the matter is that Miguel de la Madrid, the candidate favored by José Andrés de Oteyza, emerged stronger from the crisis. He had only one rival left to vanquish, a formidable opponent insofar as his personal characteristics were concerned, but easily beaten in matters of political attributes: Javier García Paniagua.

The events of June through September 1981 illustrate the thesis of succession by elimination. When a succession is handled by this method, the winner always contributes in some degree to creating a situation in which he is the only card left in the president's hand. In other words, the others are never eliminated innocently, and the winner does not prevail as a result of purely arbitrary factors. If at the end Miguel de la Madrid was the only viable candidate left, or had a dubious rival, it can be explained by the circumstances—Tello's and Moctezuma's premature departures; Ibarra's, de la Vega's, and Ojeda's various character flaws—but also by de la Madrid's own intervention. Even if we grant that Oteyza did not provoke his demise as part of a grand Machiavellian plot to pave the way for Miguel de la Madrid, Díaz Serrano's singular lack of supporters in the economic cabinet not only sealed his fate, but was also clearly a product of succession-related infighting. The attitude shown by de la Madrid, Ibarra, and de la Vega was particularly flagrant. The three knew perfectly well that Oteyza's strange insistence on maintaining oil prices at all costs was out-landish, and that Díaz Serrano was in the right, his arrogance and insubordi-nation notwithstanding. No one came to his defense because his elimination left one less candidate in the running. Moreover, if, as is widely suspected, López Portillo initially authorized the price bailout, only to back down and place the blame on Díaz Serrano, he was the one at fault for the consequences. The president became increasingly self-absorbed and conceited, which was under-standable, but laden with horrifying consequences for Mexico. Díaz Serrano took the fall for his friend's mistakes.

The incidents of June and July 1981 had a further impact on the succession, one that may have been more far-reaching than the mere fact of Díaz Serrano's resignation. López Portillo did indeed lose an option in Díaz Serrano, but the loss of his friend also signaled the beginning of his administration's decline, and of his despair over the inexorable Greek tragedy that began to envelop him. This, in turn, contributed to his increasing reluctance to listen to bad news and similarly increasing propensity to be persuaded by optimistic and illusory reports. Plummeting oil prices and soaring interest rates overturned the fiscal balance. It was necessary to redo the accounting for 1981 to calculate the new fiscal deficit and apply the corresponding adjustment in spending and revenues. Two factors helped condense the last real stage of the presidential succession in this process of defining figures and fiscal outcomes: the previous division of the Ministry of Finance into two parts, that had engendered a bicephalous number-crunching machine for the government; and the replacement, as of 1979, of José Antonio Ugarte by Carlos Salinas de Gortari as technical secretary to the economic cabinet. Throughout the summer of 1981 the two departments—

or rather the two prospective candidates behind them—confronted one another in a war of statistics, illusion, and deceit. Ibarra was by now virtually eliminated, and de la Madrid less and less concerned with details and figures and painfully aware of the danger of depressing López Portillo.

The sequence in which the figures were delivered, as José Ramón López Portillo explains, was devastating. In the first economic cabinet meeting dedicated to the matter, on August 21, the SPP presented a deficit estimate for 1981 of 490 billion pesos, a moderate increase in relation to previous forecasts. Three days later, the technical secretary to the economic cabinet, Carlos Salinas, also the SPP economic policy director, proposed a figure of 530 billion—more or less the same. The SPP had argued that a mild 4 percent cut in public spending would suffice to keep the deficit under control and to absorb the loss in revenues caused by the fall in oil prices. The Finance Ministry, on the other hand, had predicted a deficit of 640 billion pesos since August, and recommended more severe spending cuts and a currency devaluation that, added to the cuts and a domestic interest-rate hike, would balance the situation. The SPP opposed the measures, arguing that the deficit would not go so high and that devaluation would only fan the fires of inflation. The Central Bank tended to share Finance's estimates, without defending them with any great vigor. In early September, the SPP revised its estimates, raising its deficit figure to 594 billion pesos. By the middle of October the government agency from which the candidate had emerged predicted a deficit for the year of 642 billion pesos, nearly equal to the figure presented by Finance two months earlier.

In late October, the SPP adjusted its figures once again, fixing the deficit at 761 billion pesos, an increase of 271 billion pesos, or 55 percent, in about 45 days. The year ended with a deficit of 866 billion pesos. Meanwhile, on September 22, minister of planning and budget Miguel de la Madrid was launched as the PRI presidential candidate. This seemed inconceivable in this context of imminent recession, brutal readjustment of domestic and foreign accounts, and manipulation of numbers.

Was there bad faith? In his doctoral dissertation, José Ramón López Portillo cites an argument attributed to officials of the Central Bank and the Finance Ministry, which claims that the SPP had only used figures from January through April to project an estimated average monthly deficit. Based on these figures, they planned for a monthly shortfall of 35 billion pesos for the rest of the year. However, this scale was completely unrealistic. Everyone knew that spending always skyrocketed in the final months of an administration's fifth year—precisely the succession year.

One of the most costly aspects of the Mexican presidential succession mechanism has been its tendency to impose its rhythm on the economic cycle. The phenomenon of uncontrolled public spending at the end of one administration and budget austerity at the beginning of the next, in an economy that remains extremely sensitive to state activity, is a well-known feature of Mexican politics. In a recent unpublished study, the World Bank concluded, "In the election year and the year before presidential elections, growth in per capita GNP is nearly always significantly higher than in the year following the elections. In fact, this pattern of behavior can be seen in every one of the eight presidential elections held since 1950, except one (1988). The probability of this recurring pattern being mere coincidence is close to zero."

De la Madrid, Salinas, and the SPP team would experience the ravages of the exception in 1988. However, it is doubtful at best that they were empirically or conceptually ignorant of this stable and persistent cycle in the Mexican economy. All this suggests a strong possibility of statistical manipulation on the part of the SPP. The motive was simple: if the economic cabinet had reached a consensus in July regarding the real dimensions of the deficit and planned accordingly, the agency responsible for the cuts would have suffered a tremendous loss of prestige in comparison with other agencies, governors, state enterprises, etc. The agency in question, obviously, was the Ministry of Planning and Budget.

Second, such a consensus would have spelled the end of David Ibarra's Cassandra act. Either Miguel de la Madrid would have passed over into the ranks of the pessimists and shared Ibarra's fate, or Finance's analysis would have been reconsidered, reopening the succession race. Third, a consensus regarding the deficit and spending cuts would have also implied a consensus concerning the need to devalue the peso—a measure contrary to Ibarra's thinking, but also to de la Madrid's.

In light of subsequent events and the options available to López Portillo, we have to wonder whether it is reasonable to rule out the possibility that SPP and the technical secretary to the economic cabinet manipulated the budget figures to ensure Miguel de la Madrid's candidacy. The president of Mexico is the best-informed man in the country as long as the opposite is not the case—that is, provided that his sources do not dry up or go blind, and as long as the institutions that support him do not succumb to the temptation to bet on the future rather than on the present. All politicians are tempted by the opportunity to subordinate their principles to their personal ambitions. It is the essence of opportunism to do so, and the practice was by no means invented in Mexico.

However, in a more open system, where the real political forces are more diffuse and autonomous, checks on opportunism—the press, the opposition, history, the future, institutions, etc.—would appear to be more effective. All these sources of power are part of the inescapable stages that must be overcome to reach the top. Personal considerations count, but their importance is secondary.

In the Mexican system, although limiting forces such as those we have mentioned exist and operate, they are blotted out by the supreme power of the factotum. He becomes the object of all seductions, all illusions, and all conduct. In one of the most ironic and fascinating paradoxes of the Mexican presidential succession, the moment of the president's maximum power is also that of his greatest blindness. The maximum expression of his power is the act of imposing a successor of his choosing, but this exercise, the culmination of years of preparation, persistence, guile, and art, is consummated on the darkest night of his life, when no one and nothing lights the way or signals the perils that lie ahead.

The man who would be the chosen one—the seducer—knows that not all tricks work. Fatal slips include being caught in a lie, showing excessive desire to deceive or to win, and otherwise invalidating his own arguments in the eyes of the elector with excessive ambition. Under these conditions, it is hard to resist adjusting one's stance to personal interests. Conversely, it becomes impossible not to align one's official position with one's personal interests and, concurrently, to believe that one's position is informed by altruism, as in "I opposed a devaluation because it was best for the country, not because it would destroy my candidacy."

It seems hard to believe that flagrant errors such as those mentioned in relation to the fiscal deficit estimates were committed inadvertently or for lack of information. It is terrifying to think that extremely important policy decisions were postponed—in this case from July 1981 to February 1982—for lack of accurate and reliable calculations concerning the magnitude of the economic maelstrom about to sweep over the country, and that this deficiency was in turn the work of conscious, brazen, and irresponsible machinations by the winner in the 1981 succession race. In the eyes of his partisans, Miguel de la Madrid's Ministry of Planning and Budget did not oppose a devaluation, nor did it deliberately underestimate the size of the fiscal gap the federal government was generating in order to win its director the candidacy for the top job. He thought devaluation was inappropriate and was caught up in the confusion, which can be understood in light of the rush and pressure over the deficit, which in turn indeed led to de la Madrid's candidacy. However, top SPP officials—mainly Carlos Salinas—were not unaware of what was going on, and the consequences of their actions cannot be made to disappear by ignoring them. José Ramón

López Portillo mentions in a footnote that his father and Patrimony Minister Oteyza acknowledged, in interviews in 1990, that if they had been given reliable estimates in July or August of 1981, they would have adopted severe budget cuts and a currency devaluation.

Who altered the numbers? None of the individuals capable of providing an answer lack personal interests, nor are they likely to let pass an opportunity to further the same. Emilio Gamboa, chief of staff to Miguel de la Madrid; José Antonio Ugarte, López Portillo's chief adviser; and Rosa Luz Alegría, his mistress and by then minister of tourism, coincide, for different reasons, in thinking that Miguel de la Madrid did not personally mastermind the statistical fraud. Gamboa insists that the minister did not examine the numbers closely and that responsibility for verifying their accuracy lay with his team, which had already in some way been sucked into the vortex of the succession. Rosa Luz states outright: "Yes, the numbers were fraudulent, but they were altered by Salinas, not by de la Madrid. De la Madrid was also manipulated. He did not know the numbers had been changed so much. No one told him they were going to deceive López Portillo. De la Madrid would not have gone along with the idea." It is worth mentioning in this context that Rosa Luz Alegría's banishment from politics began with de la Madrid. He never gave her the top-level position she expected. As president-elect, he told her he wanted to include her in his cabinet, but never followed through with the offer. As for Ugarte, he wonders whether de la Madrid was sufficiently imaginative and perverse to come up with the idea of altering the numbers. No one, however, can doubt that Carlos Salinas—responsible for preparing briefs for the economic cabinet—indeed was, or that José Córdoba, by then already Salinas's close aide in the SPP Economic and Social Policy Division, possessed the technical expertise to conceive the scheme and carry it out. It appears entirely plausible that this was the first of the daring young duo's many masterful cosmetic operations, as profitable to them as they were costly to Mexico. In a written statement addressed to the author after the publication of this book in Mexico, former president Miguel de la Madrid denied that he had misinformed, or insufficiently informed, president López Portillo about the size of the fiscal deficit. He stated that documents in his possession show that he fulfilled his obligation to inform the president without deceit of any kind. According to de la Madrid there were differences between the relevant ministries regarding the size of the deficit, but not of the magnitude mentioned in *Perpetuating Power*. José Ramón López Portillo and José Antonio Ugarte, for their part, upon reading de la Madrid's statement and accompanying documents, maintained their point of view.

The statistical face-lift led to Miguel de la Madrid's nomination for the same reasons that the hypothetical manipulation of the 1968 student movement led to Luis Echeverría's. It helped create a situation in which there was no other possible candidate. There is, however, one objection to this hypothesis. None other than José López Portillo has argued that he had two options left at the end: Miguel de la Madrid if the main challenges facing the country were economic in nature, or Javier García Paniagua if they were issues of law and order. If we take this claim at its face value, the "shaving" of the budget figures by Salinas and Córdoba—with or without de la Madrid's complicity or omission—while still unpardonable, cannot be considered decisive. De la Madrid and his partisans still had another adversary to overcome, and a formidable one at that.

Nevertheless, an examination of García Paniagua's career and the opinions of members of López Portillo's inner circle suggest a slightly different version. The president invented García Paniagua in order to appear to hold more cards in his hand, and then kept the invention alive even after leaving office to avoid hurting his feelings. In reality, however, he was never a convincing candidate.

Javier García Paniagua, the son of General Marcelino García Barragán—the veteran defense minister in 1968—began his political career on the bottom rung of the Mexican political ladder. He acted as intermediary alongside his father during the 1968 student movement—although he officially held a modest job in the state of Michoacán—setting up contacts with the generation of military officers who would succeed the then defense minister. He probably met López Portillo in the corridors of the National Palace, when the future president was working in the Ministry of the Presidency, but they developed no significant relationship at this point. He was not a military man in the strict sense of the term, and operated, rather, in the shadows of the national civil security organization. He paid the price of the animosity that had sprung up between the two former Díaz Ordaz aides during Echeverría's term, occupying a seat in the Senate with neither glory nor shame. After Echeverría left office, he focused his ambitions on advancing in the security apparatus.

His efforts paid off. On taking office, López Portillo made sure to avail himself of two kinds of services in the confines of national security. First he needed someone to finish cleaning up the remnants of armed groups still active in the country. If the methods proved unspeakable, it was best not to know. Second, he sought to drive a wedge into Echeverría's hold on the security machine, personified by Fernando Gutiérrez Barrios, the legendary intelligence czar. No one can doubt Gutiérrez Barrios's loyalty or institutional attitude, but his ties to Echeverría were too strong and long-standing to be ignored.

García Paniagua served both purposes admirably. He knew how to follow orders without asking embarrassing questions. José López Portillo ratified Fernando Gutiérrez Barrios as deputy minister of the interior, but to strike a balance between Gutiérrez Barrios and Minister of the Interior Jesús Reyes Heroles, he positioned Javier García Paniagua as director of federal security. As Gutiérrez Barrios recalls, García Paniagua was appointed on López Portillo's express urging, and the new director consulted, as was customary, directly with the president.

García Paniagua rose through the Mexican political hierarchy during these years, from federal security director to deputy minister of the interior in 1978, followed by a stint as minister of agrarian reform, then designation as PRI president in August 1980. As party leader, his ambitions soared, and the classic misunderstandings of the succession gave rise to the confusion typical of this stage of the process. López Portillo expressed a special preference for and confidence in "Javier." On finding that he faced neither significant resistance nor vetoes, instead of deducing that this was probably due to his weak chances, he inferred acquiescence or support. He constantly reinforced his ties to the armed forces, in particular with the defense minister, a former colleague of his father's. He interpreted the pats on the back he received from the president in a strict personal sense, not as "generic," which is in fact how they were characterized by one of López Portillo's main confidants. He explained gestures on the part of the first family—including an oil portrait commissioned by his sister, Margarita, and the warm greetings José Ramón López Portillo sent him through aides—as confirming his hopes for the candidacy. When his expectations failed to materialize and García Paniagua began to feel deceived and betrayed, he vented his fury on the president's son, going so far as to threaten his life.

José López Portillo repeats time and again that, in the end, two prospects remained in the running: Miguel de la Madrid if the country's problems were economic, García Paniagua if they were political. His son corroborates the claim and confirms the viability of García Paniagua's candidacy, maintaining that to the last day, and in any event until he delivered his fifth state of the union address on September 1, 1981, three weeks before the candidate was announced, his father had not yet made up his mind. Other close presidential aides differ with this opinion, and think López Portillo created an additional option for himself as the others fell through to avoid being left with only one at the end, even though this is ultimately what happened.

López Portillo had informed the political elite of his wish to postpone announcing the PRI candidate until after the International North–South Summit to be held in Cancún in late October. One can imagine the surprise when in mid-September on returning from an official visit to the United States, the

Mexican president let fall a bombshell: "The PRI may move its decisions forward." Two days later, Miguel de la Madrid was nominated for the presidency. As in almost everything he did, López Portillo simply ran out of time.

The minister of planning and budget emerged triumphant because he understood López Portillo's overriding desire and ambition better than anyone else, and because he proved better than his rivals at navigating the quagmire of objective requisites and artifice, intrigue, and treachery that the presidential succession had become. In particular, he avoided to the last doing anything to inspire feelings of pessimism and failure in López Portillo. On the contrary, he inspired great confidence in his administrative expertise. He understood that for a man with no craving for power beyond the limits of his own term of office, but extremely vain and simultaneously endowed with an intellectual capacity without parallel in the recent annals of the Mexican presidency, his place in history was crucial. In this context, it was critical to maintain the fiction of finishing his term of office with a flourish. The upper crust of the López Portillo administration had to be made to resemble the vanguard of a new era inaugurated by "the best former president in Mexican history," as López Portillo liked to refer to his future self. De la Madrid availed himself of the same intrigues and tactics as his adversaries, but he used them better.

The president's dream was to leave an orderly, planned country, organized along clear and rational lines. More than a pure lawyer, economist, or politician, López Portillo made his start in the public sector as an administrator. He was motivated by a true obsession with administration that was healthy and well suited to the country's needs, and Miguel de la Madrid had caught his former political theory professor's fancy from the time he coordinated the internal negotiations for the government's National Development Plan. De la Madrid quickly made it clear that López Portillo's closest confidants—José Ramón, Rosa Luz, Oteyza, and Cassio Luisselli—stood a better chance with him than with the other prospects. Finally, when the crisis hit Mexico, de la Madrid understood that what mattered most was to keep the president's spirits up and stave off the severe difficulties the country would have to face at least until after the nomination, and preferably until after the 1982 elections. Whether de la Madrid himself or his subordinates were responsible for the deceit or betrayal practiced is ultimately irrelevant.

It is implicit in the Mexican presidential succession and indeed in power anywhere in the world that politicians subordinate everything else to the quest for the candidacy, then to the election, and finally to the inauguration. The special difficulty in Mexico lies in the absence of checks and balances in the Mexican system that result from the deliberately exclusive decision-making process. De la Madrid's aides, chiefly Salinas and Córdoba (assuming that they were responsible for the budget manipulation), pushed cynicism and audacity to previously unimagined extremes, although it is worth asking ourselves whether their subterfuge and intrigue were any more harmful to the country than, for example, Luis Echeverría's in 1968. Having realized that lying to López Portillo about the severity of the crisis would virtually guarantee de la Madrid's designation as candidate, for them not to proceed accordingly would have been incongruent and absurd. Others would have done so instead, thereby gaining the upper hand. The succession required that the great elector be deceived, since the truth would be unacceptable to him. The elector is in turn obliged to deceive both the chosen successor and the ineligible others. Truth revealed in advance becomes falsehood.

In the logic of our binary grouping of Mexican presidential successions, we found that when the successor is chosen by elimination, he tends to rebel sooner and more intensely than when he is designated by choice. Nothing could be more natural. The fortunate survivor of the wars of succession concludes, not erroneously, that he owes his success to his own guile and virtues, and not to the whim or imposition of his aging mentor. Obviously, his sense of proportion is not entirely obscured. The winner knows that the president has chosen him, but he also concludes that if he was chosen, it was for his political and personal superiority, his toughness and his charm, his skill, experience, subtlety, and wisdom, compared with the rest of the field. If de la Madrid's triumph was the product of his cleverness rather than López Portillo's generosity, it should hardly seem odd that relations between the two would go sour, slowly at first, and faster later on, after the unveiling of de la Madrid's candidacy. In the end, the split would spill over from the personal terrain into an infinity of other contexts, and would exact a heavy price, not only from the interested parties but also from the country.

As the former presidents mention in their interviews, López Portillo toyed with the idea of putting García Paniagua in the Ministry of the Interior in the next administration. He assumed, furthermore, that de la Madrid and the supposed runner-up would get along well, and on the weight of this assumption ratified García Paniagua as PRI president in the days immediately following the announcement. But García Paniagua's irate reaction was not slow in coming, and prevented these hopes from materializing. He began speaking out against López Portillo and his son, going so far as to issue death threats against them both. On the very day de la Madrid's candidacy was announced, García Paniagua referred to his pending ratification by the approaching PRI convention with "We'll see about that," and later he simply stopped appearing in the various campaign launching events. When López Portillo proposed to de la Madrid that García Paniagua remain in the PRI and eventually go from there to the Ministry of the Interior, the candidate reacted with skepticism and reluctance. He did not like the willingness to recur to the use of violence that García Paniagua had shown in the past. Finally, he requested a replacement, and López Portillo consented.

As the months passed, López Portillo began to discern, in the twilight of his presidency, the magnitude of the crisis he faced and its causal relationship with economic cabinet meetings. He became disenchanted with de la Madrid as a consequence of this and also because of some of de la Madrid's campaign themes—"moral renewal," for example—but they refrained from open hostilities for a while. When the time came to choose candidates for the two chambers of Congress, López Portillo once again let his guard down by failing to include his supporters among the deputies and senators. (Among the few exceptions was Jorge Díaz Serrano.)

When a devastating currency, fiscal, and psychological crisis shook Mexico in August 1982, conditions for a definitive split between López Portillo and de la Madrid came to a head. Up to this point the increasing tension inherent in a succession by elimination remained within its traditional bounds, among other reasons because de la Madrid took pains to leave open the option, or fiction, of the possibility of reappointment of the López Portillo inner circle—Rosa Luz Alegría, José Andrés Oteyza, José Antonio Ugarte, Cassio Luisselli, Rafael Izquierdo, and José Ramón López Portillo himself—in his administration. But the nationalization of Mexico's banks on September 1, 1982, and the measures implemented by the new Central Bank governor director Carlos Tello during his ninety-day tour of duty would minimize the possibility of such a happy outcome, which, moreover, too openly contradicted the logic of the succession by elimination. Miguel de la Madrid mentions that in an initial conversation on the subject in May 1982, the president warned him of the possibility of a bank expropriation, but assured him that nothing had been decided yet, and that in any event he would warn him in advance. He did no such thing. The message regarding the radical decision, forwarded by José Ramón López Portillo, reached its intended recipient on the eve of the nationalization. In part for this very reason, in part because he did not agree with the idea, and in part because such a drastic measure violated the unwritten rule of refraining from implementing measures with long-term impact during the administration's final days, de la Madrid rejected it. Moreover, when he was ordered to attend the president's state of the union address, he simultaneously applauded the measure and disapproved with complex body language; the split was complete. López Portillo in turn—like Díaz Ordaz years before and Carlos Salinas years later—regretted his choice of successor. He attempted to consolidate his act of heroism, or immolation, depending on how one wishes to look at the situation. In the end, López Portillo left office in ruin and disgrace. Commissioned by Miguel de la Madrid, Carlos Salinas warned José Ramón of the incoming administration's intention to make life hard on his father. Jorge Díaz Serrano spent de la Madrid's entire six-year term in prison, a strange cross between scapegoat and Man in the Iron Mask.

The arrogant assumption of omnipotence by de la Madrid's team, inspired by their leader's predictable belief that his triumph had been the result of the technical superiority he had displayed in the race for the nomination, had serious consequences for the country. In the first place, it narrowed the field of possible recruits for the new administration and of administrative and political élites in general. The heads of the Ministry of Finance, the Central Bank, and the Ministry of Planning and Budget took over the government because they were, in their leader's eyes, the best and the brightest. The country is still paying the price of the 1988 economic crisis that might have been averted if other candidates, with a broader range of views, had been included. Second, the manifest expertise of the new arrivals turned out to be a mirage. They committed error after error, in part due to the paltry opinions they took into consideration and in part due to the bureaucratic, ideological, and political uniformity of the authors of said opinions. Finally—and herein lies what may have been the greatest danger—the regime's political and generational narrowness limited it to the point that, when it became necessary to change course after six years of economic stagnation and a plummeting standard of living in Mexico, the only backing available was from forces outside the system's traditional power bases: the Catholic Church, the United States, and new business groups that were either formed specifically for the purpose or of mysterious or unutterable origin or purpose. Salinas sprang from the fertile ground of de la Madrid's factional politics, which in turn had been fostered by a succession overcharged with tension. As in 1976, the magical clockwork successions of the golden age succumbed to the vagaries of economics and years of wear. The two next—and final—successions would show the consequences.

# DE LA MADRID—SALINAS (1988)

The economy has always been a factor in the Mexican presidential succession. It has penetrated and permeated the succession through innumerable conduits and along diverse paths, straight or twisted. By 1988, though, two profound mutations made their presence felt in the Mexican transfer of power. The economy became the main campaign issue, and the most perverse implications and ills of the system in place since the 1940s acquired primarily economic overtones.

Miguel de la Madrid began his term of office in worse circumstances than any of his predecessors. The political crisis he inherited from López Portillo in the wake of the bank nationalization and the virtual expropriation of dollar-denominated savings not only severed the fragile strands of trust between the system and the middle classes who had thrived on the former's success but also destroyed the complicity and convergence of years past between the business elite and the political establishment. Nevertheless, the political crisis of 1982 pales next to the country's economic collapse. De la Madrid inherited a government devoid of hard currency, without reserves, and with public finances in a shambles and the country's foreign credit practically exhausted. If to all this we add a particularly unfavorable international context—soaring interest rates, recession in the United States, and the resumption of the Cold War following Ronald Reagan's election in 1980—we can understand that the new president wasn't exactly facing an easy situation. Under these conditions, it should come as no surprise that de la Madrid—at this stage of the game necessarily sensitized to the wiles and deceit that had facilitated his rise to the PRI candidacy—consciously or unconsciously avoided the harrowing dilemma that had confronted López Portillo, who ultimately resigned himself to choosing from among his prospective successors by elimination, despite considerable evidence that they were unlikely to fulfill his government's hopes and ambitions. De la Madrid allowed himself to be guided by the unwritten rule of alternating successions: after a succession by elimination, it was time for one by decision, with a small variation: all indications suggest that de la Madrid had two *in pectore* candidates and eliminated one of them less than halfway along the road to the nomination.

The new president, overwhelmed by the difficulties of getting his administration started, and without dedicating too much time and effort to the matter, placed his horses on the track in what he considered to be the two key areas: Finance, and Planning and Budget. A third contender, Manuel Bartlett, in the end won a measure of viability and headed the Ministry of the Interior for de la Madrid's entire term of office. However, Bartlett never had much chance of winning the candidacy, because, as he put it, he "was never truly a member of the 'family.'" The two real contenders were Jesús Silva Herzog and Carlos Salinas de Gortari. The former enjoyed undeniable advantages. He was born in 1934, the same year as de la Madrid; his career had paralleled the president's, except for the fact that he studied economics instead of law; and he was ideologically and politically correct since, in addition to being longtime friends and moving in the same social and family circles, Silva Herzog and de la Madrid shared identical points of view in matters of economics and finance, true to the orthodoxy of the Central Bank and the Ministry of Finance, where both got their start in public service. At first glance, the 1988 PRI candidacy belonged to Silva Herzog, unless it slipped through his fingers or was snatched away from him.

For five years, Carlos Salinas concentrated on two objectives: destroying Silva Herzog as an option and promoting himself as the only possible replacement. He did this with several aces in his hand, and with several reasons to believe that his aspirations were not overly ambitious. In the first place, since his days in the SPP and from 1979 on, Salinas had cultivated a closer, more trusting relationship with de la Madrid than had Silva Herzog. The young aide worked day and night. His contribution to de la Madrid's nomination was decisive, he played a central part in the campaign, and even in the selection of the president's cabinet. His loyalty to de la Madrid had been tested in the muddy trenches of the presidential succession, not at the elegant dinner parties and weddings of the financial and business families, or in de la Madrid's younger years at the Central Bank. Second, Salinas placed himself, or was placed, in the area closest to de la Madrid's heart: Planning and Budget, which the president had headed, and which Salinas used to weave a network of political alliances, support, debts, and commitments that the minister of finance, cut off from the spending side of economic policy, could never equal. Finally, although both Silva Herzog and Salinas put body and soul into constructing their respective candidacies, Salinas did so amidst the ruthlessness and latent violence of palace intrigue and bureaucratic infighting, and concentrated on building regional and political alliances, while Silva Herzog focused his efforts on the international arena, the media, and the business community. Salinas's strategy not only reflected de la Madrid's temperament, it satisfied an essential requisite of the process: that the candidate-in-the-making work in the shadows, and not compete with the sitting president for the weak and sporadic rays of sunlight that kept him alive.

Silva Herzog's strategy led him directly to the abyss. Salinas very quickly formed an initial alliance with Manuel Bartlett, before competing directly against Silva Herzog. He also approached Emilio Gamboa and Manuel Alonso in the Ministry of the Presidency, de la Madrid's chief staffers, and consolidated his long-standing friendship with Comptroller Francisco Rojas. Later he would acquire another valuable acquaintance in Central Bank Governor Miguel Mancera, an old and esteemed companion at arms of Miguel de la Madrid. Salinas's key ally, however, was presidential Chief of Staff Gamboa. As already stated, the president's chief of staff played a crucial role in this succession, as did his counterparts in the other cases we have examined.

In contrast, Silva Herzog opted to take a logical and accessible path, but one that placed him at an undeniable disadvantage: he tended to displace the man who, because of both his personal insecurities and institutional inertia, felt entitled to occupy center stage. Nothing does more to undermine one's chances for victory in this game than posing as *vicefactotum*, brain, star, or true source of a regime's success. Each international magazine cover featuring Silva Herzog represented a blow, mild at first, crippling in the end, to Miguel de la Madrid's ego. Each comment, from friend or foe, about the president's lack of charisma, or about the charismatic exuberance of his "second in command" further demolished Silva Herzog's chances. He now claims to have understood this, and laments that his efforts to correct the situation failed in part due to Salinas's countermeasures. Moreover, Salinas did not fail to attack this increasingly vulnerable flank that Silva Herzog had uncovered. According to Silva, when he was named "finance minister of the year" by the magazine *Euromoney*, "rumors began to circulate that I had bought the distinction. Many of these rumors came from the north end of the National Palace, that is, from the Ministry of Planning. Salinas's people encouraged these stories in the press."

The team at Planning and Budget dug Silva Herzog's grave, and the 1984 "finance minister of the year" was made a party to his own undoing. The tensions worsened as the time remaining for the succession inexorably ran out, and above all as the economic and financial situation worsened in 1986. As early as the preparation of the budget for fiscal 1984, normally negotiated between Finance and Planning in the fall of the previous year, the first skirmishes flared into open conflict, and the dispute was blamed mainly on Silva Herzog. Then, with the September 1985 earthquake, an initial fall in oil prices, and a drop in revenues caused by the economic slump, the numbers didn't balance out. Salinas pressed for increased domestic and above all foreign revenues and refused to cut the spending that he cleverly administered to further his political ends through various divisions of SPP, particularly the division headed by Manuel Camacho during the first half of de la Madrid's presidency. Salinas deliberately inflated spending in certain key areas, such as agriculture and the Mexico City government. Silva denounced his maneuvers, but his relations with de la Madrid suffered. In debates over fiscal 1985, Finance, according to its director, predicted that the economic program proposed by Planning was unsustainable. Inflation and the deficit would both increase during the midterm elections, which always set off an unbudgeted public spending spree.

Salinas, on the other hand, exposed Silva Herzog's fiscal inconsistencies, insisting that it was impossible to cut spending much more and denouncing Silva Herzog's reluctance to increase government revenues out of fear of the personal political consequences of raising taxes. SPP, in turn, claimed that Finance underestimated revenues, which in fact proved to be the case. De la Madrid sided with Salinas, although he ordered larger cuts in long-term spending. The drastic drop in the price of oil to eight dollars a barrel in early 1986 was the beginning of the end for Silva Herzog's candidacy. The resulting abrupt drop in tax revenues, and the dramatic repercussions in foreign accounts, made it necessary to overhaul public finances. The dispute between Silva Herzog and Salinas—between Finance and Planning, income and spending—worsened over the first half of the year, paralyzing a president obsessed with the need for unity in the economic cabinet, deeply irritated by Silva Herzog's growing public image, and seduced by the superficial diligence and seriousness shown by Salinas and his team. Silva Herzog's aides maintained that at the very best Mexico would be able to obtain three billion dollars in foreign aid to alleviate the damage caused by the fall in oil prices. The balance would have to come from additional internal cuts, a substantial reduction in foreign debt service, or a slightly higher fiscal deficit. Also, Finance claimed, foreign funds would flow only if Mexico took more drastic and convincing internal measures. By late spring, the team at Finance had reached a tentative agreement with the International Monetary Fund (IMF) in Washington that contemplated relatively generous amounts in "fresh funds," a more severe internal adjustment in spending, and a deficit amounting to 2.5 percent of Mexico's GNP. This agreement had already been approved in Mexico by SPP and the Central Bank, and was presented by Finance on the negotiating team's return to Mexico City in four strictly confidential yellow notebooks, one for each department involved and one for the president.

Salinas soon learned of the danger the agreement entailed and decided to break the internal consensus a posteriori. He denounced the agreement in economic cabinet meetings when de la Madrid was not present. In addition to his ally and privileged source in the National Palace, he had another "deep throat" in Silva Herzog's very office: Jaime Serra Puche, the minister's chief adviser who was loyal to José Córdoba. According to some of Córdoba's aides, Serra shared information with SPP and stopped speaking in meetings to avoid revealing his treachery. Silva Herzog does not deny the possibility of such leaks, nor does he go so far as to accuse his former aide. He does feel that by having underestimated the importance of the notes Serra prepared, he made it possible for him to transfer his loyalties to the other side of the National Palace.

The debates were soon reopened, now in a context of uncontrollable tension between Finance and Planning, and with a president growing increasingly exasperated with the conflict and with the person he held responsible: Silva Herzog. Salinas uttered his famous phrase—"We have cut spending right down to the bone. We can't cut any more"—and Silva Herzog increasingly took refuge in unilateral positions regarding the foreign debt, although never with the explicit intention of suspending payments. The financial demands grew and the crisis hit in June 1986. Salinas vanquished his opponent with two adroit maneuvers, the origins of which had everything to do with the succession and nothing to do with the crisis itself, and which were therefore devastating to Mexico.

First, Planning won the battle on the internal front in convincing de la Madrid that the accounts could be made to balance with no further adjustment by obtaining additional foreign funding and slightly increasing revenues. Salinas and his team—formed over months before with the arrival of Pedro Aspe and with José Córdoba consolidated in the Economic Policy Division—presented more consistent, and apparently better prepared, files. Moreover, they slanderously propagated an image of Silva Herzog and his aides as inexpert and careless, an effective but obviously untrue criticism. As we have seen, de la Madrid placed great emphasis on technical competence—without necessarily possessing it himself—and Salinas played on this weakness in a way for which the excellent technicians in Finance had no response.

Silva Herzog provides us with an example of the debate and the president's state of mind, in reference to the decision to make additional adjustments in allocations for six sectors of the government. Finance proposed cutting spending on the Ministry of Agriculture. The ministry in question and SPP opposed the move. The dispute was taken to the economic cabinet, where not only did the president rule against Finance, but he also granted Agriculture an increase in funding. As Silva Herzog evokes the scene, "The president turned to look at me and pointing at me said, 'I ask the minister of finance to find the money, and if he can't find it, to invent it.' Then I asked to speak and said, 'Mr. President, your orders will be obeyed, but I want it formally entered in the minutes that the minister of finance fully disagrees with the president's decision.' Miguel de la Madrid slapped his hand down on the table and said, 'The meeting is over.' " So was Silva Herzog's presidential campaign.

At the same time, Salinas was reinforcing his technical, ideological, and strategic alliance with two key individuals: Mancera, as we have seen, and Leopoldo Solís, a sort of chief of economic advisers to the president, who would uphold the macroeconomic thesis on which Salinas's victory was to rest. In fact, while Silva Herzog pressured for greater internal adjustment as a condition for obtaining the three billion dollars of necessary and reasonable foreign aid Mexico sought, Salinas insisted on the feasibility of convincing the markets and the international agencies in Washington of the uncommon magnitude of the adjustment already implemented, and persuading them that they should compensate and not demand further cuts. His team took the concept of the "operational deficit" as its battle cry to enlighten sources of funding on the subject of the Mexican budget. The concept was based on calculating the public deficit and federal spending, minus inflation and the exorbitant domestic interest rates encouraged by inflation, in turn generated by scarcity of funds. Salinas and his team sought to persuade United States authorities that, the inflationary component aside, the pruning of spending and reduction of the deficit already represented a tremendous effort that had to be recognized and rewarded. De la Madrid clung to this ingenious technical instrument fervently; the "operational deficit" made it possible to make square the circle and obtain generous foreign aid without cutting spending or raising taxes. The miraculous solution seduced the distressed president, and was even proven "correct" when, weeks after Silva Herzog resigned, Washington approved a nine-billion-dollar package for the year (from the IMF, the World Bank, the United States government, and private banks), demanding neither spending cuts nor tax increases in return.

The question of which came first, Silva Herzog's decision to resign or Miguel de la Madrid's decision to fire him, is relatively pointless. Relations between the two had deteriorated to the point where the situation was unbearable. As he remembers it, Silva Herzog had written his letter of resignation two weeks before leaving the cabinet, and carried it around in his jacket pocket. De la Madrid tends to confirm this version. Silva left, but had he stayed he would have remained in the race for the presidential candidacy. Emilio Gamboa objects that before he received Silva Herzog to request his resignation, the president had already contacted his successor at Finance, Gustavo Petriccioli, in the United States, where he was attending his daughter's graduation, in order to be able to announce his appointment immediately. The three reminiscences are no doubt accurate, and at the same time insufficient. The script had already been written.

Weeks after Silva was replaced with Petriccioli, a new Mexican negotiating mission, this time clearly handpicked by the SPP, achieved the impossible, obtaining copious fresh funding without cutting spending or making—formally at any rate—any further concession. With this backing, the government was able to weather the storm for slightly over a year, that is, until October 4, 1987, when the PRI nominated Salinas for the presidency. A month and a half later, the Mexican stock market crashed, ferocious capital flight ensued, and a major devaluation was precipitated, with the resulting inflationary spiral. In the eyes of Salinas's frustrated opponents, the government inflated the economy for a year to facilitate and guarantee Salinas's nomination. Alfredo del Mazo, a fourth contender and a stray finisher, goes even further, explaining how Petriccioli immediately backed Salinas, and how the two of them collaborated for more than a year in presenting Miguel de la Madrid with distorted figures. The president, despite Salinas's notorious propensity for failing to get even one of his predictions correct, took his advice. The cost: indispensable debt to stabilize the economy, devaluation at the end of the road, and a subsequent economic relapse in 1988. *In pectore* designation of the candidate, as we saw in the case of José López Portillo in 1975, has a high price.

Why did the Americans suddenly grant Mexico's requests, providing Mexico with vast sums in exchange for practically nothing? Three possible answers suggest themselves. The first, in general terms, corresponds to that which Carlos Salinas has offered: the situation was presented more consistently and coherently by the negotiating team, and therefore the solid arguments presented by the Mexican government were accepted. The second is a condensation of the theses offered by Miguel de la Madrid and Jesús Silva Herzog. There was no margin left for further austerity measures (De la Madrid), the Mexican government hardened its stance (De la Madrid), and the United States feared that failure to take a receptive attitude would oblige Mexico to take radical unilateral measures

(Silva Herzog). Silva Herzog's resignation frightened the Americans (Silva Herzog), three billion dollars in Mexican reserves were transferred from the Federal Reserve Bank in New York to Europe (Silva Herzog), Silva Herzog's resignation acted as a catalyst to break the stalemate. Top Federal Reserve officers consulted for this book confirm this explanation. They did in fact come to fear a Mexican moratorium on its debt service payments.

The third explanation, branded as improbable by all but one of the participants the author was able to question on the matter, is the following: A second-level but very well-informed participant claims that for several months before the financial crisis hit, emissaries from Carlos Salinas were holding parallel interviews and negotiations in Washington with the United States authorities. One can imagine the tenor of the conversations. "If you help us [SPP], by granting the government the support it needs and siding with us [Salinas's backers] in our debate with Silva Herzog, it's very likely that Salinas will be the next president of Mexico and a wide field will open up for bilateral understanding."

On the one hand, the story seems excessive. It implies a degree of Machiavellianism, calculation, and cynicism without parallel in the annals of the Mexican presidential succession. On the other hand, there are isolated facts that seem to support this outlandish version. Guillermo Ortiz, who was Córdoba's roommate at Stanford and who brought him to Mexico, was Mexico's representative before the IMF in Washington. Córdoba, already Salinas's alter ego, most trusted adviser, and covert operator, spent entire weeks in Washington in the spring and summer before the final negotiations, staying at Ortiz's residence there. On one occasion, SPP requested Silva Herzog's help to contact Federal Reserve Chairman Paul Volcker's "Invisible Man" Ed Yeo, who handled secret, dubious, and extraofficial missions for the Fed chairman. After the agreement was finalized with the international financial institutions in August, Córdoba would acknowledge that everything had come together through his informal contacts with Yeo. However, he never suggested there had been formal or informal prior secret meetings with Yeo or anyone else in the U.S. government. But doubt and suspicion persist, in view of the many unspeakable conspiracies, maneuvers, and strategies used to conquer power in Mexico. Whether or not there was a tacit or explicit secret agreement that explained Washington's astonishing willingness to disburse three times more money than before on the strength of a good "technical" argument is a question better left to the judgment of the reader and future research.

Miguel de la Madrid took an extremely close interest in the succession, and saw it through with the same meticulous deliberation—systematic if not always effective or imaginative—that characterized his administration. He knew that Jesús Silva Herzog would inevitably leave the cabinet months before his resignation, and prepared accordingly. In the spring he called his friend and *compadre* Alfredo del Mazo, already considered a presidential hopeful, with every intention of making his appointment more conspicuous and fully including him in the race for the succession. His reason: to avoid being left with only two cards, Salinas and Manuel Bartlett, who would be liable to destroy one another in a matter of minutes. To permit Salinas to reach the top, de la Madrid had to protect him. The best way to accomplish this was, as it always had been, to conceal him. The consequences of deceit were, as always, onerous and intricately tied to the feelings of betrayal and deception suffered by the manipulated losing candidates.

Alfredo del Mazo acknowledged several signs of presidential deference, many conceived with precisely this purpose in mind, and others tangled in the skein of misunderstandings and crossed signals inherent to the process. De la Madrid's first consideration was to not react negatively when del Mazo turned down an initial offer, the Ministry of Urban Development and Environmental Protection (SEDUE), just after the September 1985 earthquake. Del Mazo preferred to decline the offer, because the SEDUE wasn't part of the economic cabinet and was relatively unimportant compared with the government of the state of Mexico. Months later, when Francisco Labastida was nominated for governor of Sinaloa, de la Madrid again offered del Mazo a job, this time in the Ministry of Energy, Mines and State Industry (SEMIP), which *el compadre* accepted.

Del Mazo believes today that he lost for several reasons, with emphasis on factors related to this very promising beginning. His other arguments are inverted reflections of the reasons for Salinas's victory. Del Mazo, in his own opinion, would have been a more independent successor than Salinas, with a personal approach and independent strength. The choice of a successor, in this case, would not have been a question of de la Madrid's preference alone. In contrast, the choice of Salinas rested solely on the president's decision. Salinas owed everything he had to his mentor. The more rumors of del Mazo's supposed destiny and expectation grew among his allies, especially the least discreet, the more de la Madrid's tacit objection to the possibility grew. The president might have said, "Alfredo thinks he's got it made. He thinks he doesn't need me anymore." From this perspective, there were two further reasons behind de la Madrid's preference for Salinas. Several former cabinet members have suggested that Salinas read de la Madrid's thoughts, on his own and through Emilio Gamboa. Salinas learned what his boss's ideas or preferences were and presented them as his own, certain that they would be well received.

And the reverse was also true. The possible difficulties with Salinas, his loyalty to his family, and his ties to certain political and business sectors were never evaluated by the president, as he himself acknowledges in his interview, in part because no one fully informed him of these shortcomings.

Finally, after Cuauhtémoc Cárdenas and Porfirio Muñoz Ledo split with the PRI at the party assembly in March 1987, intransigence with dissidents became fundamental to de la Madrid. According to del Mazo, "Miguel thought I would build bridges with Cárdenas and Muñoz Ledo, while Salinas would not, and this may have influenced his thinking." De la Madrid's role in the polarization of Mexican politics from 1987 on may have been underestimated. His animosity toward the dissidents not only influenced the succession but, as we will see further on, helped to complicate or prevent negotiation with the opposition after July 6, 1988. De la Madrid came to strongly distrust the dissident PRI members, concluding very early on that there was no chance of reaching any agreement with them, and this in turn generated similar or greater suspicion toward those who favored the idea of negotiating with the renegades.

Alfredo del Mazo does not fully admit it, but if our analysis of the 1988 succession is correct, the conclusion is evident: The former governor of the state of Mexico was used by de la Madrid. For his part, del Mazo remains convinced of de la Madrid's good intentions to promote change and maintains that he didn't make up his mind until the end. He simply thinks de la Madrid made a bad choice. There was also the possibility, however remote, that Salinas would make a fatal mistake, even under de la Madrid's guidance, with consequences from which even the president would be unable to protect him. In this case, the decision between del Mazo and Bartlett could favor del Mazo. However, in the absence of an accident or error by Salinas, del Mazo's inclusion in the cabinet was more an expression of desire to cover his intentions than an authentic broadening of the field, even though del Mazo claims that Miguel de la Madrid "played fair." In his way, del Mazo understood the situation, or so his reaction, typical of disillusioned losers in successions by choice who learn late in the game of their disqualification, suggests. This does not mean that he blames or critically judges de la Madrid. One of the most frightening features of the Mexican system is the imperative, common for the great elector, of deceiving the prospective candidates, who must include even his closest friends. If in this case the president does not deceive his *compadre*, he is left with only two cards; either because he does not encourage del Mazo's candidacy or because he tells his friend in advance that it is not for real, in which case del Mazo would have probably opted out of it.

. . .

The succession mechanism inevitably involves cruelty, which is indispensable for it to function effectively—it only works if everyone believes, and no one grasps the nature of the situation until it's too late.

The other necessary object of deceit was Manuel Bartlett. More cynical, hardened, and calculating than del Mazo, the minister of the interior did not enjoy de la Madrid's friendship to the point of feeling offended at having lost. He may have felt angry and resentful, but on the surface his reaction was more political than emotional. A visceral, heartfelt outburst may have been preferable. The other—conscious or not—ultimately had devastating effects on Salinas's campaign. With greater insight than del Mazo, Bartlett warned that if Salinas were not ambushed, the race would be lost before it was run, and as a result Bartlett proved himself more willing to use negative campaign tactics against Salinas. Although, according to most of the main players involved, Bartlett and Salinas had negotiated a virtual nonaggression agreement to avoid harming one another or creating conflicts in the cabinet, the tension between them would take on an increasingly virulent tone, in part due to the maneuvers—or intrigues—of their respective allies or aides.

For Bartlett, the trend favoring Salinas was evident from the outset, and especially after Silva Herzog's ouster. Salinas's palace allies—Chief of Staff Emilio Gamboa, spokesman Manuel Alonso, and presidential guard Commander General Bermúdez—as well as countless appointments throughout the government, illustrated Salinas's growing importance vis-à-vis de la Madrid. The nomination of Fernando Gutiérrez Barrios for governor of Veracruz, and even the arrival of Jorge de la Vega Domínguez as PRI president in October 1986, can be interpreted in this context. De la Vega was an old friend of professor Carlos Hank González, in turn a longtime colleague of *don* Raúl Salinas Lozano, and more recently his boss when Carlos Salinas's father was working in the Mexican Foreign Trade Institute. Hank's ties—family, social, and business-related—to Monterrey businessman Roberto González are public knowledge, as are the links between González and the Salinas family.

However institutional de la Vega's participation in the cabinet may have been, Bartlett felt that his political history provided cause to question his impartiality. Bartlett only remembers doubting Salinas's decisive victory when Miguel de la Madrid suddenly changed the proceedings with the *pasarela*, or public appearance, of six "outstanding PRI members"—including Bartlett, del Mazo, and Salinas, as well as others—before the PRI National Executive Committee during August 17–27, 1987. It has proven difficult to determine the veracity of Bartlett's claim. On the one hand, his arguments are categorical and transparent. On the other, Mexican politicians tend to look forward, not sideways, in spite of the fact that the attacks they usually receive are oblique and indirect, never frontal and direct. According to del Mazo, Bartlett was out of Miguel de la Madrid's thoughts, but not out of the political clique in power. On the other hand, in Jorge de la Vega's appraisal of the situation, while it may be true that the minister of the interior lost the support of his natural backers—the governors—because he treated them contemptuously, as one of his fellow cabinet members claims, he won the support of the majority of the senators and deputies. All this could not fail to affect Bartlett's morale, and lead him to read the signs in his favor avidly and, naturally, to scorn his detractors. He must have been resigned to defeat until the moment when, apparently, the contest was reopened, with the idea—gradualist, moderately bold, but still discrepant with the unwritten rules of the system—of the formal, public presentation of the prospective nominees. The two real losing candidates—the others, for various reasons, were filler—coincide in their appraisal of the implications of such an exercise. Both del Mazo and Bartlett agree that de la Madrid would not have risked such open comparison if the balance had already definitively tilted in favor of Salinas.

Resentment inevitably overcame the losers. In del Mazo's case, it would manifest itself in erratic behavior on the day of the nomination, and in visible loss of enthusiasm afterward. In Bartlett's case, the symptoms were loss of enthusiasm, followed by a thirst for revenge—conscious or not—manifested mainly in an understandable passivity in his job at the Ministry of the Interior. This was simply part of the price Miguel de la Madrid, and the entire nation, paid for failing to adhere to the system's unwritten rules. Carlos Salinas was no doubt a talented prospect with a wealth of plans and ambitions, but he provoked too much complication, hostility, and frank rejection for his imposition as candidate to proceed without cost.

There are points of divergence and consensus regarding the origin of the cost in question. However, almost everyone interviewed and involved agrees concerning the biased management of the economy in the period leading up to the unveiling. According to Alfredo del Mazo, the members of the economic cabinet, the ministers of finance and planning, gave de la Madrid distorted figures. Salinas's team artificially inflated the exchange rate, the Mexican stock exchange index, and economic forecasts to promote the candidacy of the "economic czar." If we examine the minutes of the economic cabinet meetings (quoted again in José Ramón López Portillo's dissertation), the estimated inflation of 70 percent to 80 percent for 1987 turned out to be absurdly optimistic. The consumer price increase for 1987 reached 159 percent. In the categorical conclusion presented by José Ramón López Portillo (who worked closely with

Salinas from 1979 to 1982, later distanced himself from him, eventually to re-construct an amicable and respectful relationship in England in the late 1990s), "Once de la Madrid decided to designate Salinas—just before the Program for Economic Development and Growth (PEG) collapsed in late 1987—he took decisive action to give Salinas and his group a third chance to achieve the economic recovery that had eluded them thus far. It is hard to imagine how de la Madrid could have chosen Salinas after the PEG debacle. The first failure of Salinas's economic program came in 1984–1985 and the second in 1986, after his victory over Silva Herzog."

Miguel de la Madrid broke too many rules in choosing Carlos Salinas to succeed him. As José López Portillo commented to a friend—his sagacity not clouded in this case by discontent—"the president has always been the tongue of the balance. De la Madrid wanted to be the whole balance." He ignored the age rule invoked earlier by Mario Moya. He was supposed to choose a contem-porary, not skip a generation. He failed to heed the dissident murmuring of Porfirio and Cuauhtémoc, organized labor, and the former presidents. He un-derestimated the economic cost of artificially prolonging a favorable state of affairs, without which the nomination of his favorite would have overstepped the bounds of the feasible. Also, he failed to verify, or preferred to ignore, the shouts and whispers of alarm—many, it is true, tenuous, latent, or elliptical—about the Salinas clan and its concentric rings, already a topic of conversation in political circles.

On the day of the announcement, October 4, 1987, with the PRI leadership assembled at Los Pinos, PRI President de la Vega summarized the main political events in the process of selecting the candidate from the day it had begun to its culmination, and transmitted the party's resolution, asking President de la Madrid to offer his opinion and guidance. De la Madrid immediately put forth his analysis of the personality, abilities, and merits of the prospective candidates, in particular the three finalists, describing the international situation and Mex-ico's political, economic, and social circumstances. He concluded that if they wanted his opinion, the ideal candidate for the PRI was Carlos Salinas. Shortly thereafter, on arrival at his office at PRI headquarters, de la Vega contacted the six prospective candidates to inform them and start the traditional farce of the unveiling.

That morning, Salinas had contacted Manuel Bartlett to inform him of his victory and to ask Bartlett to stay on at the Ministry of the Interior. He ap-parently did so for two reasons: the convenience of keeping a true expert on the subject of elections at his post to organize the elections in July, and because Miguel de la Madrid probably made his interest in seeing Bartlett well looked after and protected known to Salinas. Salinas also sought to reinforce his existing pact with the man who would serve as his minister of public education for another reason. On the same Sunday, October 4, Salinas asked de la Madrid (in vain) to replace Jorge de la Vega with Manuel Camacho as PRI president. He could not ask for two changes of this magnitude at the same time, as the president's refusal to accept the change of command Salinas requested in the PRI shows. Salinas's problems began at this point, in part exacerbated by de la Madrid's obstinacy in retaining de la Vega, in part because of Bartlett's keeping his job, and in part due to the way the candidate created a virtual parallel party within the PRI, without the expertise and experience needed to run a campaign under increasingly adverse circumstances.

The first blow to Salinas's incipient campaign fell on October 14, when the Partido Auténtico de la Revolución Mexicana (PARM), an old state-run political party created in the 1950s, nominated Cuauhtémoc Cárdenas as its presidential candidate. For the first time since 1952, a significant split had occurred in the official party. The responsibility of "handling" the minority parties usually fell upon the minister of the interior. Moreover, as a result of recent changes in electoral law, Manuel Bartlett had developed a stronger relationship with, and control of, the small parties such as the Popular Socialist Party (PPS) and the Frente Cardenista National Reconstruction Party (PFCRN) than his predecessors had. That is why Cárdenas's nomination raised so many questions. How was it possible for a minister of the interior as meticulous and solid as Manuel Bartlett to tolerate such a slipup?

Jorge de la Vega and even Manuel Camacho insist that it was impossible to derail Cárdenas's strategy. Salinas's team unsuccessfully attempted to prevent the Cárdenas nomination by supporting an internal opposition to Cárdenas within the PARM. In Bartlett's opinion, the responsibility of handling political affairs was transferred from Interior to the PRI. It was de la Vega's responsibility to coordinate the support for the PRI presidential candidate, not the minister of the interior's. "I no longer had control; they had it," says Bartlett.

The explanation may lie in the combination of loyalty and inertia, both in a context of indolence. Nobody anticipated the enormous support Cárdenas would muster among the Mexican population. It is true that Cuauhtémoc and Porfirio Muñoz Ledo had acted astutely since before Salinas was nominated, and continued to do so thereafter. Regardless of whether their break with the party would have produced a different outcome in the PRI race, the choice of Salinas confirmed their decision and created a more favorable climate for the split. There has been a great deal of speculation about whether Cárdenas and Muñoz Ledo would have behaved as they did if, for example, Manuel Bartlett had been nominated by the PRI. But in the final analysis, the question is moot if we trust our scheme. Salinas had won well in advance of his official nomination, thanks to his commitment to the model, and his vehement anti-Cárdenism and populism. In any event, by the time Salinas and Camacho got wind of the imminent split, it may well have been too late to prevent it. To stop Cárdenas would have required an alert minister of the interior, disciplined, strong, and willing to cover every possible angle for his boss and the state and within his own field of action, tasks Bartlett had carried out for five years. His undeniable professionalism was powerless to counteract his discouragement and society's perception of his failure.

We thus return to the issue raised at the outset. It is inevitable that a defeated and deceived rival will feel bitter, even when his feelings are buried in the depths of his subconscious. Keeping the losers in the succession within the cabinet has its risks. However, removing the victims weakens the outgoing president earlier and more than is desirable. The solution lies, perhaps, in requesting the resignation of the "cardinals" well before the competition begins. Lázaro Cárdenas did it in 1940, and Echeverría considered it early in his term without becoming convinced of its merit. The fact that Jorge de la Vega and Manuel Bartlett were allowed to keep their jobs marked the entire 1988 succession, despite the gradual improvement in relations between Salinas and Bartlett. By rejecting Salinas's request to appoint Manuel Camacho as PRI president, de la Madrid condemned his candidate to conduct his campaign either with an external team or with a parallel team at odds with the party. He chose the first of the two options, and during the following months, the PRI's campaign and election experts were excluded from decisions, fund-raising, organizing events, and rallies, and from the process of preparing the election. As Jorge de la Vega puts it, "It was no longer a traditional PRI campaign with the party's customary efficiency, it was the campaign of a new candidate seeking the presidency with a new strategy that I didn't share, implanted by Salinas and his team, less PRI and more candidate." Relations between Bartlett and Salinas improved notably toward the end of the campaign. This was not the case, however, between Salinas and de la Vega. The PRI president asked to be relieved of his duties on several occasions, but Miguel de la Madrid insisted on keeping him to the end.

When Manuel Camacho turned down the consolation prize of being appointed PRI general secretary, he also passed up the opportunity of assuming a central role on Salinas's campaign team. Gradually, José Córdoba and Patricio Chirinos displaced Camacho in decisions. Campaign manager Luis Donaldo Colosio assumed operative responsibility. With the support of a close, loyal, and dedicated minister of the interior, or with less formidable rivals than Cárdenas and Manuel Clouthier, or safe from the new economic catastrophe that battered Mexico in late November 1987, the inexperience and lack of support from the party hard-liners that handicapped Salinas and his team would have been less important. In the context of these further calamities for Salinas, the results were devastating.

The key, no doubt, lies in the true nature of the electoral process in Mexico until 1997, and in any event during the 1970s and 1980s. Elections were not just held, they were organized. The state guaranteed the victory of the official party through the Ministry of the Interior, the National Voters' Registry, and, to a lesser degree, the governors. The official voter registration list, in particular, served this purpose. In it were entered, actively or by failure to purge them, hundreds of thousands or more "dead voters." They were "false guests" at real addresses, in the operators' slang, and were used to deliver voter registration cards to PRI district delegates and candidates. Thanks to these voting cards, the "floating brigades" of faithful party members who voted five or six times each, and the use of certain codes—as of 1982 "little dots" in the voter registration lists used to identify the "dead voters"—the PRI guaranteed the necessary votes to reach the desired totals. These totals were based on the opposition's presence in a "dangerous" district or on using various calculations, such as the number of votes for the previous presidential candidate. Each district representative or delegate appeared before the authorities at the Ministry of the Interior to negotiate their respective "contributions"—i.e., how many votes they had and how many they wanted. The state delivered the corresponding voting cards, in an amount calculated from a vast compilation of political, social, and demographic data for each district, including perfect knowledge of the district's PRI membership. The governors also had their part to play. They coordinated, proposed, and organized, but always with prompting from the center, without which chaos would reign. The authorities—the minister of the interior, the director of the National Voters' Registry, the director of political and social investigation at the Ministry of the Interior—negotiated the election district by district, candidate by candidate, and delegate by delegate. Nothing was left to chance. Attention to detail was deservedly legendary. This and other factors enabled the PRI to win all elections in which it participated by large and acceptable margins.

But someone had to do the job, and in 1988 no one did. Therein lies one of the crucial elements of the debacle that unfolded on July 6, 1988, the day of the most hotly contested and questionable election in Mexico since 1940. Needless to say, without bold, consistent opponents with a strong appeal to the social imagination of the Mexican population, nothing would have occurred. But with only the appeal of Cuauhtémoc Cárdenas, it is possible that nothing would have happened either. A vacuum was created when Manuel Bartlett lost the race for the candidacy and remained in his post; Jorge de la Vega was not replaced, failed to win Salinas's full confidence, and proved unwilling to go the extra mile for someone whose first act as candidate had been to ask for his head; and Manuel Camacho, lacking the necessary experience, failed to impose his will as Salinas's campaign manager. Bartlett, resigned and understandably irritated, must have concluded, "Let them see what they can do to get their own damn votes!" De la Vega, who was no specialist in elections, did not exactly put his all into the campaign. And the members of Salinas's circle such as Chirinos, Colosio, Córdoba, and Granados limited themselves to pursuing upper-level accords, without solidifying the deals on which the election would depend below. Under these circumstances, it was little wonder that the votes disappeared, that the traditional *ex ante* electoral fraud proved insufficient, and that Salinas and his group got the surprise of their lives when it came time to tally votes at the polls.

Much has been written about the events leading up to and after July 6, 1988. The events of those days—from the computer system crashing to the mass demonstrations of support for Cárdenas in the Mexico City Zócalo—have been repeated elsewhere. It would be pointless here to go over the entire chain of events. We will limit ourselves to examining elements directly related to the presidential succession, or that warrant further scrutiny. In the chapters that discuss the presidential successions prior to 1988, the space dedicated to the election day is nil for an obvious reason. Power was not won at the polls, but through the secret dealings described in these pages. As of 1988, not necessarily because the system willed or planned it so, but because of the strength of Mexican society, power began to be contested at the ballot box. According to José Newman, director of the National Voters' Registry, and operator of the official electoral apparatus until shortly before the 1988 elections, the problems began with a sudden, unthinking, and partly inexplicable change of opinion by Manuel Bartlett. For weeks, the ex officio chairman of the Federal Electoral Commission (CFE) had refused to accept one of the opposition's main demands. At issue was the public delivery of preliminary, partial early election results, as soon as the polls closed on July 6, and as data was received at the Ministry of the Interior. While the opposition's formal request referred to the creation of a custom-made system for delivering data, the petition was really focused on demanding transparency in what already existed, specifically the National Political-Electoral System (SNIPE), an immense machine designed by Oscar de Lasse, the minister of the interior's chief adviser. The opposition had already got wind of its installation in the basement of the Ministry of the Interior building, thanks to numerous indiscreet contracts into which de Lasse had entered in order to organize it. Bartlett, however, resisted giving in to the opposition demands for several reasons. First he was under no legal obligation to do so. It was not easy to gather data rapidly, and, as the opposition well knew, the interval between the time votes were deposited in the ballot boxes and the official announcement of the results offered ample opportunity for manipulation.

Suddenly, in the last CFE session before the elections, Bartlett changed his mind and finally gave in. He announced that results would be made available as early as possible on the evening of the elections, although still unofficial and with no guarantee that there would be a flow of abundant and reliable figures. He immediately passed the ball to Newman, instructing him to meet with the political parties on the following day to explain the workings of a supposed additional computer system to be installed at the Voters' Registry offices, where terminals would be provided for each party, giving them direct access to the results as they were received. Newman knew that there was no such system. The terminals would be limited to reproducing the numbers received by the Ministry of the Interior's central computer, the UNYSIS machine at its headquarters on Avenida Bucareli. There was never any other at the Ministry of the Interior, at PRI headquarters, at the National Archive, or anywhere else.

At the end of the meeting, Newman asked Bartlett and Deputy Minister of the Interior and CFE Technical Secretary Fernando Elias Calles, "What am I supposed to explain about a system I haven't got? What should I say?" Bartlett called de Lasse, ordered him and Newman to reach an agreement on the matter, and departed. In the presence of Calles, de Lasse explained the real mechanism to Newman. "We're going to put a monitor for each party at Insurgentes Sur [the Voters' Registry]. I'm going to send them the most convenient information I get at the SNIPE. The rest stays here." Newman warned, "You'll have a problem on your hands if it doesn't work. Either they'll turn on the machine and there will be no data, or compromising information will get out. What am I supposed to tell them if they ask me to show them the data compilation center on Insurgentes?" De Lasse retorted, "Tell them you can't for reasons of security and time." Newman again explained the various complications to Calles and then to Bartlett, but de Lasse convinced his superiors to remain unconcerned. In response to Newman's skepticism regarding so much presumed ease and precision, de Lasse calmed them with assurances that everything would turn out well. The old-style magnetic telephone system connected to the different district seats to send information would work perfectly. The Ministry of the

Interior's computers would record the data with no problems and it would be retransmitted to the political parties in politically predigested doses.

In the course of the week, Newman described the workings of the system to the parties and the press. He was hounded with questions. He equivocated and gave evasive answers, and, when he had no other alternative, he lied. At what time would the information be available? Where were the tabulation center and the computers? He faced the public and propagated the myth that information would be released as it was received in the course of the evening after the polls closed. However, he understood perfectly well that a risk had been created when Bartlett had agreed to deliver results and confirmed the existence of a computer center for compiling preliminary figures. Either the data would fail to flow adequately, in which case the opposition would begin to suspect and then protest, or the results collected by the Ministry of the Interior would come in skewed—arriving first from the most urbanized states and those closest to Mexico City, that is, those favorable to the opposition—generating all kinds of distortion, conflict, and misunderstanding. Precisely to prevent the problem of a biased data flow, which could result in an apparent Cárdenas win based on returns in urban areas, de Lasse thought the software should include a safeguard to bifurcate the flow. The "good" precincts or districts—where the PRI candidate was in the lead—would be transferred to the file accessible to the parties. The "bad" precincts or districts—where the PRI was losing—would remain in the file accessible only at the Ministry of the Interior, until the totals leveled off as a result of the eventual arrival of additional data from "good" sources. According to Manuel Camacho: "As the information for Mexico City came in, entirely favorable to the FDN and negative to the PRI, the government decided to administer the information it released to prevent these first unfavorable reports from Mexico City from creating a snowball effect."

Newman assumes today that Bartlett acted in good faith in agreeing to provide election results in advance with no legal obligation to do so, and with deficient technical capacity for the purpose. He recalls that Bartlett believed almost blindly in de Lasse's promises. Although Newman attempted to conceal results that were damaging to the PRI, he tried not to make them disappear, but only to "keep them under his hat" and/or disguise them until they were compensated for by more favorable data. Newman also refrains from accusing Bartlett of having assumed the commitment to advance numbers knowing that the decision would cause endless problems for the PRI and its candidate Salinas, but he cannot avoid a murmur of suspicion. He still fails to fully understand why the minister of the interior and Federal Electoral Commission chairman changed his mind.

When asked directly, Bartlett replied, "I didn't change my position. That's not true. I wasn't obliged to grant their request. I did them a favor because they asked me to. The information was public property from the first instant at the polling station to the final moment in the district committee. The information was available to the parties in accordance with the law. Therefore, the favor was to give them the totals computed by the Ministry of the Interior and make them participants in an arithmetical exercise as the data came in, and in the understanding that the information was unofficial." In fact, Bartlett gave in to the pressure from the opposition as part of the give and take of negotiation, and also, perhaps, because he never imagined that the procedure in question would cause unmanageable difficulties. He trusted that it would work and never expected such favorable results for Cárdenas and Clouthier. Finally, he may have unconsciously been not entirely adverse to the idea of limiting Salinas's margin for manipulation, not for ethical reasons or fondness for the opposition, but to prevent the PRI from surpassing the results obtained in the 1982 elections, which he had directed.

The rest of the story is more or less well known. At around 5:00 PM the first "good" results, from a few dozen Hidalgo state precincts, began appearing on the parties' monitors. Unfortunately, according to Newman's to-date unpublished narrative, a PAN technician trying to open the more complete "closed" file entered a password he had detected that very morning during a demonstration of the system in the terminal room. Suddenly the screen flickered, and results from the "bad" precincts in Hidalgo appeared. The PAN technician printed the list and attempted to get further information. One of the PRI representatives removed him almost forcibly from his terminal, contacted de Lasse at the Ministry of the Interior, and seven minutes later the system "crashed." The screens went blank. Party representatives at Insurgentes Sur got in touch with their colleagues at the Ministry of the Interior and told them what had happened. Immediately, at 7:50 PM, protests begin in the CFE plenary session. Bartlett ordered Newman to leave the room, find out from de Lasse what was going on, and above all not return to the table. De Lasse, true to his style, informed Calles and Newman, "All hell's broken loose here now. But don't worry, we'll take care of it right away." He was not entirely able to fulfill his promise. The protest in the CFE grew, and the three opposition candidates— Cárdenas, Manuel Clouthier, and Rosario Ibarra de Piedra—set out for the Ministry of the Interior. Bartlett suspended the CFE session, went to his office, and, furious, interrogated Oscar de Lasse, Newman, and, Calles. "What happened? What numbers are there?" De Lasse, the only one with any real figures, confessed. "I have plenty of numbers. They suck." He referred to the 1,100 precincts that would be delivered hours later to the opposition, when there was no other alternative. Bartlett ordered that a clarification statement be prepared for Newman to deliver. Newman replied, "I don't know how to explain. Let Oscar [de Lasse] explain." Bartlett left them. At this point Bartlett contacted the president at Los Pinos and informed him of the situation, as Miguel de la Madrid describes in his interview. Bartlett described the poor results reported and proposed, according to de la Madrid, delaying the release of further data until the figures "evened out," that is, until the numbers came in from the "strong" PRI states of Veracruz, Oaxaca, Chiapas, Campeche, and so on. De la Madrid authorized the measure and Bartlett returned to the Juárez room where he reported that a "technical deficiency" (saturation of telephone lines) had arisen. He assured the members of the CFE that Calles and de Lasse would soon offer a detailed explanation and a tour of the data tabulation facilities at the Ministry of the Interior. Meanwhile at PRI headquarters, Jorge de la Vega Domínguez delivered a speech about Carlos Salinas's "clear and decisive" victory. Thereafter, the debate in the CFE focused on the inevitable refutation of the proclamation of PRI victory issued by the authorities.

Bartlett's motives are evident. In a climate of distrust and accusations, and in light of the plethora of electoral anomalies observed during the day, the fact that the first numbers came from the capital city and surrounding areas—the states of Mexico, Morelos, Michoacán, etc.—and therefore pointed toward victory for Cárdenas, could turn the tide irreversibly in favor of the opposition candidate. Disclosure of this information, once combined with the results from the strong PRI areas, would encourage a generalized impression that fraud had been committed—manipulated or not. The dilemma Bartlett faced was whether to allow the information to be released as it came in, conscious that this would further the perception of a victory for Cárdenas before the deadline for the domestic and foreign newspapers, or to interrupt the flow, wait for favorable numbers for the PRI to come in, and only announce a partial result that was close or favorable to his party. He chose the second option, without weighing all its consequences. The interim had seen an inopportune visit of the three opposition candidates to the Ministry of the Interior and a protest by them. It was the beginning of the end of the world for Carlos Salinas. The longest night in the history of the PRI, and probably in the life of its candidate, had begun.

As an experienced participant of the day, with scant affection for Bartlett, recalls, "Bartlett opted to hold the information, because if the trends persisted, the PRI would lose. And it saved the election. Things improved, by natural or unnatural means." Carlos Salinas persists in reproaching his former rival, more or less tacitly, for having handled the events of the night of July 6 ineptly, if not in his basic approach, at least in his style. For Bartlett, however, the rumor whereby he deliberately marred the election as vengeance or reprisal against Salinas was invented and spread by Manuel Camacho.

In any event, Bartlett took the fall, and perhaps deservedly so. In the words of José Newman, a psychologist and close colleague of Bartlett's for many years and, in spite of the conventional wisdom, largely a distant spectator to the post-election fixing of results, "If Manuel had been the [PRI] candidate, he would have been as obsessive about the details of the election as he was in the elections he directed" (e.g., in 1985 when he was minister of the interior, or 1982, as PRI general secretary and Miguel de la Madrid's campaign manager). We come back to unconscious betrayal. A losing prospect filled with bitterness is unlikely to be the best standard-bearer for his erstwhile competitor. Human nature imposes itself. Even then, Salinas has a far from insignificant debt of gratitude to Bartlett. Granted, were it not for Bartlett's error of promising results on an ongoing basis, part of the July 6 fiasco would have been avoided and the electoral fraud, regardless of its magnitude, would have passed, if not unnoticed, at least removed from the spotlight. But without Bartlett's bold move to interrupt the flow of information, however, political events would probably have overwhelmed the government.

At the same time a tense scene was being played out at PRI headquarters that night. The Plutarco Elías Calles auditorium had been packed since the early evening. Fourteen hundred devotees, labor leader Fidel Velázquez among them, awaited the proclamation of the official candidate's victory and his victory speech. But upstairs, in Salinas's offices, the mood was not one for celebration or proclamations. There were two electoral information systems at PRI headquarters, according to Jorge de la Vega. One was the traditional party system in which each state committee chairman reported the results received from the polls. The information was entered on large sheets of paper by district and by state. The other, according to de la Vega and Manuel Camacho, was in a small room next to Salinas's offices where the candidate had assembled a parallel system, operated by José Córdoba and Patricio Chirinos, that never worked with the desired efficiency. From 4:00 PM on, the official PRI apparatus had gathered information that painted a discouraging picture. At 9:00 PM de la Vega knew that the PRI had lost Mexico City and the states of Mexico, Michoacán, Morelos, and perhaps Guerrero and Baja California Norte. Notwithstanding, according to de la Vega, there were also data guaranteeing a nationwide victory for Carlos Salinas.

At this point, the PRI president made the first of several unsuccessful attempts to convince Salinas to go downstairs to the auditorium to deliver his victory speech. Salinas remained holed up in a small, dark office on one of the PRI building's top stories. In a beam of dim light, Salinas leaned on his desk, jacket and tie off, disconsolate. At 10:00 PM, de la Vega contacted President de la Madrid, who already knew that Bartlett would release no further figures until after midnight, and asked whether the PRI had sufficient grounds to proclaim victory. According to his interview, when de la Vega warned him that "if we don't go out and announce our victory, it's going to make us look bad," de la Madrid ordered him to go ahead and do it. De la Vega has confirmed his constant contact with de la Madrid, and that all his decisions were discussed with the president.

On the five or six occasions when de la Vega entered Salinas's office, he found him in the company of Camacho, Córdoba, Chirinos, and Granados. They went in and out of adjacent offices. All but Córdoba and, in particular, Camacho were opposed to a unilateral declaration of victory. Salinas's response to de la Vega's persistent urging was always the same. He would accept no such invitation if the minister of the interior did not first announce his victory, in his capacity as chairman of the Federal Electoral Commission. He failed to realize that such an official recognition was simply impossible at that point. At 1:00 AM, de la Vega went upstairs again to exhort Salinas to go down to the auditorium. The PRI candidate persisted in his refusal. De la Vega then informed him that, with or without his presence or consent, he was going to fulfill his responsibility as party president and declare the PRI's victory. It was not yet daybreak when de la Vega slammed the door of the gloomy office, delivered his speech, and departed. Countless disconcerted party members had already abandoned the auditorium. According to de la Vega, this situation would provide Salinas's political enemies with grounds to consider his government illegitimate. During the night, the candidate reconsidered. In the morning he contacted the party president, admitted that de la Vega had been right and informed him of his intention to give a speech on the "end of the era of the virtually single party [system.]" He did so, however, without the presence of various important party leaders, whom it was impossible to assemble.

Why did Salinas turn a deaf ear to the repeated pleas of his political organization? He no doubt preferred to wait for the CFE to legitimate the process as a whole, but he may also have been influenced by a desire not to owe his victory to the PRI, especially in the absence of institutional endorsement. Camacho corroborates his opposition to any show of triumphalism. He thought any such premature action would lead to harsh questioning later on and complicate or prevent subsequent negotiation with the opposition. He maintains, however, that he did not have all the data. "Salinas didn't share the results with me. He left the room and went into another with Córdoba where the numbers were. I had some numbers, but the governors were calling to inform us that the numbers weren't what we had expected." Camacho's opposition to declaring victory immediately, as de la Vega suggests, was accompanied by a recommendation for Salinas to prepare a speech acknowledging what had occurred, in order to preserve credibility in the future. Salinas made sure to do just that the next day, with his speech to a PRI audience dazed by the pummeling it had taken at the polls.

After this speech, the Salinas team, so far comprised of a compact and close-knit group of peers—Camacho, Córdoba, Chirinos, Colosio, and Granados—split in two. One faction, headed by Córdoba and Chirinos, allied with the PRI machine, and a large part of the government, including Manuel Bartlett, planned to guarantee a result of 50 percent or more of the vote, to avoid negotiating with the left-wing opposition and Cárdenas and facilitate the subsequent work of the government. The other faction, headed by an isolated Manuel Camacho, was in favor of dialogue with Cárdenas, Clouthier, and Rosario Ibarra, to examine the electoral information and thereby determine the real results. Thus, according to Camacho, "even if the figures were lower (for example, 42 percent instead of 50 percent), their acceptance by the opposition parties would legitimate the election and open the possibility of reaching a political pact between all the parties, similar to the Moncloa agreement in Spain." Camacho even presented this proposal to de la Madrid, but the president also showed little disposition to negotiate. He thought, according to Camacho, that it would be impossible to reach any agreement with Cárdenas and Muñoz Ledo: "He didn't trust them." However, the two factions had one thing in common: their certainty that Salinas had won, and their refusal to surrender power that, in their opinion, was rightfully theirs.

At the same time as he encouraged efforts to "straighten out" the election and negotiate his rise to power with the real sources of power—the business community, the Catholic Church, the PAN, the United States, and part of the old political establishment—Salinas accepted Camacho's July 12 suggestion to meet with Cárdenas. The idea of clarifying the figures emerged in this meeting. Salinas accepted in principle, but Cárdenas insisted that it was imperative to annul the elections. In his unpublished memoirs, Camacho, at the time minister of urban development and environmental protection, describes this meeting: "I proposed that within the law, and in a spirit of absolute professionalism and good faith, a technical team of trustworthy people from the different parties review the election results." According to Camacho, he never claimed that the elections had been completely clean, as Salinas maintains in his interview.

Neither the FDN nor Cárdenas accepted the idea of "cleaning" the elections. The PRI and the group close to Salinas also rejected the proposal. They preferred the option of an adjustment to around 50 percent of the vote and a majority in the Chamber of Deputies in the single-member districts. Thus was the presidential investiture won in the months of August and September 1988. There was no negotiation with the FDN, or the PAN at this point, only later. Mexico is still paying the price of this decision. The last attempt to reach an agreement was completely pro forma in character. On September 12, Salinas instructed Camacho to offer Cárdenas the Mexico City mayoral seat. The offer never reached the opposition leader, since Camacho didn't speak with him before a huge FDN demonstration on September 14, and afterward moods and positions had become polarized.

The 1988 elections were the first since 1911 in which the presidential succession and the constitutional elections shared moments of interaction and simultaneity. This has not been repeated since. Despite the hopes and illusions of many people—the author included—power was never in dispute in 1994. This peculiarity of the 1988 succession obliges us to take a significant detour in our narrative. It is impossible to ignore the topic of the elections, but it is not an inherent part of the normal chain of events in the Mexican presidential succession. To preserve narrative, political, and personal symmetry, I have elected to relegate the reflections, testimonies, and conclusions that are the fruit of my research on the subject to a brief appendix. There isn't room enough for them here, but they can't be suppressed. The reader interested in numbers, conspiracies, and historical issues can consult the appendix. Readers whose interest is confined to the mechanics of the presidential succession can calmly skip it.

The conclusion to the drama can be summarized in a single question. Would Carlos Salinas have been president without resorting to widespread electoral fraud? An affirmative answer suggests that Mexico might as well have spared itself the damages and injuries that this painful and harrowing succession entailed. Negotiation with the opposition would have been entirely feasible and enormously beneficial to Mexico. A negative response means that Córdoba and the faction that opposed negotiating were correct, since without a change in the voting margin—to pad the figures or revert an unfavorable decision—the 1988 succession would have produced a major disruption in the institutional order. We know that the Salinas group, along with Cárdenas and Muñoz Ledo—the former opting to calm his furious followers and send them home and the latter unable to convince him to do otherwise—the PAN, which preferred shady negotiations to full-fledged confrontation, the Church, the business community,

Washington, and the armed forces all concluded that the risk was too great. Ten years later, the denouement seems inevitable and contradictory. Time lost in the Mexican transition is invaluable, and may be impossible to recover. Many of the reforms implemented during the Salinas administration, directly derived from deals with the real sources of power during those stressful months, pushed the country to the brink of the abyss. However, it is also true that the inexperience and ineptitude shown by opposition groups, including a radical inability to negotiate, had their own costs and consequences.

We are, therefore, ignorant of whether some of the necessary and desirable reforms begun during these years would not have come up against the barrier of tradition and inertia if Salinas had not reached office as he did, in a succession that was mismanaged and sloppy—in a word, failed. We are still paying the price of this failure.

# SALINAS—COLOSIO (1994)

The shipwreck of the 1988 succession should have sufficed to teach Carlos
Salinas to prevent another disaster from befalling the system he had inherited. Protecting the succession mechanism had become over the years the
principal responsibility bequeathed by each president to his descendant. More
than the economy, foreign relations, or social stability, the acting president's
top priority had to be protecting the procedure used to ensure an orderly
transfer of power. Therefore, it seems odd that a man as rooted in the norms
and mores of the Mexican political system and as imbued with its vices and
virtues as Salinas should have underestimated the importance of certain recurring themes in the presidential succession.

If we give free rein to speculation and imagine an inauguration of Luis
Donaldo Colosio on December 1, 1994, and the first few years of a Colosio
regime, parallels with the 1976 succession leap to mind. But the formidable
challenge Salinas faced remains striking: to repeat, nearly twenty years later, in
completely different economic, political, international, and cultural circumstances, Echeverría's headstrong feat of making his friend president, paving the
way with all necessary brazenness and impudence, despite myriad objections
and entreaties to the contrary. Still, the gamble might have succeeded. It is
conceivable that Salinas's schemes to retain his hold on power beyond his own
mandate—equally complex, Florentine, and ambitious as Luis Echeverría's, and
far more sophisticated—had a strong chance of succeeding and were destroyed
by, and only by, the fatal shooting of Luis Donaldo Colosio in Lomas Taurinas,
Tijuana, on March 23, 1994.

Among its many other incomparably more significant consequences for Mexico, Colosio's assassination prevents us from presenting a narration of the succession identical to, or even symmetrical with, the other cases analyzed herein.

We obviously lack the testimony of the protagonist, Luis Donaldo Colosio, and in consequence, certain voids, vagueness, and a greater degree of speculation than in the other situations we have examined will inevitably limit our reconstruction of this transfer of power.

We have seen how the relentless logic of each succession acquired a rhythm of its own, completely independent from the deliberate actions of the participants, but which seems simultaneously to have permeated their unconscious behavior, thereby producing a nearly perfect alternation over the three decades discussed herein. Each succession by elimination was followed by a succession by choice, which was in turn the prelude to another succession by elimination. The sequence the succession had followed thus far—and the human desire to spare close friends and loved ones from the ordeals one has oneself undergone—augured a succession by elimination in 1993–1994. In accordance with the established sequence, the next PRI candidate should not have been chosen from the outset, precisely to avoid the contradictions and birth pains that beleaguered Salinas's rise to power. The young president, however, more ambitious and Machiavellian than any of his predecessors since Echeverría, conceived a different plan. From the very beginning of his term of office, he would prepare a successor from his own generation, endowed with undeniable political talent but also riddled with serious defects. At the same time, he sought a candidate who would have a good chance of reaching the presidency intact and who would fit in with his plans after leaving office.

Nevertheless, Salinas had learned several important lessons from his own debacle in 1988. Several of these can be inferred from his interview, such as the need to take excruciating pains to keep the ruling party united, not promoting *pasarelas* or publicly parading the candidates, to avoid encouraging feelings of defeat or open manipulation among disappointed hopefuls or their followers by refusing to place losing prospects in delicate positions, and to ensure that the real sources of power in Mexico got to know the possible candidates and would be willing to applaud whichever of them he chose. The problems, however, resurfaced very quickly, due to the very nature of the system and the peculiarities of the political situation in the 1990s.

Salinas's attitude toward the succession and his behavior in regard to his three final prospects—Manuel Camacho, Pedro Aspe, and Luis Donaldo Colosio—reflected the conclusions he had presumably drawn from his own experience. As with the other cases, it would be pointless to digress into a disquisition on the reasons why the losers were not chosen. They were defeated because the winner won. The first and foremost reason why Manuel Camacho and Pedro Aspe did not succeed Carlos Salinas was because Salinas chose

Colosio. Salinas does not lie when he says he did not choose the others because he preferred Colosio, which neither diminishes the importance of the concrete circumstances, nor overrides the president's more specific motives.

As his term got under way, Salinas de Gortari gave Fernando Gutiérrez Barrios the administration's top job: the ministry of the interior. It appeared to be an intelligent choice, but it suddenly inflamed multiple stress points in the president's inner circle. Despite Don Fernando's experience and skills, he lacked two crucial attributes for a minister of the interior: he was not a member of the president's inner circle, nor was he seen as a convincing prospect for the PRI candidacy. If we add to these factors the re-merger of the Ministry of Planning and Budget with Finance in 1991, the two ministries from which four of the last five presidents had come became marginal to the race. Their exclusion was rife with consequences.

The first to protest the appointment of Gutiérrez Barrios was Manuel Camacho. In his memoirs, Camacho relates how Salinas entrusted the task of preparing cabinet lists to four of his aides: Camacho himself, Luis Donaldo Colosio, José Córdoba, and Patricio Chirinos. Only a few days before his December 1 inauguration, the president-elect notified Camacho that he was to be mayor of Mexico City. Camacho recalls that he replied with a question— "Who's going to the Ministry of the Interior?"—and various protests. Salinas shrugged off his insistence and Camacho formulated three conditions before accepting the Mexico City government. He demanded that he be given complete control over the district attorney's office and police as well as permission to participate in the political reforms and preserve his relations with the opposition. Finally, Camacho wanted full political responsibility in the city. Salinas acceded, perhaps without realizing the danger of being suddenly left without an effective minister of the interior and with an overqualified mayor in charge of the country's main city. Camacho insisted that Salinas offer him the option of "moving anyplace else" after three years in the nation's capital, but the offer only highlights yet another element in this comedy of errors. Salinas used the offer of the Mexico City government to send an ambiguous and somewhat discouraging signal for the succession in 1994, but despite this first, barely coded message, Camacho never lost hope.

As has already been noted, the great pitfall when the successor is chosen in advance is always deceit. To prevent the preselected candidate from being devoured by his rivals, the press, or enemies of the regime, it is necessary to have several contenders in the running, and they in turn must remain wholeheartedly convinced of their chances. The only way to achieve this result is presidential encouragement, using implicit codes and explicit messages to persuade the interested parties that they still have a chance. By definition, the overwhelming majority of the signals are false, but their recipients believe them to be authentic and act accordingly. This was how the first of several misunderstandings between Carlos Salinas and Manuel Camacho began. Camacho showed himself to be completely convinced that the president approved of his political adventures outside the strict incumbency of his cabinet position. Salinas, on the other hand, could neither hinder nor dissuade his friend. To do so would have either led Camacho to stop believing in his chances, or obliged him to desist from his indispensable extrabureaucratic functions. A skilled and ambitious politician like Manuel Camacho would have angrily cut short his participation in matters outside the strict scope of his responsibilities, or cut his ties to the opposition as soon as he either discerned or received an indication from the president to such effect. The only problem was that Salinas would then be left without a minister of the interior possessing the strength of a credible candidate and with no alternate aide to fill the void. An example raised by Camacho himself became more relevant over Salinas's term of office. Camacho could meddle in a thousand affairs unrelated to his official responsibilities, but his unflagging insistence on promoting encounters, understandings, agreements, and convergence with the opposition in general, and with Cárdenas and the PRI in particular, provoked limitless irritation in Salinas's circle. In addition to the so-called concessions attributed to Camacho by his enemies and generally related to the extralegal solution of electoral disputes, especially with the PAN in state elections, the mayor played into his adversaries' hands. After having promoted and organized Salinas's meeting with Cárdenas immediately after the 1988 elections, and himself meeting several times with Cárdenas and Muñoz Ledo, Camacho resumed his offensive. In late 1990, with Salinas firmly established in the presidency and with Cárdenas in an evident slump, Camacho launched yet another attempt at a meeting and compromise between Cárdenas and the president, but this attempt also failed. Camacho narrates the events with a strange blend of candor and realism: "The president called a meeting of his closest advisers to discuss the matter. The attitude toward the proposal was one of generalized rejection. Some said it might be a trick, others claimed it would weaken the government. The aggressive tone used in reference to Cárdenas was visceral. . . . At the end of the meeting, the president did not close the door on the possibility of maintaining communication with Cárdenas or even negotiating a meeting. He entrusted the matter to Gutiérrez Barrios. I felt the opportunity had slipped away. From then on, any contact with Cárdenas would have an even higher political cost for me."

Thus, the consequences of the indispensable succession charade made themselves felt almost from the beginning of the Salinas administration. Camacho thought he was in the race, not despite his extrainstitutional escapades but in large degree because of them. He acted on orders and with the *ex ante* and *ex post facto* approval of the great elector. Salinas could not curtail his activities without undermining the credibility of the succession mechanism, nor could he control the consequences of letting Camacho continue unchecked with his constant ambitious political projects.

Like Silva Herzog before him, Pedro Aspe seemed to be a natural candidate for the presidency, although there were obviously considerable differences between the two ministers of finance. Silva had enjoyed a long-standing friendship with Miguel de la Madrid, while Pedro Aspe was a newcomer to the Salinas inner circle. Silva was obliged to administer during times of austerity and crisis, while Aspe ran the Ministry of Finance during a relative economic recovery. For three years, Silva suffered the pains of his department's rivalry and conflict with SPP. Aspe, in contrast, by the administration's third year had presided over the submersion of SPP under the control of the Ministry of Finance. However, in one aspect they were as similar as two grains of sand. A president as battered by circumstances as de la Madrid, or as vain as Salinas, would hardly be attracted by the exceptional international credentials Silva Herzog and Aspe had acquired. Carlos Salinas's minister of finance quickly became the "architect" of the administration's economic reforms, and a tendency emerged among the international news media and in certain sectors of the Mexican business community, in part independently of Aspe himself, to glorify the MIT economics graduate. This adulation was not particularly disturbing to Salinas. His own image was excellent—while he was president and Aspe his loyal and efficient subordinate. However, the idea of handing over his legacy, his place in history, and his own and his family's integrity to an individual endowed with a personality and international recognition of his own has never been a seductive one to any Mexican president.

A second handicap hindering Aspe was the need to nominate a candidate who would draw votes, a need that became increasingly acute with the PAN's dramatically improved electoral results in the mid-1980s and the Cárdenas juggernaut in 1988. It was no longer sufficient to win the nomination—the candidate had to win the elections as well. In the PRI tradition, this meant two things: first the need to be familiar with and able to mobilize the "live wires" of the apparatus—that is, the PRI, the Ministry of the Interior, and the state governors—to "organize" the elections; and, second, recruiting a charismatic candidate, whose personal—as opposed to strictly political—traits would draw votes.

In both cases, there were real, although not insurmountable, objections to an Aspe candidacy. He not only clashed with the PRI, the operatives at the Ministry of the Interior, and the so-called *mapaches* (experts in electoral acrobatics), but, despite his unquestionable talents for public speaking and debating, he lacked experience and the charm apparently needed to bewitch voters. Salinas had suffered the effects of the machine's animosity and its reluctance to get behind its candidate. His insight led him to believe that, while with discipline, time, and presidential authority Aspe could become a viable option, he also posed certain potential problems, such as discontent in the PRI, the hostility of the political old guard, possible resistance from organized labor, or a split-off by a losing prospect with the support of significant sectors of the party. He concluded that the candidate would have to be steeped in PRI ideology, with less technocratic, more party-related credentials. The job description required a PRI politician with technical training and ideological, regional, personal, and age-group affinity with Salinas. Aspe did not fit the bill, Camacho did, but less so than Colosio, and although he would not easily acknowledge the consequences of his own lack of charisma as an orator and proselytizer, Salinas was not naive about his unfamiliarity with the political scene and the PRI's political customs in 1988. Aspe's potential weakness grew in the light of a probable repeat run for the presidency by Cuauhtémoc Cárdenas in 1994.

Carlos Salinas may have exaggerated in confessing—supposedly—how he resolved to prepare Luis Donaldo Colosio to succeed him from the moment he made him his campaign manager in 1987, but only by a matter of degrees or months. The only case in this saga of a Mexican president choosing his intended successor so far in advance is Echeverría's decision to nominate López Portillo—hardly comparable with Salinas's decision. Salinas remains cautious in his public pronouncements. In reference to Colosio's designation, in an interview granted to the Mexico City daily *Reforma* in late 1996, the former president asserted: "In this sense—and in this sense only—can it be said that [Colosio's] candidacy was painstakingly constructed over several years." The reason for such prudence is identical to that which we have discerned in the analogous cases: to reduce the feeling of betrayal and victimization in the hearts of the competitors who were never really in the great elector's thoughts in the first place. Exaggeration aside, however, Colosio satisfied the requisites for an *in pectore* candidate, chosen years in advance and led by the hand by the great leader. He was placed at the head of the official party to complete his PRI indoctrination at the beginning of Salinas's term, and at the same time acquired a seat in the Senate to round out his political image. After the PRI's landslide victory in the 1991 midterm elections and its XIV$^{th}$ assembly, where it proved impossible to implement party reforms decorously, Salinas took the orthodox route and placed his favorite in the perfect cabinet position for him to acquire the attributes he lacked ... but just barely.

Thus, in the Ministry of Social Development (SEDESOL), Colosio came in contact with the economic cabinet, without himself heading a strictly economic government agency. He dabbled in international politics through SEDESOL's participation in international environmental conferences without getting seriously involved in Mexico's foreign political, financial, and commercial affairs. Through the *Solidaridad* program and social interest spending in the states and municipalities, he became familiar with Mexico's problems of inequality and poverty, without controlling the administration's new machinery, which was entrusted to Carlos Rojas and the National Solidarity Program (PRONASOL). Thus, Salinas achieved two objectives at once: teaching Colosio about the country's main problems, of which he was palpably ignorant, and "hawking" him to the country's various administrative and political groups so that he could neutralize any significant resistance—without allowing him to gain complete control of any given group or outfit himself with an independent, competent, and complete team of specialized aides that would enable him to fly on his own when the time came. Colosio would accede to the candidacy supported by or known to all, but with no real power of his own. He would owe his victory exclusively to his mentor, and above all would rely on him implicitly to establish his foreign, economic, and financial contacts and to strengthen his ties to sectors outside the PRI and the system.

Colosio honed his exceptional political intuition and his remarkable gift for pleasing Salinas. Instead of committing more frequent errors as he approached the finish, he dodged them with increasing acumen. Similarly, as Echeverría had done for López Portillo, Salinas looked out for his heir, picking him up when he stumbled and shielding him when he came under attack. An example of this protective behavior can be found in the early days of the Salinas administration. Salinas was leaving a state wedding in the company of Emilio Gamboa, who had more influence over the media than anyone else, and warned him that, "[Luis] Donaldo's being treated pretty roughly in the media. Anyone who messes with him is messing with me." The implication was clear: Gamboa must press all his media wizardry into the service of Colosio's vulnerable image. Similarly, when Colosio stumbled in the wake of a severe gas explosion in Guadalajara on April 22, 1992, underrating the magnitude and repercussions of the tragedy, Salinas intervened to amend the faux pas.

This leads us to reflect on successions by choice and on the nature of the Mexican political establishment as it has evolved over the years. We have attempted to show that the typology outlined herein is not only useful to order historical events and trends, but also to elucidate the implications of the different types of Mexican presidential successions. Foremost among these are the implications related to the different participants' reactions. Successions by elimination spawn and nourish tensions between the incumbent and the chosen successor. Successions by choice cause conflict and resentment between winners and losers. Nevertheless, events unfold in the sphere of human acts and passions. Nothing is pure, simple, or easy to classify. To argue that in a succession by elimination, such as that in 1993, the acting president plots from the beginning of his term of office to impose his chosen successor does not mean that the fortunate beneficiary of his predilection remains immobile, awaiting the gift to fall from the sky. On the contrary, the anointed must maintain the support and approval of the factotum in the process for three, four, or five long years. He has to make the charm last for the entire six-year term, keeping his seductive gaze fixed on its object through all storms, through all his rages, humiliations, and triumphs. He has to persevere in his efforts to read the president's mind, without relaxing his effort for an instant. A single slip could be fatal. The rules are clear and categorical: there is only one sun in the sky and only one personal virtue that matters—loyalty. The favorite has to share all the president's battles and defeats, but none of his triumphs; all the executive's enemies are his, but not his friends.

Winning in a process of elimination is a feat of survival and luck. Completing the entire race unscathed constitutes a triumph of discipline and ambition. Colosio and his advisers guessed this. His preliminary campaign documents testify to their determination to respond to the (accurate) criticism of the prospective candidate's "lack of ideological definition and independent personality, overly protected career, and weak candidacy." For José Luis Soberanes, one of Colosio's most loyal and valued aides, it was "a deliberate ploy on Colosio's part to have no personality of his own and present the ideal personal traits to Salinas. It was a pragmatic strategy to win: never upstage Salinas, avoid expressing definite opinions."

Needless to say, these strategies are not unique to Colosio, but have been shared by all the competitors in all the successions, some more than others. The three successions in this category (Echeverría–López Portillo, De la Madrid–Salinas, and Salinas–Colosio) involved relatively fewer contradictions and conflicts between the outgoing and incoming presidents—without this implying that they were entirely in harmony—and produced a far greater tension between winner and losers. Of course we can only hypothesize about how the relationship between Salinas and Colosio might have evolved, but if we reject the hypothesis that Salinas was responsible for Colosio's death—we later suggest that the idea is incompatible with a rational explanation of the second succession of 1994—a peaceful coexistence would have been plausible, regardless of the wishes and prophesies of their respective aides.

The dynamic of modern electoral systems is well known: The talent needed to win votes does not necessarily equate with talent for resolving current domestic or international problems. On the contrary, the education, training, and concentration needed for meaningful government tend to alienate voters and activists. The examples mentioned above conform to this rule in terms of the preliminary selection of possible competitors. Not just anyone could win at this game, although many tried. The virtues necessary to compete and triumph were opposite to the ideal traits for governing, as is true in any other political system, democratic or not. Thus, Carlos Salinas knew how to conceal his propensity to megalomania as well as his penchant for clan-oriented politics. Similarly, Luis Donaldo Colosio, who lacked the time and the power to see the depths of his own soul flourish, cleverly concealed his bouts of depression, as well as his occasional frivolity. We will never know what other characteristics he might have demonstrated once in power. The charade leaves its mark on the psyche; no one gets off lightly. Power unmasks, liberates, and transforms those who wield it, but always from the basis of the available material, in this case the genetic code of a political class shaped by several decades of systemic inertia.

The traditional Mexican separation of administration and politics, business and government, highly organized party constituencies and disorganized masses, combined with the succession rules described herein, was responsible for the existence of two further divisions—often imperceptible, but possibly more damaging—between politics and substance. Significant issues were banished from Mexican politics by the succession mechanism—the kind of tabula rasa that it made of the cabinet and all the lower echelons of the government—and by the system's de facto division of labor. Politicians specialized in graft, administrators in bureaucracy, businessmen in making money, and intellectuals—apparently— in thinking.

By the time they got near the cabinet, politicians had left substance behind them, and administrators, though better trained, confused technical competence with argumentative posturing. When they entered the presidential race, pure politicians did so with a pseudolegalistic, rhetorical, and shallow discourse, entirely devoid of substance. Administrators, on the other hand, entered politics well equipped with technical expertise, but without the personal criteria necessary to apply their technical skills in a meaningful way. Once they reached the cabinet—and they entered the race for the presidential succession—what little substance remained would evaporate completely, leaving only the skills and instruments suitable for the contest at hand: seductiveness, discipline, loyalty, and hypersensitivity to the president's opinions. All these traits were accentuated over time; Colosio epitomized the phenomenon.

The culmination of this trend was manifest in a unanimity of positions among the candidates to succeed Salinas that would be otherwise incomprehensible given the tremendous upheaval in Mexico's economic, cultural, and international traditions caused by the Salinas administration's policies. Fully aware of the personal and long-term motives behind the reforms the administration promoted, Camacho, Aspe, Zedillo, Colosio, and all the others backed—or failed to express their disagreement with—overnight trade liberalization, the lock-stock-and-barrel privatization of Mexico's state enterprises, the North American Free Trade Agreement (NAFTA), the reopening of relations between the state and the Catholic Church, and a difficult and burdensome amendment to the *ejido* regime of collective ownership of land in the countryside. Camacho may, as he claimed in 1992, have mentioned to the president his concern about the corruption that was already enveloping the "royal" family, in particular the president's brother Raúl Salinas. Some top- and midlevel functionaries in the economic and financial apparatus may have guessed the existence of Salinas's tacit agreement with the United States as of early 1993, whereby he would refrain from devaluating the peso either before or immediately after NAFTA's ratification, and deduced that it precluded any exchange-rate adjustment before late 1994. (Harvard professor Jorge Domínguez recalls his former colleague Lawrence Summers, then assistant secretary of the treasury, dropping a hint at a 1994 dinner party to the effect that the Mexican government had promised to defend the stability of the peso and that Washington supported this policy.) And finally, some of Salinas's older and more experienced cabinet members may have sensed that the country completely lacked the necessary regulatory framework to manage a massive transfer of public assets into private hands with honesty and integrity. But none of this mattered: meaningful dissent had been forever banished from the struggle for power in Mexico. The cabinet, formerly the place where dissenting opinions were expressed, was transformed first into a bastion of unanimity and then into a hotbed for complicity.

By late 1993, the various prospective candidates' chances had become clear. The field had narrowed to two: Colosio and Camacho. Moreover, time was running out. The postponement of the elections to the middle of August 1994 and of the president's state of the union address to the first of November moved the succession calendar back somewhat, but the traditional calendar—with the nomination falling in September or October of the year before the presidential election—was still a factor. The window available to Salinas was narrow and fleeting. He had to act after the 1993 presidential address, after the NAFTA vote in Washington, and before the traditional Mexican year-end festivities began on December 12.

As the decisive dates drew near, Salinas was attentive to the acute contradictions the process entailed. Camacho, more confident every day, still provoked violent resistance in sectors of the political establishment and the business community. This would not have prevented Salinas from imposing Camacho as his choice if he had wanted to do so, however. The author personally witnessed a sign of Camacho's confidence—and also of his imprudent behavior—early that October, when I launched a new book in Mexico City. Camacho, aware that Cuauhtémoc Cárdenas was likely to attend, and that news of his presence would probably leak to the press, attended the restricted celebration I offered at my Mexico City home. A few months later, as was made public a few years ago, Salinas shared his irritation over Camacho's gesture with novelist Carlos Fuentes and the author: "Why was Camacho so visibly meeting with critics and adversaries of the regime?"

Colosio was improving his position also, but personal problems, including his wife Diana Laura's illness, did not help matters. In February 1990, Diana Laura Colosio was diagnosed with cancer and was operated on with apparent success. In October 1992, pregnant for the second time, she suffered a relapse. Diana Laura and Luis Donaldo Colosio decided not to interrupt the pregnancy, despite the obvious consequence that all chemotherapy or radiation treatment would have to wait until after the child was born. Diana Laura underwent further surgery and her illness was monitored at the National Nutrition Institute in Mexico City, where Salinas could be accurately informed of her condition on a regular basis. The couple did not fully accept the inevitable outcome, although doctors they consulted in the United States explained the situation to them bluntly and less euphemistically than had their Mexican colleagues. The Mexican authorities were also kept fully informed of the situation. In connection with this and undoubtedly other factors, a proliferation of succession-related signals emerged. Some came from Salinas, others from Colosio himself, directed toward his entourage.

Early in September of 1993, Colosio allowed himself an excess that provides a clue to his mood. Normally extremely careful to avoid ostentatious spending or opulence, he decided to give Diana Laura a luxury automobile for her birthday. Aides to both members of the couple were startled by the gesture. Given his sensitivity to the president's moods, Colosio must have begun to grow increasingly sure he was "the one." Nevertheless, the imperative to deceive the unfavored rival grew as the critical dates approached. With even greater care and malice than before, Salinas continued to weave a web of false or misleading messages in which he enveloped Manuel Camacho between early September and late November. The feat was complicated even further by the fact that the date for unveiling his candidate was out of Salinas's hands; it would depend on NAFTA's ratification in the U.S. House of Representatives.

A first demonstration of Camacho's standing was staged for his benefit at a September 2 luncheon at Los Pinos, organized by the president. With labor union leader Fidel Velázquez and half of his cabinet on hand, Salinas spoke so highly of Camacho that, despite vehement disagreement from several of the luncheon guests, at least two present were led to predict that Camacho would be the nominee. In the following weeks, however, the climate for his candidacy deteriorated. Salinas refrained from consulting with Camacho on the content of his fifth annual address, and was nearly convinced by several aides to simply remit his message to the Congress instead of delivering it in person. Not perceiving Salinas's liking for the idea, Camacho opposed it vigorously. Alongside skeptical or frankly critical references to Camacho, columns praising Colosio began to flood the Mexican press. Today, Camacho grudgingly acknowledges that "Salinas had already chosen Colosio by the November 1 presidential address."

In what was possibly the most visible hint of all, Colosio contacted Camacho days after the presidential address—on the eve of the NAFTA vote in the United States and therefore of the unveiling. It is difficult to imagine that Colosio would take the initiative of meeting with his main rival at this point without having been instructed by the president to do so. According to Camacho, Colosio ended the interview by affirming his confidence in Camacho's imminent victory. Any interpretation can be given to this meeting and the conversation that ensued. José Luis Soberanes, Colosio's friend and deputy minister at SEDESOL and subsequently one of the people in charge of his campaign, recalls how Camacho and Colosio did in fact meet on a monthly basis. In one of their last such conferences before the unveiling—possibly the same one Camacho mentions—Colosio expressed an assessment of the situation to Camacho that favored the latter, and gave him a list of five aides for whom he wanted Camacho's support.

But Camacho's disagreement with the president over the presidential address, together with Salinas's evident need to prepare Camacho for defeat and Colosio for victory, generated increasing friction between the two former college friends. The tension peaked on November 20, at the traditional Revolution Day parade, two days after NAFTA's ratification in Washington and one week before the PRI announced its presidential candidate. On the balcony of honor at the National Palace, Camacho appears to have felt the president's chilly attitude toward him, and realized that Salinas had made his choice. After the parade, Salinas called a cabinet meeting in the National Palace to celebrate the approval of NAFTA, and extended public recognition to Trade Minister Jaime Serra and Presidential Chief of Staff José Córdoba for negotiating the treaty. NAFTA ceased to be an instrument of economic policy, subject to approval or rejection, to become the centerpiece of a plan the dimensions and ramifications of which would only emerge later on, although some of its ingredients—such as the repeated test balloons sent up during Salinas's term to evaluate his chances for reelection—provided clues to the scope of the project.

Camacho, like all vanquished finalists, weighed his alternatives on the eve of the denouement. Time was short for Salinas, since he would surely have to unveil his candidate before U.S. Vice President Al Gore's approaching visit, scheduled for late November. Time was also running out for Camacho, whose appearance before the Chamber of Deputies on Wednesday, November 24, represented his last chance to publicly influence the presidential succession, one way or another. He decided to seek a private confrontation with Salinas, to present the arguments in favor of his candidacy and against the political line that he felt Colosio's designation would reflect. He also attempted to put forth his objections to certain declarations Salinas had made and to respond to some of the criticism to which he had been subjected. He recalls how, "before talking with Salinas that Monday, I thought seriously about launching my bid for the presidency on the day of my [congressional] appearance. I decided that it would be best to consult with Salinas first. Everything suggests that what followed was deception [on Salinas's part, intended] to control the situation." In fact, it is probable that one of Camacho's close aides informed Salinas of the mayor's intention to take matters into his own hands with a classic coup or, more novelly, an advance announcement of his aspirations. For someone as obsessed as Salinas was with preventing a split in the PRI, the omens signaling Camacho's discontent could not have been more ominous. If anything were lacking, the next day's conversation convinced Salinas of the enormous danger facing the tidy and painless succession of his dreams.

In his unpublished memoirs, Camacho reproduces the script of the comments he intended to present to Salinas. In his interview for this book, the former president limited himself to corroborating the essence of the conversation, without admitting that the details Camacho provides necessarily coincide with his recollection. Where Salinas does agree with Camacho is in regard to his blunt, unpremeditated response to Camacho's central thesis—self-serving and debatable—that the Salinas years were characterized by two contradictory lines: one of increased political tolerance, and another of backward authoritarianism; one hard and another conciliatory; one intent on opening the political system and another equally determined to keep it closed. Salinas concluded the conversation with an indisputable parting shot: "There's only been one line in this administration, Camacho—the president's line." Camacho still remembers the president's parting words as he was leaving the office: "As he was seeing me to the door, Salinas said, 'The decision regarding the candidate has not yet been taken.'"

The truth was otherwise, but Salinas had to move swiftly and adroitly to outflank his friend's offensive. He went into action that very Monday. In the afternoon, Minister of the Interior Patrocinio González invited Camacho to dinner with the president's closest aides the following evening. The conversation that night took a predictable course: José Córdoba's supporters, particularly Minister of Education Ernesto Zedillo, offered a cogent and intelligent defense of Córdoba's role in negotiating NAFTA. Jaime Serra pointed out that the attacks on the negotiating team were due to fundamental differences of opinion regarding the administration's economic model. Camacho limited himself to presenting the same arguments he had outlined to Salinas at the National Palace on November 20, with a minor variation—that it was not right to give credit for NAFTA to Córdoba rather than to Salinas. At this precise point in the conversation, Salinas arrived. He was attending the dinner party to perpetuate the charade and thereby prevent Camacho from using the congressional podium to announce his own candidacy the next day. He had but one objective, to convince the mayor that his candidacy was still alive, thus insinuating that if he stuck by the rules he could win, while a break with tradition would condemn him to defeat and ostracism. Salinas employed his entire repertoire of seduction and dissimulation to achieve this objective. He repeated Camacho's arguments in his conversation as though they were his own, and expressed his unconditional admiration and respect for Camacho. In speaking of the prospective candidates, he reserved special praise for Camacho and made vaguely denigrating remarks about Colosio. In Camacho's words, "At dinner, Salinas said of Colosio that 'his greatest merit is having worked with Camacho.' Salinas left for a moment and Colosio slouched and started watching the candlelight through his wineglass. He felt offended." We do not know whether Colosio at this point was already an anointed candidate, playing his part with absolute certainty of his impending victory and determined to conceal his joy, or a depressed prospect, co-victim of Salinas's deception of Camacho.

In any event, that very Wednesday Colosio and Camacho accompanied the president to an event in Mexico City's Magdalena Mixhuca district. There, according to Camacho, Colosio referred to the dinner party the evening before, saying that "these things are too hard, Manuel. This kind of thing shouldn't happen in the future." From the event, the two finalists traveled to the airport in the president's car. En route, according to Camacho, "Salinas did nothing more than congratulate me for my congressional appearance (that morning) and ask Colosio if he didn't think it had been magnificent." Salinas had cause to congratulate himself—Camacho had lost his last chance to defy him. From this very moment, as he kicked off his Pacific Coast tour, Salinas turned his mind to the other half of his two-sided endeavor: appeasing Colosio and unveiling him as the chosen candidate. On Wednesday evening he dined in Ciudad Obregón, Sonora, with Luis Donaldo's father and the entire family of that state's prodigal son.

Colosio was officially nominated by the PRI on Sunday, November 28, 1993. That morning, Camacho tried to contact Salinas, and refused to congratulate Colosio until he had spoken with the president. Salinas granted him an audience, but refused to offer any explanation. He asked Camacho to resign as mayor, offering him the same two positions Camacho mentions having been offered at the beginning of the administration: in foreign affairs or education.

Camacho considered the proposal, consulted with his closest aides, and accepted the appointment to the foreign ministry. In response to concern in Colosio's camp, the president would offer an explanation three weeks later to a close Colosio aide: "I know Manuel well. It's better to have him in the cabinet than out. Someone who holds a cabinet position six months before the election can't be president." Indeed, Salinas still feared Camacho's reaction to the defeat and deception inflicted on him, because he had suffered the effects of a similar reaction by Manuel Bartlett six years before. This was his reason for relieving Camacho of the Mexico City government. Under no circumstances did he want to leave the job of organizing the elections in the nation's capital to a frustrated and embittered loser. In the event, however, it seems that his own guilty conscience at his excesses of manipulation and malice vis-à-vis Camacho would lead him to irrational extremes of reconciliation and compensation that were to result in infinite misunderstanding.

Before delving into the confusions and disputes that arose owing to Salinas's guilty conscience on account of his friend, and the eventful consequences they entailed for Mexico, it is worth reviewing the main events of Colosio's first month of campaigning and the indications of things to come that it contained. The first dilemma originated in the debate over whom to appoint as the newly minted candidate's campaign manager, a position that, although no one knew at the time, was destined to be occupied by Mexico's next president. Several possibilities existed for promoting contact and understanding between the outgoing and incoming presidents. One, the most readily available, consisted of designating a new PRI president. Nevertheless, Salinas never considered it, nor was it an easy proposition for Colosio, shaken by the vicissitudes of his own party and bewildered by the evidence of his own weakness. What remained was the approach taken by Bartlett in 1981 and by Camacho in late 1988: making one of the candidate's men PRI general secretary, under the tutelage of a party president with no real power. This was, give or take a few details, the solution Salinas proposed to Colosio, either on Saturday, November 27—that is, the day before the unveiling—if we trust Salinas's memory, or Monday, November 29, if we go by the recollection of Colosio's people, in particular the three of the candidate's close aides interviewed for this book: Alfonso Durazo, Samuel Palma, and José Luis Soberanes. According to these three, that Sunday afternoon, during the first private meeting with his top aides after his unveiling, Colosio announced that his campaign manager would be Carlos Rojas, his deputy minister at SEDESOL, national *Solidaridad* program director, a staunch Salinas supporter, and skilled organizer of communities and social groups.

According to Salinas, Colosio requested Rojas, and the president refused. The real question, however, lies behind the formal sequence. Why did Colosio propose Rojas? The answer may lie in the procedure Colosio opted for—which can be detected, incidentally, in all the successions—of resorting to the perfect middleman, the loyal messenger, the brilliant interpreter of the chief's thoughts, whose tips and predictions never fail. In this case, the man indicated was José Córdoba, who had in fact opposed Colosio's candidacy from the start, but who became a resigned convert after the collapse of Ernesto Zedillo's campaign, eventually holding a privileged position in Colosio's network of alliances. Colosio's aides admit that Colosio did take the initiative of proposing Carlos Rojas for campaign manager and that Salinas did indeed reject his request for the reasons he gives. However, according to Alfonso Durazo, the idea of appointing Rojas was based on Colosio's desire to make a gesture of reciprocity toward Salinas, rather than on Rojas's intrinsic merits. Rojas would provide a conduit for information from Colosio to Salinas, on which Salinas could rely implicitly. Colosio may have tried the suggestion out on Córdoba, and Córdoba in turn ventured that Salinas would reject him, but would consent to an alternative proposal: Ernesto Zedillo.

The same former Colosio aides confess that when the candidate settled on Ernesto Zedillo, he was seeking, above all, to placate Salinas. Also, he wanted to maintain solid ties to the financial community and the rest of Salinas's top staff, all of whom got along well with Zedillo. The fact of the matter is that Zedillo, while he may well have been designated with Salinas's prior and real—not merely formal—approval, was not Salinas's first choice for the second choice, nor was he cast as Colosio's understudy with this function in mind.

Thus, Colosio launched his bid for the presidency with a campaign manager he respected and esteemed, but who was, through Córdoba, totally subordinate to Salinas. He was neither Bartlett in 1981–82 nor Camacho in 1988, nor even Muñoz Ledo in 1975–76. He launched his campaign, moreover, with a precarious security team, limited funding, and all the shortcomings his lack of preparation as candidate entailed. Months later, on the eve of Colosio's death, his campaign manager would put his finger on the sore spot: in a letter to Salinas dated March 19, Ernesto Zedillo lamented "the deficient quality of the human resources in the campaign team." Colosio's team was made up of representatives of the various currents in the cabinet and in the succession. The candidate sought above all to build his strength by uniting all factions behind him, and perhaps this explains his campaign's exceedingly slow start.

The honeymoon between Salinas and Colosio lasted through December, but ended violently on January 1, 1994, with the Zapatista rebellion in Chiapas. In the opinion of his friends and aides, Colosio made his first serious mistake on this issue: He left Salinas alone, instead of sticking to him like a leech. Swiftly and relentlessly, the losers in the race for the candidacy surrounded the president, and their traditional conspiracy did not take long to materialize. Colosio uncovered his flank in the capital, where his defeated adversaries did not rest in their efforts to avenge their loss. The transition from subordinate to independent actor, always abrupt, was more than Colosio could handle, and a shadow fell over his relationship with Salinas as a result. The normal strain began to take its toll, but prematurely. Colosio tried to act on his own accord. He issued his peace plan for Chiapas—which lasted only half a day—alone. His proposed mediators simply got nowhere in the media. Worse yet, José Córdoba, who strictly speaking did not belong among the losers, joined forces with them, due, perhaps, to his own fears and Colosio's rudeness to him, including a serious altercation over the inclusion of ideas of Córdoba's in the candidate's acceptance speech. Exasperated by Córdoba's suggestions, Colosio exclaimed, "Include them, but for the last time." As a Colosio aide recalls, the friction dated from some time earlier. On September 16, 1993, Colosio had sworn to the governor of his home state, "If I make it [to the presidency] Córdoba not only won't have a place in my government, he won't have a place in the country."

Whether Governor Beltrones's memory is accurate or not, the hostility toward Córdoba in Colosio's camp could not remain hidden from or insignificant to someone so close to the security apparatus, the polls, and the inner workings of the official residence. Thus, the only authentic and effective link between Colosio and Salinas, between outgoing and incoming presidents, vanished. The ensuing misunderstandings multiplied rapidly. As political damages from the crisis in Chiapas began to accrue, two separate issues contributed to souring the relationship between Salinas and the appointed successor, or, to be more precise, between the candidate and Salinas. The less important dispute involved the new electoral reform, undertaken as a result of the Zapatista uprising. As of January 24, Colosio had attempted to take the lead in promoting the reforms, and Salinas dragged his feet over convening a special session of the Congress. Colosio accepted Salinas's reluctance, but the president then changed his opinion, leaving Colosio in the lurch and creating the impression that he opposed the vaunted reform. By late February, Colosio's irritation was palpable, but it would pale in comparison with the fury Salinas provoked by his behavior in regard to Chiapas.

The uprising headed by *Subcomandante* Marcos had an effect on Salinas similar to that of other major setbacks mentioned previously. The president nearly collapsed, as he had on July 6, 1988, and when, earlier during his 1988 campaign, he was practically run out of the Comarca Lagunera area of Mexico City by a population whipped up by the imminent arrival of Cuauhtémoc Cárdenas, or as he would once again in the days immediately following Luis Donaldo Colosio's assassination. The blow dealt to the government by the Zapatistas warranted nothing less. Salinas's dream of Mexico entering the First World, a painless succession, and a legacy that would continue after he left office in an atmosphere infused with tact, sensibility, and conviction, had gone up in smoke. Lacking accurate information—the most powerful and best-informed man in Mexico is also the most lied to and misled—and distressed by the surprise, Salinas was at a loss. The combination of the uprising in the state of Chiapas with bombings in Mexico City and at various electrical facilities near the capital, and intense media coverage of the rebellion, magnified the impact, if not the reality, of the events in southwest Mexico. It was not merely a local insurrection, deficiently armed and commanded with tactical genius but with no strategy, that Salinas saw emerging before his very eyes. He saw a massive conspiracy to destroy his government. His first clumsy attempts at a solution failed. His blaming foreigners did not do the trick, and his efforts to resolve the conflict locally got nowhere. In this context, sending Manuel Camacho to negotiate offered a twofold solution. It provided a package of coherent and viable initiatives *and* acted as a balm for Camacho's ego to heal the wounds of November. If Salinas had discharged his obligations to his companion of a thousand battles in the succession with disloyalty and treachery, he could now expiate his sins, if not his omissions.

Any explanation for the events of the first few months of 1994 that overlooks these two factors will be incomplete or unconvincing. The devastating impact of the events of New Year's Day 1994 explains Salinas's enthusiasm for fanciful solutions. His guilty conscience regarding Camacho explains his willingness to embrace the then–foreign minister's ideas and oblique maneuvers. The measures Camacho proposed were sensible and relevant: a unilateral cease-fire in Chiapas, the opening of negotiations, a change of command at the Ministry of the Interior and the attorney general's office, a new official policy and attitude toward the leftist opposition, breaking the PAN's monopoly on dialogue with the government. The designation of Jorge Carpizo as minister of the interior made it possible to organize the elections on more amicable terms with the PRI, and the choice of Diego Valadés as attorney general guaranteed that the agreements reached in Chiapas would not be offset by arrests and police excesses in Mexico City. Finally, Manuel Camacho's appointment as negotiator or mediator fulfilled several objectives simultaneously. It put his undeniable skills to use, prevented him from breaking with the regime by removing him from the Foreign Ministry in acceptable circumstances that he himself had suggested, and put him back in the limelight. Chiapas became a kind of consolation prize for his loss in November.

Thus far everything had proceeded smoothly. The first signs of disagreement between Salinas and Colosio over the accords Camacho proposed appeared easily surmountable at first, but the rift between them, predictable as it was, augured the worst. Colosio never entirely assimilated Camacho's move to the Foreign Ministry, nor did he ever entirely get over the string of inconsequential but hurtful tricks Salinas had used in achieving his ends in the succession. When the president presented Camacho's ideas to Colosio as his own, Colosio limited himself to expressing his disagreement with the idea of placing the former mayor in the Ministry of the Interior. It would have been an aberration for Salinas to entrust the task of organizing the nationwide elections to the man who had been relieved of responsibility for performing the same task in Mexico City. The Carpizo-Valadés duo was probably not to the candidate's liking either, in view of both officials' affinity with Camacho, but he did not object to it. Also, the president's decision to recur to Camacho, while it did not exactly please Colosio, obeyed political criteria that he himself could understand and grant as valid. But the last straw was probably the legal subterfuge Camacho and Salinas created for Camacho to take over the negotiations in Chiapas: the title of "peace commissioner." The problem was that, carrying no salary or cabinet position, this position made Camacho eligible to be a candidate for the presidency. This was so because Article 82 of the Mexican Constitution requires that any candidate for the presidency must have resigned any cabinet post at least six months before the election. The elections were scheduled for August 21, 1994; if Camacho had remained in the cabinet until February 21, he would have been ineligible to replace Colosio; by declining a cabinet post, he was automatically reestablishing his eligibility.

Camacho recalls, "I proposed that I receive no salary, but it was a symbolic gesture. I didn't want to depend on any cabinet member. I would not have agreed to go to the Ministry of the Interior." And it is possible, despite the former mayor's penchant for political infighting, half-truth, and sophism on ominous occasions, that he had not at this point contemplated a succession showdown, reopening the presidential race. The possibility of Salinas removing Colosio as PRI candidate and replacing him with Camacho was remote at best at this point. Camacho's public reasoning, confirmed by Salinas in his interview, appears to be true. If he remained in the Cabinet, his credibility with Marcos and the Zapatistas would evaporate. Furthermore, where was he to go? The symbolic contradiction inherent in negotiating a domestic conflict from the Foreign Ministry was intolerable. The Ministry of the Interior was out of the question. His options were limited. Furthermore, the entire plan for the succession depended on Salinas's prestige, which had been severely undermined by the uprising.

Salinas's conduct poses many enigmas. He either miscalculated and failed to anticipate Colosio's reaction or deliberately reopened the presidential race by effectively reviving a discarded option in appointing Camacho as peace commissioner. Colosio's anger and bewilderment reached the extreme that, according to José Luis Soberanes and Palma, the candidate wondered, "What if I quit?" When the author explicitly asked Salinas whether he had informed Colosio of his intention to entrust Camacho with the negotiations in an unpaid, non-Cabinet position, the former president declined to answer.

Colosio's adherents, later to become adversaries or accusers of Carlos Salinas, would profit from Salinas's silence. During the next two months, they repeatedly urged the candidate to stop naively and systematically believing the president. Salinas's speech on January 17, with its famous statement, "Don't get me wrong, Colosio is the candidate," was not a response to public opinion or the political establishment, but rather an attempt to appease Colosio and his camp. Until mid-March, when signs of change began to emerge, there was no way to convince Colosio and his aides that Salinas did not harbor among his hidden intentions the perverse plan of trumping him with Camacho at any moment. Everything fit: Camacho's poor media image and the difficulty Colosio's campaign was having getting across to the public; Colosio's desire to visit Chiapas and Salinas's reluctance to let him go; the simultaneous appointments of Camacho, Carpizo, and Valadés coinciding with the formal launching of Colosio's campaign; difficulties within Colosio's inner circle, languishing electoral reform; a lack of campaign funding; and Colosio's problems forming an independent security and intelligence team.

Whatever their real intentions may have been, the impression Salinas and Camacho created was clear and devastating to Colosio's people. A plot, conspiracy, or "campaign" was being hatched against the Colosio campaign from Los Pinos. Once the specter of Colosio's removal or substitution was loosed, nothing seemed able to stop it, although there was ample cause to disbelieve or challenge the perception. Salinas ignored or deliberately aggravated the problem until late February, after the first round of Chiapas negotiations had ended. Finally, Salinas made a clean break of it and demanded that Camacho explicitly renounce any designs on the presidency. Camacho granted the president's request on March 22, the day before Colosio's death. To date we have neither a coherent explanation for Camacho's withdrawal nor a categorical answer as to whether Salinas wanted to remove Colosio. If we draw on the history of conflicts and misunderstandings between presidents and candidates outlined herein, we should arrive at a double conclusion. Like his predecessors, at several junctures Carlos Salinas both wanted and intended to change his mind. But—as also occurred in the other cases—he never put the plan into action, because he could not do so without paying an exorbitant political price.

At the same time, another drama was unfolding in Colosio's campaign, derived I believe—insofar as has been possible for me to untangle the snarl of passions, interests, and moods of those fateful weeks—from the problems inherent in the succession and from the candidate's mental state. A friend of Colosio's recalls having contacted him in Querétaro in mid-January to ask him to act as witness, alongside Manuel Camacho, in her daughter's civil wedding ceremony. She found Colosio alone at night in a hotel, with a cold and an untouched dinner on the table, in a state of deep depression. His family was suffering increasingly from the curse that seemed to hang over it. Diana Laura's cancer ravaged her body. Less terrible, but also lacerating, illnesses afflicted Colosio's mother and sister. The heir apparent did not even seem to be enjoying his recently acquired power. If we add the incomprehensible maneuvers of his friend Carlos Salinas to our analysis of Colosio's moods, we find ourselves contemplating a candidate who must have given vent to expressions of desperation, resignation, anger, and resentment. The crisis peaked in early March as Colosio struggled to take control, or, as his aides and Salinas would put it, to relaunch his campaign. He would dedicate the month of March to this objective.

The task would be divided in three parts. The first was defining the traditional break with the president. Second would be draconian changes in his campaign team. Finally, he needed to solve the problems of Camacho and of his own relationship with Salinas. The cutting of the umbilical cord between president and candidate has always been a traumatic moment in the succession. No truly opportune occasion ever really presents itself for the outgoing president. Any distance, however inevitable and healthy it may seem, is dangerous. For the candidate, every opportunity is hazardous. The balance of forces is always unfavorable, and the danger of the president's overreacting is never entirely absent. This contradiction, which figures in all the successions we have examined, is heightened in cases of what we have called successions by choice, for the same reasons discussed in previous chapters. The president feels, in part correctly, that the candidate owes him everything he has. By what right does he dare distance himself from the regime, question its errors, or propose remedies? The candidate, on the other hand, develops an extreme sensitivity to the president's humors—honed during the preliminary stage of the race—which he must use to identify the moment, issue, and circumstances that will allow him to affirm himself and respond to the clamor born of the inevitable discontent accumulated during the six difficult years of the outgoing administration. If, moreover, the administration closes with severe mishaps—devaluation, repression, social unrest—the task of deciding when and how to make the break becomes even more arduous, bordering on impossible.

The correspondence between Colosio, Salinas, and Ernesto Zedillo—who acted as Colosio's campaign manager, but also acted as go-between for Colosio and Salinas—reflects the complexity of the issues in question. An exchange of private and public letters took place in the context of the imminent changes in Colosio's team, which the candidate had been planning since January, transcribing lists of substitutions among his top aides on index cards. His resolve to make these changes grew stronger as the campaign progressed and internal tensions peaked. His planned replacements included Ernesto Zedillo, who, to use Colosio's own words, simply "didn't fit in."

Colosio wanted to appoint Zedillo mayor of Mexico City, with apparently three goals in mind. The first was to make the campaign team more united and efficient, a task to which Zedillo was not suited. The second objective was to deprive Manuel Camacho of support in the capital, on the remote chance that he should run on an independent ticket or as candidate for one of the opposition parties controlled by the PRI. Manuel Aguilera, who had been appointed mayor in December to replace Camacho, was one of Camacho's oldest and most loyal friends. Colosio's camp came to believe so strongly in a possible challenge from Camacho that Zedillo, in the aforementioned letter, attributed such an intention to Camacho. "His options also included running as candidate for a party other than the PRI." Zedillo's virulent dislike for Camacho would guarantee Colosio's interests in Mexico City. Finally, although it was not the "reason for the proposal," as Alfonso Durazo recalls, rendering Zedillo ineligible for the presidency by returning him to the cabinet was also "a conscious, planned consequence." Another possibility that Colosio considered was making Zedillo deputy governor of the central bank, where he had gotten his start in the government, placing him in line to succeed incumbent Governor Miguel Mancera when the latter was to resign in 1997. In either event, Zedillo would cease to be Colosio's campaign manager with no conflict or break between them. Colosio would conserve Zedillo's friendship and admiration, but from a distance. To the extent that the PRI general secretary, who was close to Córdoba, would also be transferred, Córdoba's presence in the campaign was effectively annulled. From this point on, the powerful presidential adviser's influence would be greatly diminished, if not eliminated. This may explain why Salinas was never thoroughly convinced that removing Ernesto Zedillo was appropriate, necessary, or correct.

This was the situation when Zedillo wrote a (subsequently leaked) letter to Colosio on March 19: He was faced with his imminent removal from the campaign staff, Córdoba's eviction from the campaign, and Colosio's desire to cautiously but firmly separate himself from Salinas. The president, as he assures in the full version of his interview, had sent a letter of his own to Colosio (a copy of which he failed to provide the author), recommending that he distance himself from the Salinas administration, but clearly defining the limits of their separation. Two meetings apparently helped delineate the balance of power, in turn aggravating existing tensions. According to some sources, Salinas and Emilio Gamboa—more and more Colosio's emissary to the president—spoke on Saturday March 19. The subject of the tense meeting was Salinas's intent that Colosio feel the effects of Salinas's power, and Salinas, not Colosio, would set the terms of their separation. The intent, and even the language, resemble Zedillo's letter, especially in the "political alliance" it proposed between Salinas and Colosio. Several of the main players involved at the time suspect that this letter was really intended for Salinas. If so, the reason would be Zedillo's (and

Córdoba's) desire to leave proof of their loyalty to Salinas, and to position themselves as the champions of a lasting, strategic convergence between the president and the candidate.

After many setbacks, and a possible final meeting between Córdoba and Colosio on March 19, an easing of the tensions between the two camps could be felt. The main event, of course, was Camacho's public withdrawal from the race on March 22, which occasioned two announcements by Colosio for his aides: first, no one was to ever again discuss Camacho with Salinas; second, Colosio himself planned to have dinner and a bottle of wine with the president when he returned from his trip to northwestern Mexico, before Holy Week. They would then be able to clarify matters, agree to the changes to be implemented, and plan the relaunching of the campaign for after the April holidays.

Luis Donaldo Colosio was, in more ways than one, the last of the Mohicans. There would be no more candidates guaranteed an easy victory, and no one ever again would accede to the presidency by "caping the bull backwards." In nearly every way, the first succession of 1994 exaggerated the characteristics of the earlier successions. In particular, it accentuated the contrast between the losers—who seized a not-insignificant measure of independent power—and a victor bereft of personal power. Pedro Aspe and Manuel Camacho, each after his own fashion and in different or even diametrically opposed areas, won considerable autonomous (though not always spontaneous) political backing. Camacho's popularity among social organizations, in the intellectual community, and with the opposition greatly exceeded the power acquired by previous prospective candidates, except perhaps for Mario Moya Palencia. The fact that Camacho's success has often been the result of his own machinations—even to the point of creating, promoting, or subsidizing nongovernmental organizations—in no way alters the importance of the strength he achieved. Moreover, Aspe's appeal to the international financial community and the Mexican business community left little to be desired in comparison with similar support won by Antonio Ortiz Mena in 1970, or Jesús Silva Herzog in 1986, for example. The importance of the distribution of privatized public assets in Aspe's gaining such popularity in no way dims his accomplishments. Colosio, on the other hand, reached the candidacy with less popularity and political power than any of his predecessors, except, possibly, López Portillo. However, Luis Echeverría's successor's age, political experience, and bureaucratic résumé gave him political clout that Colosio had yet to display.

It would be absurd to suggest a causal relationship between these weaknesses and Colosio's tragic fate in Lomas Taurinas. Nevertheless the temptation exists to conclude that Colosio died partly from a feebleness imposed not by the individuals involved, the executioners, or the circumstances, but by the logic of the succession. His urge to awake popular sympathies, to get better media coverage, to break free from the constraints imposed by Salinas (identical to those set by Díaz Ordaz, Echeverría, López Portillo, and de la Madrid in their times), to gain the upper hand against his formidable opposition rivals for the presidency led him to take risks of all kinds, and he grew reckless regarding his personal and political security. The tragedy of his assassination was not an entirely inconceivable outcome of this attitude.

The Mexican presidential succession mechanism arose indirectly from the death of Álvaro Obregón in 1927, because conflicting ambitions could no longer be sorted out with bullets. Its decline began with Colosio's assassination, when it became clear that it no longer worked properly. It is not the purpose of this work to determine who masterminded the killing. Nevertheless, in the next, and last, chapter we argue that the theory holding that Salinas planned the assassination is incompatible with a coherent explanation of the events of the darkest year in modern Mexican history. The explanation lies in the sad epitaph to Carlos Salinas de Gortari's political career. He did not lose everything because of his perversion toward the weak, but because of his weakness for the perverse.

# SALINAS—ZEDILLO (1994)

The last Mexican presidential succession examined here—and perhaps the last of the traditional successions—offers a broad spectrum of epistemological and research-related difficulties that distinguish it from others. In the first place, decisive documentary material is lacking: the author refrained from requesting an interview with President Ernesto Zedillo, out of respect for his investiture and to avoid false symmetries. Second, in part by prior agreement and in part due to increasing reticence, former president Carlos Salinas de Gortari was especially reluctant to discuss the presidential succession that occurred in late March 1994, immediately after Luis Donaldo Colosio was assassinated. Thirdly, it is important to consider the weight of the theory, to date unproven but significant notwithstanding, of a supposed link between Zedillo's designation and Colosio's death. Even if one rejects the premise, as the author does, its very existence complicates historical inquiry, facing us with an unknown element that is for the judicial authorities, not the academy, to elucidate. Finally, understandably, the main characters in the drama that unfolded in the spring of 1994 have been much less willing to tell their stories than their counterparts in the previous cases.

This does not imply, however, a dearth of information, hypotheses, or narrative elements. It simply requires a different approach. I have deemed it preferable to proceed on the basis of questions rather than statements, presenting my findings as what they are: speculation lacking the kind of corroborating cross-reference found in the other chapters. The material presented here is supported by testimony that is equally serious and as reliable as that drawn upon above, but it is less abundant and definitive.

Our first question, already hinted at, is whether Salinas—Zedillo was the epitome of the succession by elimination. Was it really a condensed, accelerated process including investigation, elimination, and decision that squeezed a normally drawn-out and elaborate rite into a five-day span? This is the version Carlos Salinas has taken pains to maintain, especially as the antagonism between the former president's family and the sitting president grows, and as the current administration enters its final phase without the luster many had hoped and wished for. In this version, Salinas proceeded by eliminating prospective replacements for Colosio by stages. First he explored the possibility of amending Article 82, paragraph VI, of the Mexican Constitution, which, as previously stated, stipulates that cabinet members or governors must resign from their posts six months before the federal elections to be eligible for the presidency. Salinas consulted the leadership of the PRI and the PAN on the issue, and received a categorical negative in reply. Neither the state legislatures controlled by the PRI nor the PAN's deputies would approve such an amendment, since it would have opened the door to the third member of the original trio from 1993, Pedro Aspe. Aspe's viability as a candidate has acquired such credibility that sources close to Aspe mention a conversation with Salinas in which the president asked him whether he would accept the nomination, and Aspe replied in the affirmative. Another version, from a privileged source, involves a dialogue between Fidel Velázquez and Salinas, in which the elderly labor leader expressed his unconditional approval of Aspe, arguing that he was the first man in many years to head the Ministry of Finance who had defended labor's purchasing power. Salinas, reportedly disconsolate, replied, "I can't do it, *don* Fidel, I just can't." In any event, any attempts he may have made were for naught. Salinas closed the file and proceeded to consider the remaining options.

Unfortunately, this elegant script contains too many imperfections. First, some sources shed doubt on Salinas's account. For example, it has been possible to corroborate the story according to which at 2:30 AM on the night of Colosio's death, that is, just following his assassination, Jorge Alcocer, an adviser to Minister of the Interior Jorge Carpizo, telephoned PAN president Carlos Castillo Peraza to ask whether the PAN would agree to amending Article 82 of the Constitution. The reply—"Certainly, we don't want to be the buzzards around the corpse"—was so clear that a "whereas" clause to the relevant article suppressing the problematical requisites was drafted forthwith. Concerning the question of an apparently personal intent, the problem could easily be solved by excluding Pedro Aspe, although of the prospects the proposed constitutional amendment would render eligible, the minister of finance appeared to be the most palatable to the PAN. Moreover, such an amendment would not be evidently personalized, since it would have brought several prospects into the race, including cabinet members Jorge Carpizo, Emilio Gamboa, and Emilio Loyoza, in addition to Aspe and state governors Manuel Bartlett of Puebla and Manlio Fabio Beltrones of Sonora.

The same source mentions another important objection: that on at least one occasion Salinas resorted to "go-betweens," who were practically obliged to give him biased opinions. His remarks on the subject are an almost literal repetition of López Portillo's recommendation to avoid formal polls, when he insists in his interview that inquiries should be conducted personally by the chief investigator, that is, the president himself. In this case, the source reports, PRI president Fernando Ortiz Arana, one of the strongest prospects, was commissioned to consult with the PRI militancy. Logically, he reported a negative reaction to Salinas's query regarding constitutional change, expressed mainly in the state legislatures' unwillingness to pass a constitutional amendment—thereby improving his own odds. Salinas dispatched José Córdoba to inquire into the PAN's position. The president's adviser, as we have mentioned previously, was firmly behind Zedillo, so it came as no surprise when the PAN's reaction was also negative. Finally, the president entrusted Carpizo with discussing the issue with the PRD. The response was an equally categorical rejection of the proposal. The source in question recalls that Carpizo may have supported Manuel Camacho, his former mentor in the cabinet who had been partly responsible for his rise to the Ministry of the Interior. Thus, each emissary Salinas entrusted with conducting his inquiries presented him with results that favored their own interests or preferences, and Salinas must have suspected that they would all present biased reports. Also, Colosio's death would have been more than sufficient cause for Salinas to exchange views with the PRD presidential candidate, and Salinas acknowledges that he had no conversation with opposition leaders Cuauhtémoc Cárdenas or Porfirio Muñoz Ledo at this stage.

In light of these considerations, it seems reasonable to wonder whether Carlos Salinas in fact practiced only a pro forma consultation, into the possibility of amending the Constitution, settling for the more expeditious solution of choosing Ernesto Zedillo to step in as the PRI's new presidential candidate.

The second option Salinas considered was to postpone the federal elections by five weeks. This tactic would leave a sufficient margin to allow certain cabinet members or governors, including any of the prospects mentioned above, to resign from their posts with six months remaining before the election, and thereby become eligible to contend for the presidency. This procedure would have made a constitutional amendment unnecessary, since the Constitution sets no fixed date for holding the elections. Consequently, the measure would require neither a two-thirds majority in the Chamber of Deputies nor approval in the state legislatures. However, the measure would most likely have required the consent of the opposition parties (or at least one of them), the IFE (Federal Institute Electoral) citizen counselors, and the minister of the interior, a virtual elections minister.

According to Salinas, the president consulted with Jorge Carpizo, and Carpizo confirms Salinas's claim that Carpizo opposed the proposal on the grounds that it would entail a series of insurmountable technical complications, including the date for installing the new Chamber of Deputies, the duration of the "interregnum," and so forth. His main objection was: "In 1994, we fought for legal, impartial elections and made considerable progress toward our goal. Postponing the elections would have shown that the process was not an impartial one and would have revealed a preference for a particular party. Would anyone have proposed postponing the elections if an opposition candidate had been assassinated?" According to both men, Salinas did not pressure Carpizo, nor did he explicitly link the option of postponing the election by forty days with the probable consequence of not doing so: that Ernesto Zedillo would become Mexico's next president.

Salinas may have avoided forcing the hand of his minister of the interior because he felt it would be to no avail; another possibility is that he wasn't particularly keen on the idea himself. Carpizo was one of the president's closest aides, and would have been able in full confidence to express a negative opinion of Zedillo as a possible candidate. Salinas never formulated the issue as "we either move the elections, or it's Zedillo." We can only surmise how Carpizo might have reacted if Salinas had put the matter to him in these terms. Once again, the option was not discussed with the PRD, which might have agreed to rescue Salinas from his plight in exchange for other democratic reforms.

There are two possible explanations for the idea of a merely superficial, formal inquiry into the options for avoiding Zedillo's candidacy. The first rests on a fact that figures in all the versions available, even those provided by sources unencumbered by any fear of, or affection or respect for, Carlos Salinas. That is, Salinas was devastated on the night of the assassination, and remained so through the first few days of the following week. His entire political, personal, tactical, and strategic plan for the short- and medium-term future was collapsing. This is the most powerful argument for Salinas's innocence. It seems highly improbable that he would have engineered so overwhelming a personal and political debacle. Just after news was received of the shooting, before the formal announcement of Colosio's death, a cabinet member who had to discuss with the president how to handle a state dinner that evening in honor of the Canadian prime minister found Salinas in pieces. According to one of his friends, who visited with him several times during the week, he lost eleven pounds in seven days, drastic for a man of moderate stature. Another person who visited Salinas several times during this period describes him "in a near-fetal position."

Both Miguel de la Madrid, whose familiarity with Salinas dates from 1979, and Jorge de la Vega—less close to Salinas, but equally perceptive—have emphasized one character trait in Carlos Salinas. Under fair and even mediocre conditions he is a formidable politician and adversary, but he lacks the capacity of, for example, a Bill Clinton, to rise to the occasion and perform brilliantly in the face of sudden and unexpected situations of extreme adversity. Salinas, normally vivacious and resolute, was stunned, blinded, and paralyzed. Therefore, it is not entirely surprising that none of his interlocutors got the impression that the president was pressing for a constitutional amendment.

A second explanation fits with this line of reasoning. Zedillo represented not only the most painless and expeditious solution, but also the option promoted by José Córdoba, the palace confidant present in all the successions, who on this occasion took advantage of his chief's distress to recover lost ground and, in a tacit and successful act of vengeance, to place Ernesto Zedillo in a position that he could not handle.

If Zedillo's designation was indeed the epitome of the succession by elimination, it was not so because Salinas considered all the possible options. He resigned himself in the face of a situation that, although difficult to change, might have proved elastic in the face of greater effort or persistence than the president brought to bear during the critical days.

However, the idea of designating Zedillo to succeed Colosio was neither as natural nor as simple as we might imagine. Salinas had to persuade himself, or be persuaded, of Zedillo's advantages over the alternatives, and soothe the hard feelings or hostilities some people harbored toward him. Before examining this wealth of speculation, we would be well-advised to explore the viable options available to Salinas. Having discarded the idea of postponing the elections and eliminated variants involving a constitutional amendment, the spectrum of available candidates lacked breadth, diversity, and, above all, prospects not hindered by technical impediments or objections. First were former Salinas cabinet members Fernando Gutiérrez Barrios (in first place) and (second) Manuel Camacho. Some social leaders proposed Camacho. In his interview, Salinas assures he never so much as considered him, because it would have been impossible, as was demonstrated by an anti-Camacho demonstration at Colosio's wake in Mexico City. However, others claim that the uproar against the peace commissioner was not a spontaneous outburst but an orchestrated event. From this perspective,

Salinas might have had sufficient strength to impose Camacho if he so desired, but this brings us back to square one. In what state of mind would Camacho have assumed the candidacy after having been passed over the first time around, with the tensions and resentments Salinas describes in his interview, and with the need to test his independence from the outgoing president? Moreover, how would Colosio's people, from the deceased candidate's inner circle to his wife Diana Laura, have reacted on seeing the martyr replaced by his presumed tormentor?

Gutiérrez Barrios was in a similar position, only more so. A former minister of the interior and legendary security czar, he had not stepped down from the cabinet on the best of terms. He maintained ties to various political groups hostile to Salinas from former days, and his age and style were out of step with Salinas's. Thus, the only remotely viable options available to Salinas were members of the—constitutionally unimpeded—extended cabinet with whom he had long-standing relations, and PRI president Fernando Ortiz Arana. The first group was reduced to two: José Francisco Ruiz Massieu, director of the National Housing Institute, former governor of the state of Guerrero, and former brother-in-law to Carlos Salinas (Ruiz Massieu was to be assassinated later in the year); and Francisco Rojas, PEMEX director, former federal comptroller, and brother of Carlos Rojas, minister of social development and erstwhile leading candidate to take over the job of managing Colosio's campaign from Zedillo. According to some versions, Salinas discussed with Ruiz Massieu the possibility of nominating him, but Ruiz Massieu alerted him to a possible legal obstacle involving his father's nationality, thereby excluding himself from the race.

Along with Ortiz Arana, Rojas was the only real alternative. His relationship with Salinas was close and long-standing. He had been the young Harvard graduate's colleague in the public sector in the mid-1970s and his first companion in the bureaucracy. Rojas's administrative experience was all that could be desired. His political expertise, while not optimal, was hardly negligible. Such was the opinion of Miguel de la Madrid, who was probably more explicit in his support for Rojas when he breakfasted with Salinas on Saturday March 26 than he acknowledges in his interview. How could the man have run PEMEX for nearly seven years if he lacked political skill?

Four preliminary reasons help explain why Salinas did not choose Rojas, a candidate closer to his career, his heart, and his future interests than was Ernesto Zedillo. The first has been put forth by some of Rojas's aides, who claim that Rojas himself was convinced of its importance. A fatal explosion in Guadalajara on April 22, 1992, had become an unbearable burden for the PEMEX director, the institution responsible for the tragedy. Nominating Rojas would have been equivalent to reopening the file, the wounds, and the scandal. Salinas recoiled at the thought. Salinas himself has suggested a second explanation: the backup had to be someone farther from the president than Colosio had been, not closer. Otherwise the suspicion—already on the rise—that Salinas had planned Colosio's assassination would spread with even greater virulence. Rojas's main asset—his closeness to the president—became his principal liability. If he was chosen, there would be no lack of speculation regarding a plot against Colosio masterminded by Salinas, in order to replace him with a member of the "happy family," as Salinas's inner circle was known. The third objection rested on more substantial arguments. Since his days at PEMEX, Francisco Rojas had disagreed vehemently with José Córdoba and Jaime Serra over the state enterprise's future, as well as the energy provisions in NAFTA. After the Guadalajara explosion, Córdoba tried to remove Rojas from PEMEX, blaming him for the accident, but the scheme failed, partly due to Manuel Camacho's defense of Rojas—the kiss of death as far the 1994 succession was concerned, given Camacho's enmity with the slain candidate. Worse yet, Rojas surrounded himself with advisers with little liking for Salinas's policies, and the fundamentalist circle saw him as an enemy of the economic model in its purest expression.

Finally, Salinas knew Rojas well and recognized two essential attributes in his character. First, he maintained a relationship of equality with Salinas—no doubt tempered during the former's presidency, but destined to revert to its former level thereafter—and second, the president was fully aware of Rojas's toughness: He was a hard nut to crack, and would be a difficult successor to control, a president who, though he might lack political and intellectual stature, would nonetheless be hard or impossible for Salinas to manipulate after he left office. A friend and former aide to Rojas summarizes the dilemma confronting Salinas in a succinct formula: "Rojas was his pal; Zedillo was his employee."

Finally, Salinas considered Fernando Ortiz Arana, who presented various complications, such as a scant affinity with the Salinas economic model and team (in age or professional affiliations), and the possibility of a negative reaction to him on the part of the international financial community. By Saturday, March 26, when Salinas began to drop hints that he was leaning toward Zedillo, Ortiz Arana had ceased to be an option, either because of his apparent intention to launch his own bid for the candidacy or for other reasons for which his attempt to take a hand in fate merely provided an effective and credible alibi. To conclude, Carlos Salinas did in fact entertain options, but without having been particularly enthusiastic about any of them. Nevertheless, some of the rejected prospects were endowed, from the point of view of the nation and within the classical terms of the succession, with virtues at least comparable to those offered by Zedillo. The president was left with only one card to play because the others were not to his liking, because they were ambushed, and because he convinced himself of the intrinsic advantages of the one in his hand. Before we attempt to elucidate what merits his ultimate choice may have possessed, we should pause to consider a problem that is always a key factor in the succession, and which was especially so on this occasion: the necessity of haste.

Due to their heightened complexity, the alternatives discussed above required time for consensus building or forceful imposition. Salinas was not in a frame of mind at this point for complex, chesslike strategies calculated five or six moves in advance. The fast solution was also the easiest. Salinas himself on several occasions has described one attempt to wrest control of the process from him: a conspiracy involving faxes sent from PRI offices expressing support for Ortiz Arana. The president attributed this attempt, perhaps in retrospect, to the group of entrenched old-school politicians with ties to Luis Echeverría. Regardless of its origin, the attempt had a chance of success, because it had the consent of the interested party—Ortiz Arana was himself actively involved in the plot—and corresponded to an understandable desire on the part of sectors displaced by Salinas's policies to take matters into their own hands. Salinas managed to scotch the intrigue, but with an evident cost that probably left him concerned about his ability to neutralize other such attempts on the succession. When evidence of two other such plots appeared—at least in Salinas's imagination, and probably in reality—the president decided to define the issue as quickly as possible, more to prevent the worst than for the sake of speed itself.

The first of these additional attempts at a coup may have crystallized during a meeting at Guerrero governor Rubén Figueroa's house on or around Saturday, March 26. Rumor has it that several governors attended, to discuss the possibility of nominating Minister of Communications and Transport Emilio Gamboa Patrón as PRI presidential candidate. They were aware of the constitutional impediment to his candidacy, but believed that a means could be found to overcome it. From this meeting, on the very same or the following day, the governors in question traveled to Gamboa's office, where they presented their plan and verified that he had no objection. They took his reticence as a sign of approval, and one of them passed the idea on to Salinas or to a close presidential aide who in turn forwarded it to his boss. Logically, the president was furious. He defused the situation, but once again was weakened by the ordeal, and may well have concluded that he was nearly out of time.

It is difficult but not impossible to credit the existence of a plot by the governors. Dazed by recent events and stunned by the collapse of his succession scheme, Salinas saw traitors at every turn. It is also possible that he saw two conspiracies in one, believing some of the same individuals to be involved in both, and since the second attracted supporters much closer to the official residence, paid more attention to the second plot. At issue was the trend—that may or may not have gotten past this stage to become a movement—in favor of Manlio Fabio Beltrones, the governor of Sonora and a confidant of Colosio's. Too many sources have coincided—in the research for this book and countless editorial spaces—in affirming that the president's brother Raúl, later jailed on murder and corruption charges, supported and promoted Beltrones's bid for the candidacy in order to head off this second aborted coup. Whether Raúl conceived the plan out of liking for Beltrones or to cut off Zedillo is irrelevant in this context. The idea was far from absurd. Beltrones, from Colosio's home state, was a close friend of the fallen candidate. If not for Colosio's death, he would have been destined to hold an important position in the coming administration. He maintained excellent relations with his former boss at the Ministry of the Interior, Fernando Gutiérrez Barrios, and, through his friendship with Emilio Gamboa, had solid ties to many politicians from Miguel de la Madrid's administration. He was young, possessed of administrative and political experience, and likely to be well received by the majority of the real sources of power in Mexico except one: the United States government, which purported to have information linking Beltrones to drug trafficking (that in fact was to appear in the U.S. press months later).

There are two possible explanations for the apparent indifference shown by Beltrones's supporters regarding the constitutional limitation that affected him, still a sitting governor. First, many politicians were ignorant of the fact that governors were included among the officials excluded under Article 82 of the Constitution. Among others, both a former cabinet member and a former PRI president—even five years after the events in question—were uncertain whether a sitting governor could have been the candidate. The second explanation may have to do with Raúl Salinas's conviction that through some sophism or other it would be possible to override the constitutional restriction in the case of his friend Manlio. He was "the one." The confusion regarding twin "plots"—one favoring Gamboa and the other Beltrones—may in turn have arisen from the close friendship between the two supposed pretenders and their equally close personal and political ties to Colosio. Therefore, in hours of high tension and scant information, the president's suspicion, well-founded or not, that Gamboa supported Beltrones or Beltrones was backing Gamboa—or that they were each acting on their own account—was hardly unreasonable. If, moreover, certain aides exaggerated minor indications into major intrigues it only increased

Salinas's feelings of persecution and convinced him that it was urgent that he resolve the matter immediately.

From this second, tentative conclusion we can move on to the main question concerning this succession. As in the others we have examined, we must ask ourselves, Why did the winner win? We have suggested that the elimination of the other prospects was a decisive factor, but not to the point of precluding other explanations. We have shown how two different parallel processes unfolded: the elimination of other options and the construction of the "Zedillo option." We will now turn our attention to a second phase, once again underlining the precarious nature of our conjectures, the accounts offered, and the deductions hazarded.

Several sources have contributed to the theory that the key figure in this drama was the president's chief of staff, José Córdoba. This was possible not because Córdoba manipulated the president or conspired for or against any given candidate, but simply because Carlos Salinas, deprived by this point of some of his main advisers from earlier times—Colosio, Camacho, and his brother Raúl, who had a clear favorite—and brooding over the collapse of his long-term project, relied as never before on the man who had proven since 1981 to be his most loyal and efficient aide. According to Salinas, Córdoba presented the most "convincing and relevant" arguments in favor of Ernesto Zedillo.

From this angle, the succession by elimination became in part a succession by choice. Salinas eliminated options and Córdoba encouraged him to make a choice that he felt was intrinsically superior to other alternatives, both comparatively and on its own merits. Córdoba had backed Zedillo as a prospective candidate since before Colosio's unveiling and the tragedy in Lomas Taurinas. It is not hard to imagine that when Colosio died and a new candidate had to be found, Córdoba would understand perfectly that if he left matters to fate, to the process of elimination and to Salinas's decisions and moods, anything could happen. This may have led him to speak out for Zedillo more than against other alternatives. It seems reasonable to suppose that Córdoba employed various arguments to persuade Salinas. These, to be considered "convincing and relevant," needed to differ—at least somewhat—from those presented by other advisers, and to be strong enough to rebut the arguments against Zedillo that were rife among Salinas's other aides and confidants.

The first and most obvious argument in favor of Colosio's campaign manager may have been the prospects for the continuation of the Salinas administration's economic policies. Although an Aspe presidency would also guarantee the perpetuation of the model Salinas had implemented, none of the others could promise the same. Francisco Rojas and Fernando Ortiz Arana in particular offered no such assurance.

Closer to Córdoba's interests was that only Zedillo guaranteed the continuity of the Salinas *team*, which was in turn the best possible proof of devotion to— and identification with—the Salinas *project*. None of the other prospects offered any guarantee that the "hard core" of the president's inner circle—Córdoba himself, Jaime Serra, Ernesto Zedillo, and Guillermo Ortiz in the first circle; Francisco Gil, Carlos Ruiz Sacristán, Adrián Lajous, Juan Rebolledo, and others in the broader field—would remain intact. Zedillo was the only one likely to renew this team's lease on life, and he rewarded the confidence placed in him, until the collapse of the economy and the currency, in late December of 1994, upended everyone's plans and ambitions.

Another argument in his favor may have invoked Zedillo's commitment to the integrity and peace of mind of the former president and his family. By this point, even in the unlikely event that he lacked accurate information, Carlos Salinas knew trouble was brewing. Rumors were rife concerning his brother Raúl's shady dealings and excesses. According to Colosio's aides, Colosio had mistrusted Raúl, according to his aides, and Camacho also shared his suspicions with the president. Therefore, in as untimely and improvised an undertaking as replacing Colosio was bound to be, it would be fundamental to guarantee that the former president and his family be protected from scandal or prose- cution in accordance with the unwritten rules of the system. Normally, this guarantee was implicit in the succession process as a whole. Given that in this case one process—involving Colosio—was cut short, and the other—with Ze- dillo—never began, Córdoba's predictions, vouchsafed by his inclusion in the next administration, were very attractive to Salinas.

Finally, Zedillo satisfied the requisites regarding distance from Salinas and closeness to the deceased candidate, factors far from irrelevant in view of the prominence the widowed Diana Laura Riojas de Colosio subsequently acquired.

At this juncture unfolded a delicate and enigmatic episode in the tragedy plot of the spring of 1994. Some brand it betrayal, others misunderstanding, but its harshness aside, it was able to end one of the most intense and significant collaborations in recent Mexican history—that between Salinas and Córdoba. Very shortly after the announcement of Zedillo's nomination—perhaps on the afternoon of March 29—Salinas met with Diana Laura Riojas de Colosio and heard her complaint, lament, or outburst of irritation at the ordeal she had undergone. In particular, she deplored the regime's insistence on associating the newly proclaimed candidate with her late husband, reminding the president how Colosio had already decided to dump Zedillo as his campaign manager before he died. Zedillo had not fit in with the other members of Colosio's team, and while Colosio liked and respected him, he still opted to put him in another job, as we saw in the last chapter. He had planned to request Salinas's approval for the move at their next dinner date, scheduled for that very Monday or Tuesday, before Easter week. Perceiving Salinas's perplexity, Diana Laura alleged that Colosio had sent Salinas a message about the matter through José Córdoba— that is, through the same channel as always. Salinas protested that he had never received the message. Córdoba had misinformed him.

The president complained about the omission to his top aide. According to some sources, a bitter verbal altercation ensued and a few days later Córdoba was relieved of his duties and appointed Mexico's representative before the Inter-American Development Bank in Washington. According to sources close to Salinas, but also in contact with Córdoba, Córdoba would not admit to having stifled the message, claiming instead that the president had misinterpreted the report he had presented. Relations between the two were partially repaired in December 1994 when Córdoba coordinated Salinas's campaign to head the World Trade Organization from Washington, speaking on the telephone with ambassadors and high-level officials commissioned by the Zedillo administration to lobby for the former president, but he never recovered the trust of earlier days.

A final general reflection is in order here. The presidential succession un- leashes abnormal ambitions and greed for many reasons, but one is foremost: there is too much power at stake. It is, or was, all the power in the entire country, all the time, for six years. This power—of decision, placement, gain, transformation—well rewards fighting, cheating, stealing, and killing for, not to mention ceaseless conspiracy if you are successful. The only way to curtail the passions and interests involved is to limit the power at stake, making such recklessness and desperation unwarranted. Until this is achieved, any substitute system employed unleashes the same furor and delirium, with similar results.

Beyond the anecdote concerning José Córdoba's supposed treachery, which in any event reflects only one facet of the succession, by the weekend of March 26, Salinas had revealed a clear disposition toward Zedillo, although his pref- erence in fact became firm almost immediately after the tragedy. People who spoke with Salinas on Saturday March 26, from former president de la Madrid to Jorge de la Vega, remember receiving the impression that Salinas was so convinced and vigorous in his defense of Zedillo in comparison with the other alternatives that he appeared to have thoroughly resolved the dilemma. In any event, Salinas undertook very quickly to build a consensus in favor of Zedillo.

Several of Salinas's aides expressed opposition to Zedillo's nomination. However, because Zedillo did become the president, many of those then opposed to him now deny having so lobbied. Among the most active Zedillo opponents were Finance Minister Pedro Aspe, Minister of the Interior Jorge Carpizo, and the president's brother, Raúl Salinas. The tensions between Aspe and Zedillo became evident in November of 1994 when the former opposed a devaluation and Zedillo refused to keep Aspe as his minister of finance after the inauguration on December 1. Raúl Salinas supported Sinaloa governor Manlio Fabio Beltrones, one of Zedillo's main rivals for the nomination. In addition, Raúl Salinas and Zedillo apparently had personal conflicts dating back to 1992. At the time, the governor of Guerrero invited then Minister of Education Ernesto Zedillo to spend the end-of-the-year holidays in Acapulco. The house rented by the governor belonged to Adriana Salinas, sister of the president and Raúl. On December 28, the presidential guard came to vacate the house, so that Raúl Salinas could occupy the premises with his new wife, Paulina Castañón. Apparently Raúl Salinas did not know the identity of the family that had been asked to leave the premises, nor did the Zedillos know who came to occupy the house, but it is not altogether implausible that Raúl Salinas believed Zedillo still resented the use of the presidential guard by the president's brother.

Despite the qualms expressed by his various counselors, Salinas went ahead with his plan. According to some sources, he found Zedillo fully willing to be chosen. Other sources suggest he encountered a shy, reticent individual, hurt or offended at having been passed up twice already by Salinas, once when Colosio had been the president's first choice, and again during the first few days after Colosio's assassination, when Salinas seemed to be leaning toward the idea of making Pedro Aspe the candidate through a constitutional amendment or Manuel Camacho without one, even at the risk of a possible rebellion in the PRI. Some of Zedillo's people claim the former minister of education held out for several days, adducing that he was not going to help Salinas solve a problem that he was not responsible for creating. In any event, in the end he consented. The rest is history. With all due cunning and delicacy, Salinas incited Ortiz Arana's explicit withdrawal and Zedillo's nomination by the governor of Colosio's home state, Salinas's friend and aide Manlio Fabio Beltrones.

Beltrones recalls an initial talk with Salinas in the helicopter between Magdalena de Kino and Hermosillo on the afternoon of Friday, March 25. He expressed himself openly in favor of the constitutional amendment, adducing that Colosio's death was not an accident, but an assassination. Even if fortune smiled on a candidate who would be eligible without the amendment, it would be preferable to nominate him with one. Beltrones landed in Mexico City early on March 26, and had another interview with the president the same day. Salinas lamented the lack of support for an amendment, and insinuated that the field had shrunk to only three prospects: Zedillo, Ortiz Arana, and, less promisingly, Rojas and asked him for his opinion: "What did Colosio think of his campaign manager?" He went on to elliptically reconstruct a public remark Colosio had made about Zedillo, on the occasion of his appointment as campaign manager, and ask whether there was any record of Colosio's words. Beltrones answered in the affirmative, and promised to find it. Finally, Salinas suggested a visit to his friend Diana Laura to inform her that a decision was imminent, and that the alternatives appeared to be Ortiz Arana and Zedillo, but most likely the latter. Beltrones visited Diana Laura's home in Tlacopac on Saturday, March 26, gave her the president's message, and elicited her opinion. Salinas spent that afternoon in the company of Colosio's widow, accompanied part of the time by his wife, Cecilia. Part of the conversation focused on an exonerating letter Manuel Camacho had asked Salinas to extract from Colosio's widow. From the testimony of Colosio partisans who met with Diana Laura after Salinas did, it appears that the widow and her husband's aides thought that despite the president's encoded messages he was again considering Camacho. Through a television station he owned in Sonora, Beltrones obtained a video with Colosio's declarations concerning Zedillo and, acting on Salinas's tacit suggestion, invited a group of fellow governors who were also friends of his to breakfast at his home on Tuesday morning, in the knowledge that the "unveiling" would occur a few hours later. From there, they proceeded to Los Pinos to go through the formalities of designating Colosio's successor. They first discussed the method, and then the different options. Once they were installed at Los Pinos, in the company of Salinas, and the PRI *nomenclature*, the saga's final episode began. Salinas announced that PRI president Fernando Ortiz Arana wished to make a statement, and Ortiz Arana formally waived his claim to the candidacy. Thereafter, Salinas gave Beltrones the floor, for the governor of the deceased candidate's home state to share a posthumous suggestion from Colosio with all present. On video equipment he had installed in the hall, Beltrones played the scenes of Colosio praising Zedillo and closed his presentation explaining his proposal: Ernesto Zedillo should be the party's new candidate. Salinas asked if there were any other proposals, and after more than twenty seconds of sepulchral silence, announced that Zedillo himself would be with them soon for the PRI leadership to make their decision public. According to Beltrones, Salinas never told him what to do. He merely encouraged him to do what he did.

Process of elimination or choice? If we judge the matter in retrospect, on the basis of its repercussions, the conclusion is self-evident. The degree of antagonism between Salinas and Zedillo during the campaign and the "interregnum" and, obviously, after Raúl Salinas's arrest on homicide charges in February 1995, compares only with the splits between Díaz Ordaz and Echeverría in the first succession by elimination, and between López Portillo and de la Madrid in the second. Zedillo believed that he had prevailed on his own merits, and Salinas felt betrayed by someone who broke his promises, and failed to live up to the expectations he had aroused. This is not to say there were no frictions with the losers, but these were relatively insignificant, and in any event, the animosity or disillusionment of the prospective candidates ruled out in March 1994 does not appear to have arisen from this succession.

At the same time, it is difficult to ignore the volume of evidence suggesting that Salinas made a more active, conscious, and deliberate choice, opting for Ernesto Zedillo from the outset. This may explain why we are faced with an idiosyncratic succession, in which all the characteristics of both types of succession were accentuated by the accelerated pace of events. The process included random elimination, but it also involved a relentless effort to speed and guarantee the exclusion of some prospects and the promotion of one in particular. It included choice, but also a deliberate strategy to eliminate the remaining alternatives as quickly as possible and place a preordained candidate in the presidential seat. There was, in the end, conflict between rivals, in the best style of the *in pectore* successions, and also a brutal rift between the outgoing and incoming presidents, after the tradition of the successions by elimination. Mexico experienced the worst of both worlds: the row between Aspe and Zedillo that led to the December devaluation, and the war between Zedillo and Salinas that marked and poisoned the last Mexican presidency of the century. The frailty of the mechanism and its inability to withstand the passage of time were more clearly in evidence than ever before, sending out a double message. There was an urgent need for change, but the nebulous nature of any alternative system outweighed any will for change.

# The Ex-presidents

# LUIS ECHEVERRÍA

L uis Echeverría Álvarez was born in Mexico City on January 17, 1922. He studied at the Universidad Nacional Autónoma de México (UNAM) School of Law and Social Sciences, where he graduated with a law degree in 1945. Echeverría entered President Gustavo Díaz Ordaz's cabinet on December 1, 1964, when he was appointed minister of the interior; before that he had enjoyed an uneventful career as a midlevel government official. He was nominated for the presidency by the PRI general convention on November 8, 1969, elected on July 5, 1970, and took office on December 1, 1970. Echeverría passed the presidential sash to José Lopéz Portillo on December 1, 1976.

In 1970 Mexico was a country with a population of 48.3 million inhabitants and a per capita GNP of 690 dollars. During Luis Echeverría's six-year term, the Mexican economy grew at an average rate of 6.1 percent per year. Average annual inflation was 13.7 percent, but reached 27.2 percent in the final year of Echeverría's presidency. Per capita GNP reached US$1,670 in 1976.

Luis Echeverría faced two real rivals for the 1970 PRI nomination: Minister of the Presidency Emilio Martínez Manatou, and Mexico City Mayor Alfonso Corona del Rosal. Early on during Díaz Ordaz's term, Minister of Finance Antonio Ortiz Mena had also been identified as a possible contender. However, in part because Ortiz Mena had also contended for the 1964 nomination against Díaz Ordaz and lost—but retained his post as minister of finance from 1958 to 1970—and because he was seen as the favorite of the United States and the business community, Ortiz Mena's chances diminished as the term ended.

What was to be simultaneously Echeverría's stellar and darkest moment in the cabinet came as a result of the 1968 student movement in Mexico City. As minister of the interior, Echeverría successfully maneuvered to both preside over and avoid being blamed for the massacre of student protesters at Tlatelolco Plaza on October 2, which brought the student movement to an end and allowed the Olympic Games to take place unperturbed.

Martínez Manatou went on to serve as minister of public health (1976–1980) and governor of Tamaulipas (1980–1986). Alfonso Corona del Rosal retired from politics; Ortiz Mena served as president of the Inter-American Development ment Bank from 1971 to 1988. Alfonso Martínez Domínguez, the PRI president in 1969 and 1970, was named mayor of Mexico City (1970–1971) and then served as governor of Nuevo León (1979–1985) and senator from Nuevo León (1988–1991).

In 1975, Echeverría selected José López Portillo as his successor over rivals such as Interior Minister Mario Moya Palencia and Labor Minister Porfirio Muñoz Ledo. Echeverría's term was characterized by a breakdown in the traditional cozy relationship between the government and the business community, and, in response to the student movement of 1968, Echeverría increased public spending, foreign indebtedness, radical rhetoric, and scattered reforms. That is, Echeverría saved the PRI system from collapse, but at a price. Toward the end of his term, he was forced to devalue the currency and to hand over power in the midst of an economic crisis, charges of attempting to control his successor, and rumors of a pending military takeover.

*When you were elected president in 1970, did you discuss your choice of cabinet members with your wife María Esther or anyone else?*
Absolutely not. I want to emphasize this point: the solitude of the man in the National Palace. The president-elect's moment of greatest solitude comes when he sits down with pencil and paper to select his future aides. It is a decision that will be decisive in their lives and his own, and it carries hope and a risk. The only moment he is really alone is when he chooses his cabinet. Much has been said about the solitude of the man in the National Palace, his solitude in the midst of aides and friends. There's always someone to talk with throughout the years of the presidency and, when the time comes, for farewells. The real moment of solitude is when the president-elect becomes the focus of everyone's aspirations and expectations, and, unaided, takes a pencil and a sheet of paper and starts to write: Minister of the Interior, Defense Minister, Foreign Affairs Minister, and so on. He must do this alone, because anyone else could influence his decisions or commit an indiscretion; even a trusted, lifelong secretary could go right out and tell an interested individual, "You're on the short list." It is a moment of absolute solitude.

*Were you already thinking, "One of these men will be my successor"?*
The issue was present in the back of my mind. At the time, the main questions I considered were who would help me, who would offer support, people's family lives—that matters a lot, doesn't it? Faced with serious unrest or a scandal, you have to know who your friends are and how far you can rely on them.

*Did you investigate any of your prospective aides or have anyone investigated?*
No, I wasn't in a position to. The president-elect lacks the resources to have people investigated because the president is still in power.

*With regard to your relationship with Gustavo Díaz Ordaz, did the two of you ever become friends or did your families ever socialize?*
No, never. He was very formal, straightforward, honest, violent with sluggards, distant, and alone in the cabinet, because he didn't have a likable, amiable personality.

*What, in retrospect, were your rivals' strong and weak points in 1969?*
There were several prospective candidates. We can add two to the most well known, because they were possible options, although with much less of a chance: the director of the Department of Agriculture, Aguirre Palancares, and Alfonso Martínez Domínguez, who was party president at the time.

As the years passed, the prospective candidates were Minister of Finance Antonio Ortiz Mena, Mexico City Mayor Alfonso Corona del Rosal, Minister of the Presidency Emilio Martínez Manatou, and myself. What happened? Circumstances started to put us in the spotlight. One day the chairman of the Mexican Business Council called me: "Would you like to come and have lunch with the Council?" I already knew he had invited Ortiz Mena, who was a good friend of theirs, to speak with the Council. "A group of [longtime national labor leader and influential PRI militant] Fidel Velázquez's colleagues has invited you to breakfast." "Well, let's go to breakfast with them and talk politics," I replied. The National Peasant Confederation, a group of senators and deputies, and other party sectors were doing the same with the three prospects. I was the last, and also the youngest.

What happened? Alfonso Corona del Rosal was my candidate in the final series. I thought, "How nice, I'm going to go on working in the government." He had always done well for himself. Why wasn't he the candidate if he had support in the Senate from all the states? I've thought since that perhaps it was because he was a military man and there was a civilian tradition.

*And why did matters turn out differently? Why do you think General Corona ultimately was not chosen?*
I still can't figure it out. Corona was a man of great experience.

*Did he negotiate, or try to negotiate, with the students in 1968?*
Evidently, since the original demands were matters for the Mexico City government to handle [not the national government] and he did receive some commissions [to negotiate]. I think he always showed great loyalty to Díaz Ordaz.

*Don't you think that the reappearance of the military in Mexico's political affairs in 1968 made it more difficult for someone from the military to become a presidential candidate?*
It probably did. There is a phase of civilian government in Mexican history, which was consolidated under Alemán (1946–1952), continued with Ruiz Cortines (1952–1958), and culminated with López Mateos (1958–1964) and Díaz Ordaz (1964–1970.) It imposed the obligation or condition that the next president also be a civilian. This political climate was probably one of many factors.

*Would it have been difficult in terms of public opinion to have someone with a military background as candidate and president after 1968?*
I don't think so.

*You don't think the fact that things hadn't gone well in Mexico City in 1968 was a factor in Díaz Ordaz's decision not to choose Corona?*
No. He thought very highly of him, and they were very close friends. Corona del Rosal's relationship with Díaz Ordaz may have grown closer over the years. It is probable—and I emphasize the word *probable*—that, in the degree militarism returned to Mexico with the army's intervention in the events of 1968, Díaz Ordaz felt that it was best not to choose a military man, without Corona's having been in any way directly responsible.

*Was he less likely to be nominated after the army intervened?*
Probably.

*What about Minister of Finance Antonio Ortiz Mena?*
Ortiz Mena was in contact with the same kind of people he invited to a dinner party at his house just five years ago, the richest people in Mexico, on the Forbes list, people like Telmex owner Carlos Slim, Televisa's Azcarraga: "Gentlemen, twenty-five million dollars for the party," with the president on hand. When the president of Chase Manhattan Bank came to Mexico in 1969, there was a bankers' meeting at the Camino Real Hotel and [Ortiz Mena] gave a speech: "Bankers and businessmen of Mexico, I'm the minister of finance and a candidate for the presidency." There were three months left before the nomination and the president of Chase said, "Let's hope Mr. Ortiz Mena is nominated; you all seem to think very highly of him."

*Was this praise a negative factor for him?*
Yes. Shortly before the PRI was to nominate its presidential candidate, he was recommended as a result of the prestige he had gained in the United States financial community.

*What about Minister of the Presidency Emilio Martínez Manatou? Was he weakened or out of the running before or after the 1968 movement?*
In 1969, after the movement. He established a dialogue with distinguished intellectuals, something happened in the talks, and he was no longer a candidate.

*They spoke harshly of Díaz Ordaz and he didn't respond?*
He didn't respond well.

*Do you think Díaz Ordaz might have entrusted Martínez Manatou with this mission precisely because he wasn't his candidate?*
No, because that wasn't why he did it. They were very close. [Martínez Manatou] was the closest to him in the cabinet. He had been his friend for many years and was constantly spending time with him.

*How explicit did the conversations about the presidential succession get in meetings you held with labor leader Fidel Velázquez?*
Not very explicit: "Counsel, how are you, how are things going?" There was no conflict; we beat around the bush because the group of politicians knew the president would decide in his self-appointed role of "tongue of the balance," to use López Portillo's expression.*

*Did Fidel Velázquez support you?*
No, because the president would have been irked if he had ultimately chosen someone else.

*How do you think the events of 1968 affected the succession? How did they influence Díaz Ordaz's mood and his decision?*
I don't really think it influenced him much at all. He handled every aspect of state security. The 1968 student movement leaders truly wanted him to be obliged to resign. There were fifty or seventy thousand students asking him to come down and dialogue. In the worst moments, they wanted to burn down the door of the National Palace. It was a very personalized conflict.

---

*Fiel de la balanza* (tongue of the balance): López Portillo uses the metaphor of a balance, or a scale, to describe the process of selecting the PRI candidate, assigning himself the role of "tongue of the balance," in reference to the stem rising perpendicular from the beam that, when the beam is horizontal, points to the top of the handle from which the balance is suspended.

*You had no contact with the students in 1968?*
No.

*You did not negotiate?*
I did not negotiate. On one occasion, I issued a message calling for a very orderly dialogue in response to the insistence of the multitudes asking for the president to come out of the National Palace into the Zócalo, to speak with them.

*You had no negotiator or back channel?*
No, I had no contacts; quite the contrary.

*And why not?*
Because I had received no instructions to that effect.

*You never held secret meetings with members of the National Strike Council in 1968?*
No, I never received instructions to do so.

*Because you weren't instructed or because you didn't undertake to?*
Neither one nor the other.

*Why do you think you weren't instructed to negotiate? As minister of the interior, it would have been logical for you to negotiate with the students. . . .*
Well, [Díaz Ordaz] used several channels, and did what he felt was appropriate, or else he thought he had the right person for the job, and that it was important to protect me.

*Why protect you?*
Precisely because, although he doesn't always manage it, the president always needs to have a few prospective candidates that haven't had problems with certain sectors.

*For example, you had a contact that could have been utterly natural: your daughter-in-law, Rosa Luz Alegría. . . .*
Yes, she was very well-liked at the university, in the School of Sciences. Then she got married in the midst of the movement, and went to Paris with my son Luis Vicente.

*Did you ever discuss the movement and October 2, 1968, the day of the Tlatelolco massacre, with Díaz Ordaz after the fact?*
We really discussed the matter very little. It became a question of the army's intervention and a police problem.

*Did you ever think of resigning during 1968?*
No.

*What is your opinion of the debates that have arisen over 1968 and October 2? Two important facts have now been confirmed. One is that the army didn't enter the square with weapons in firing position, and did not intend to open fire. Do you believe this?*
Yes, yes I do believe it.

*Did the army have rubber bullets?*
I don't know.

*You have said that the first shot fired was intended for Colonel Hernández Toledo, the commander of the army batallion, and that it came from above. From where and from whom did it come?*
The shot took a descending path. Members of the Strike Council have told me that they think there were people with instructions to shoot at the soldiers to provoke the massacre. The squad stationed on the roofs of the adjacent buildings was a military squad the Defense Department had organized to guarantee security during the Olympic Games.

*To whom did this squad report? From whom did it take orders?*
It reported to the Defense Department. They were soldiers.

*Why were there so many contradictory orders?*
It wasn't a matter of contradictory orders. The situation was that the army was there and the *Batallón Olimpia* [Olympic Battalion] was present.

*But why would the* Batallón Olimpia *have fired at Hernández Toledo?*
No, that's what has been alleged.

*What do you think?*
I think they did not.

*Who shot Hernández Toledo?*
There were always a lot of armed men at these events.

*Do you think it was the students?*
Someone. The students were in very heterogeneous groups, with very different ideological backgrounds and of different ages.

*How did the year 1969 take shape?*
With great expectations. Corona del Rosal, Ortiz Mena, Martínez Manatou, and I were discussed as possible candidates. I was far behind, in fourth place. I was the youngest of the group and I hadn't formed my own political base.

*Did Defense Minister General Marcelino García Barragán have a candidate?*
He did nothing other than what his boss, the commander-in-chief of the army, ordered him to. He was a great soldier.

*Did PRI President Alfonso Martínez Domínguez have aspirations?*
He was known as the top politician in Mexico. He really started out in the Mexico City government with high ideals and very little schooling and managed to form a very important relationship with the labor union. President Miguel Alemán used him and he became a congressman. Then President Ruiz Cortines gave him a job in his administration, President López Mateos promoted him again, and Díaz Ordaz, who had had considerable difficulties with the entire cabinet under López Mateos, hired him. When Díaz Ordaz was nominated he brought in new groups, and that was when he made Alfonso party president.

*When did you begin to feel that things were going your way? What were the first signs?*
Around the time I was nominated by the National Peasant Confederation. Thinking about it now, in retrospect, during the first half of 1969, I received a series of invitations to talk from the Mexican Business Council, with prominent businessmen among its members, and from leaders of organized labor.

*There were no low blows from your rivals?*
No, I don't remember anything significant. Perhaps because I was the youngest and—at least apparently—had less of a chance, they didn't concern themselves much with me.

*In the end, why do you think Díaz Ordaz finally decided to choose you?*
Because he saw no opposition to my candidacy. It's a subjective question that history may reveal some day, or he may have left some written recollections. Later on, during my campaign, his attitude toward my candidacy began to change.

*How did he inform you of his decision?*
With great simplicity, after a meeting that had not been held in the National Palace, but in Los Pinos; one afternoon, after discussing other relatively unimportant matters, he told me.

*When?*
It must have been in mid-July 1969. He announced my candidacy to me in June or July: I was nominated by the CNC in October. He said, "You're going to be the PRI candidate for the presidency; are you ready?"

"I'm ready."

"See you later."

"Good-bye."

*Nothing further?*

No, nothing. There wasn't even a promise or any special, effusive show of emotion. He told me with the utmost simplicity.

*He didn't say, "Don't tell anyone else?"*

No, there was really no need to.

*You didn't mention it to your wife María Esther?*

Absolutely not. Not even as August and September passed, and the four finalists began to be mentioned in the newspapers.

*Why do you think he told you so far in advance, in July, when the candidate was to be announced in October?*

Evidently because the man who was going to emerge as candidate had to start thinking about his situation, his personal affairs, and his family, and examine his conscience to see whether he was ready to work intensely, take risks, and possibly face danger. It requires preparation. A presidential candidate has to take precautions. In the first place he needs to look after his health. Some need to talk with their families. I did not. Some go over their wardrobe, others invent or rediscover illustrious ancestors, or make sure the children behave, because things start appearing in the newspapers.

*How did your antagonism with Díaz Ordaz evolve?*

I deduced that it wasn't going to be very ostensible. There were some demonstrations as a result of a rally during my visit to the Universidad Nicolaíta in Morelia. The trip to Michoacán included, by tradition, placing flowers at the monument to Hidalgo in the university's main patio. I arrived, the university was packed, with an atmosphere of great expectancy. After being attacked by three youths, I spoke, and declared before the portraits of Fidel Castro and Che Guevara, whom I admire, that the students should not ask for heroes borrowed from abroad, with the traditional example of the fathers of the nation, and others such as Melchor Ocampo and Lázaro Cárdenas. Half the university applauded these remarks, and as I was coming down from the stand, a young man surnamed Sandoval, of the Communist Youth, shouted, "A minute of silence for the students killed in Tlatelolco." The minute passed and I continued on my way, having won the sympathies of a considerable part of the university population after this incident. In Mexico City, there was commotion over what had happened in Tlatelolco and on the next day at PRI headquarters there were instructions to stay put, and rumors began to circulate that there would be a change of candidate. I was told in Michoacán that the climate was building for a change of candidate. I said, "They're going to have to work hard to hold another national assembly." A few days later the doubts cleared and there were no further problems thereafter.

*Where did this come from, from Díaz Ordaz or the army?*
Probably from a misinterpretation on the part of some immature, lower-ranking army officers, and probably in political circles. The candidate could still have been changed in October, because there was more than enough time left for the necessary proceedings.

*Did you speak with PRI president Martínez Domínguez that day?*
No, there was no need to because the shadows had cleared.

*Did you have any contact with the president or with the army?*
No.

*Did anyone call you to inform you that Defense Minister García Barragán was irritated?*
No, no one.

*I'm going to read the notes from my interview with a former aide of yours who held an extremely sensitive position at the time, and who granted me an interview with the condition that I would not mention his name in this context: "García Barragán called me, very upset over Echeverría's imprudence in having gone to the university. He asked me to act as go-between with Díaz Ordaz to inform him of the irritation or anger the matter had aroused in the armed forces. President Díaz Ordaz ordered me to speak with Echeverría by telephone and make him understand the problem with the armed forces. I told him Díaz Ordaz had asked Echeverría to dedicate his next speech to the armed forces, and that's exactly what he did. Later, Echeverría asked me to arrange a meeting with García Barragán in Jalisco for him." Is this true?*
I stopped to greet him at the entrance to his ranch.

*This top government official didn't ask you to give the speech in question?*
We spoke frequently and he may have dropped some kind of hint, which would have been logical to me, but not as a critical issue.

*And you didn't speak with President Díaz Ordaz that day?*
No.

*You don't remember in detail your conversation on the evening I mentioned?*
Well, we talked.

*Alfonso Martínez Domínguez, who was PRI president at the time, has claimed that he had a conversation with you, that he went to meet you at the airport on your arrival from Baja California. You started talking and he mentioned that he thought you were ignoring the president, that adverse sentiment toward your campaign was building, that your trips were too long, that your defeated rivals for the candidacy were still in Mexico City and were misinforming the president, and that he thought you should report to the president more often. You replied, "President Díaz Ordaz knows everything, I'm not going to distract him with trivial matters." Is this true?*
That's how the conversation must have been, among other issues we discussed. It was a surprise to the party and bothersome to many people, because of the work it meant for them, that I wanted to travel through Baja California. We started the trip by crossing most of the desert.

*To continue with Martínez Domínguez, in the same month of January 1970, a few weeks after this conversation, he says that he went to visit President Díaz Ordaz, with whom he was very good friends. When he entered the president's office, Díaz Ordaz said, "What does your damned candidate have to say?" He says that he answered, "Stop it, Mr. President, he's your candidate as well as mine."*
*"Then why," replied Díaz Ordaz, "is he going around saying there's going to be a change? What change? We're through with him, he can go to hell. We're going to make him ill, and he's going to get really sick. The PRI can still hold a convention, we're still in time. Start getting ready, stay at home for three or four days, stay in touch with PRI headquarters by telephone."*
*What comments do you have to offer?*
It must have been after the incident in Morelia. It doesn't strike me as improbable. I can't be sure, because Alfonso didn't tell me, but it doesn't seem unlikely, because it's true that I wasn't very well received at the National Palace after I had said we had to move onward and upward.

*You never received any reports during those January days that President Díaz Ordaz had thought of replacing you of his own accord?*
No, but—and I want to emphasize the point—I don't think it unlikely. Not to justify myself, but he didn't like my campaign or my administration. After taking office, I never discussed anything with him.

*Never?*
I never spoke with him again for the entire six years. Never. He hadn't liked my campaign and he disliked my administration. He didn't like the fact that I

included a lot of young people. The incident with Martínez Domínguez doesn't strike me as improbable, but its very probability includes the possibility that it was merely a way of letting off steam, in a manner of speaking.

*Now, if you had in fact been displaced as candidate, Martínez Domínguez would have been your replacement, wouldn't he?*
Well, that's what he always hoped.

*Would you mind discussing your first cabinet members one by one?*
There was no doubt in my mind that Moya Palencia was going to be minister of the interior. I asked Gómez Villanueva to head the Agrarian Affairs Department and I told him, "And we're going to make the department a ministry because of the importance of the countryside." And that's how it was.

*You obviously thought that Moya was a prospective candidate for the presidency from the first days of your administration. . . .*
I thought his name would come up, and Moya had a brilliant background. He had been a classmate of Carlos Fuentes and was a member of the so-called class of 1950, who were all very intelligent, and he kept in touch with them.

*Whom did you think of from the start as possible candidates?*
I considered Carlos Gálvez Betancourt, who had shown excellence and honesty as my director of the Mexican Social Security Institute (IMSS). He did an excellent job as governor of Michoacán, had been my chief of staff in the Ministry of the Interior. Being designated IMSS director obviously opened up possibilities for him.

*Who else?*
Among my several very accomplished aides, I saw that Porfirio Muñoz Ledo had considerable abilities. He was much younger, and had affinities and differences with the cabinet.

*And Minister of the Presidency Hugo Cervantes del Río?*
Let's say he was another lesser prospect, very close but lacking the cold, calculating nature that many people assume is necessary.

*Had you already thought of José López Portillo at the beginning of your presidency?*
I had a liking for him because of our long-standing friendship, notwithstanding which I hadn't really been his candidate in 1970. But that never clouded our friendship. He was already working closely with Dr. Martínez Manatou, and

our friendship always remained unalterable, but each of us with his own destiny and activities.

*But you think, rather, that he supported Martínez Manatou [in 1970]?*
Let's say it was a matter of inertia. He had started working with Martínez Manatou in the Ministry of the Presidency: Díaz Ordaz came to like him very well because of his extensive studies. He became undersecretary under Martínez Manatou. When, as was always the case, the country's financial situation took a turn for the worse, I thought it would be recommendable, after working as director of the Federal Electricity Commission, that he be minister of finance and have contact, as an independent person, with the financial sector—with the bankers, and with the private initiative. Then I did begin to think he might make a good presidential candidate.

*By the time you appointed him minister of finance?*
Yes.

*Did you appoint López Portillo to the Ministry of Finance because you thought he needed more opportunities and should have more contact with financial circles, which he was unfamiliar with, or was it the other way around?*
No, it worked both ways.

*When you brought him to Finance, were you already clearly considering him for the candidacy?*
As a possibility, and it was recommendable to have someone with certain ties and experience with those people.

*That's why you put him in Finance?*
So he could learn the ropes, in the event that he worked out and no serious problems arose.

*Did you protect him during those three years?*
No, quite the contrary. I told him he would have to handle very serious problems.

*When did you stop considering Mario Moya Palencia?*
When I realized that financial problems were the most pressing items on the agenda. When poverty, unemployment, and international trade convinced me that they are the essential problem, more than the question of politicians and their respective ambitions per se. When I realized that the other part is essential—social inequality, population growth—I began to think of finance as essential to public policy. Mario Moya was an excellent and loyal minister of

the interior, talented and brilliant, and was the candidate of important political groups both within the PRI and nationwide.

*What do you think of Mario Moya's theory of generations, according to which he knew he wasn't going to be [the PRI candidate], because it would have implied a generation gap at an inopportune moment?*
No, he assumed he was going to be nominated. I had the utmost confidence in him. He was extremely efficient and talented. We saw one another on rare occasions for coffee at Los Pinos with groups of friends. I had visited his house often before I became president and appointed him minister of the interior. Our wives were friends in those days.

*He did assume that he might be the one?*
Of course, but Gálvez Betancourt and Hugo Cervantes del Río also entertained the same assumption.

*You don't seem to think age was a factor. If you had wanted Moya to be the candidate, would you have chosen him?*
Certainly, with no problem whatsoever.

*When did you finally decide?*
After talking with the party sectors. I insist that you can't underestimate the importance of this stage of the process. Those of us who make our careers in the party know that our votes come from the party sectors* and there may be sectors that are obliged [to vote for the PRI]. But if nothing expressly or tacitly awakens voters' enthusiasm and support, you can't have a solid, firm candidacy.

*Did PRI president Jesús Reyes Heroles favor any of the prospective candidates?*
No, he did not. He was interested in creating a platform for the party, which he presided over at the time, to choose its presidential candidate. However, circumstances precipitated López Portillo's candidacy, and he felt it was inconsistent with his convictions for there to be a candidate before the platform was complete. My thinking was that the candidate would prepare his platform during his campaign swing across the country.

*Was he opposed to the idea of López Portillo being the candidate, or did he simply think it was not feasible?*
It was more a functional than a personal issue. López Portillo's candidacy was decided. Reyes Heroles didn't like that and had already demonstrated his re-

---

*The term "party sectors" refers to the PRI's traditional organized constituencies, which are three in number: organized labor, the peasantry, and the "popular" or lower-middle-class sector.

luctance to participate in the campaign. Muñoz Ledo became party president and Reyes Heroles went to the IMSS, because Gálvez Betancourt had left his job there to be minister of labor. Afterward, López Portillo appointed him minister of the interior, and he held the job for slightly less than half of López Portillo's term.

*When did you finally take the irrevocable decision to go with López Portillo? On approximately what date?*
In September or October of the fifth year of my term.

*You allowed for a lapse between when you informed López Portillo and the unveiling similar to that which Díaz Ordaz gave you?*
As a matter of fact, I did, only I wasn't very explicit. I started putting the pieces in place and he understood.

*But you did inform López Portillo explicitly of your decision in advance?*
Well, I did say near the end, "It's decided, they're going to nominate you, go to work."

*You didn't inform him weeks or months in advance? Why didn't you inform López Portillo that far in advance?*
Because there was no need.

*Mario Moya Palencia has told me that on one occasion with López Portillo at a government house in Ixtapa, López Portillo told Moya, "I'm very fond of this house, because this is where* don *Luis [Echeverría] informed me of his decision."*
It was probably one of the conversations that made him feel his time was near. We never had as open an understanding as Díaz Ordaz had with me. But there were some very tangible things.

*Such as . . . ?*
Well, connecting him with certain people, discussing issues that went beyond his specific incumbency as minister of finance, issues in world politics.

*And when did you start discussing these topics with López Portillo?*
Two or three months before.

*And he understood?*
Obviously, if it was something important enough for him to perceive. Because of our long-standing friendship, we understandably conversed on a number of topics that went beyond any specific function he may have had, which was as it should be.

*Did you ever have the kind of conversation you had with López Portillo with the other prospective candidates?*
No, but I did make them participate. I put them to the test.

*But you didn't start saying "prepare yourself, get ready"?*
No, because it would have given the impression that there was a very serious commitment on the president's part.

*Who were the finalists?*
The process advances, the president has to weigh the alternatives. Moya Palencia was in it until the final round, Porfirio Muñoz Ledo, those four.

*Who was the fourth?*
López Portillo, Moya Palencia, Muñoz Ledo, and Gálvez Betancourt.

*And why wasn't Muñoz Ledo the one?*
Well, because the minister involved with finances was the one. López Portillo was in touch with financial problems.

*What about the rumor that Porfirio had been vetoed by the Americans or the business community?*
No, Porfirio was not then—and to this day is still not—a radical element. He was liked by a lot of people. Many people were frightened by his so-called European socialism, but it was the socialism of Willy Brandt and other European leaders.

*Porfirio says that on one occasion, you summoned him to Los Pinos and said, "Listen, don't socialize with the other cabinet members at parties."*
That's right.

*It's true?*
I'm sure of it. Also drinking. . . . I told him they shouldn't be drinking and never at meetings. I had a practical-minded Puritanism.

*But also you didn't like them partying. . . .*
Not at all.

*What information did you get from the business community about its preferences regarding the succession? Did they have a clear candidate?*
No, I really think there was no emphatic objection to anyone. They liked López Portillo because he was in contact with the banks and with a lot of businessmen. Gálvez Betancourt, in Social Security, was in touch with the essential forces of

production. Gómez Villanueva was also mentioned in those days. He had very close ties to the peasant sector, to which he was completely loyal.

*You wouldn't say they had a candidate, or even reservations or disagreements about any of the prospects?*
No, no negative opinions were expressed about any of them. I think not. I think they would have accepted any one of the prospects, even Muñoz Ledo, who had fought tenaciously for an economic development strategy that included expanding the market.

*The Church?*
No, there was never any problem, quite the contrary.

*And labor union leader Fidel Velázquez?*
*Don* Fidel, who was always very prudent, was on the alert.

*He expressed no opinion at all?*
Some people have told me Muñoz Ledo's candidacy was to his liking, although he supported the party with complete loyalty afterward.

*Your colleagues have given me different answers to the question of how much they wanted to know, and how much they did in fact know, about their prospective successors' personal affairs. Miguel de la Madrid said, "No, I didn't have anyone investigated from that angle, and even failed to learn things I should have learned." In your case, there was a peculiarity, at least as regards López Portillo. You knew him better than anyone else. You knew his strong and weak points. Did none of these seem sufficient to make you decide against his candidacy? His family life, for example?*
No, no, no. Objectively speaking, while he was a top-ranking member of my administration, I perceived nothing more than the confirmation of what I had observed since his early youth: that he was brave, determined, with an agile mind. That's what I had always thought of him, since we were students.

*López Portillo had a reputation for being a womanizer. . . .*
One way or another we all have, or more or less. For me it is entirely secondary. It was not a relevant issue.

*Did you ever have any doubts about López Portillo?*
None, and I think he had a very successful campaign, and that Muñoz Ledo managed it well as PRI president.

*Porfirio maintains that you were somehow thinking in terms of two successions. . . .*
Two successions?

*Yes, he claims you were thinking of López Portillo in 1976 and Porfirio in 1982, and that's why you put him in the PRI. He didn't want to go to the PRI. He even thought that if you sent him to the PRI, you would be forcing him on López Portillo, and that in the medium term they would fight and he would have to quit.*
In the first place, it would have been extremely naive to think about what might happen twenty years later. It wouldn't have occurred to me, and I would not have been so naive. Secondly, I considered it my responsibility to manage things so that López Portillo's campaign would be a success, and Porfirio, who is very intelligent, is a good public speaker, and has a 100 percent political temperament, could be [a good] party president. Porfirio is not someone who says "yes sir, no sir," even to the president and much less to a candidate. He's a person with ideas, with education, that give him the ability to propose alternatives to recommendations from the president.

*He didn't resist your sending him to the PRI?*
Not at all, he's a politician. What did happen is that he didn't get along with López Portillo.

*They didn't understand one another?*
They were both consummate politicians.

*But you don't think they clashed partly because López Portillo saw him as one of your people, more loyal to the president than to the candidate?*
They may have given that impression, but it wasn't like that at all.

*Did any of the prospective candidates get angry with you?*
None of them did. They went to give López Portillo a hug, and we went on working and, because of the harmony that had prevailed during the campaign, they probably had hopes of staying on in his administration.

*You didn't offer any of them an explanation?*
Of course not. I told them neither why they had not been chosen nor why they had a chance in the first place. The issues are very subjective and subtle, and you can't get into too much explanation, in the first place because it's not necessary.

*You haven't talked with Mario Moya about why he wasn't the one?*
I've talked with him, but never about that.

*How did your relationship with López Portillo evolve during the campaign, and once he was president?*
He had the idea, from interested rumors, that neither Díaz Ordaz nor Echeverría should give the impression of participating in politics after leaving office. He

asked Díaz Ordaz to be ambassador to Spain, and me to be ambassador to France. I immediately told him that I didn't speak French and that I was going to leave for China in mid-1977. I had already made my travel arrangements, and my wife and four of my children were ready to go. I explained that I didn't think I was the right man for the job and that I was planning to travel on my own account to different parts of the world. He picked up the telephone and ordered Minister of Foreign Affairs Roel to issue me a diplomatic passport, to allow me to travel freely, and to assign me an adviser. I went quickly to China and then to Paris. While in Paris, I noticed that the small embassy to the UNESCO was vacant. I called Roel on the telephone, and twenty minutes later I had been appointed. I stayed on there for a year.

*According to López Portillo the interested rumors were from Minister of the Interior Reyes Heroles. Do you agree?*
There was something special. I think I've mentioned before that as PRI president, Reyes Heroles did not support López Portillo. He assumed that a tax collector could not be a presidential candidate. Then López Portillo, surely remembering that Reyes Heroles had been very studious as a political ideologist, took him to the Ministry of the Interior, where he stayed for two years. They became very distant.

*López Portillo says that he no longer thinks that you tried to control him after you left the presidency, but that Reyes Heroles exaggerated the activity here at your San Jerónimo home.*
He was very concerned, because I had friends and family. How were we to isolate ourselves? It was impossible. I entertained lifelong friends, aides who had worked for me for many years. Why not? After being president, it would have been naive to try to intervene in any decisions of the executive branch.

*You left Porfirio in the PRI and Gómez Villanueva in the Chamber of Deputies. . . .*
I didn't leave them, [López Portillo] invited them.

*You put Porfirio in the PRI. . . .*
But not until the end of the campaign.

*And you also put Gómez Villanueva in the Chamber of Deputies. . . .*
I did so with López Portillo's full knowledge and consent. That's how it was, no different. As to Muñoz Ledo, López Portillo asked him to be minister of education. That was his affair altogether.

*Did you tell López Portillo to include anyone in his cabinet?*
No one. I know how it is. He included people from my cabinet and close friends.

*But you didn't intercede on anyone's behalf?*
No. He even very kindly and generously appointed my two eldest sons, who are economists, to manage para-statal firms. Then he came here, to San Jerónimo, and was the main witness at the birth of a grandson of mine in 1978.

*Did friendship in any way influence your decision to favor López Portillo, or lead you to think that having been your friend for so many years he would look out for you?*
That "look out for you" seems to have little value compared with the risks the president runs with the candidate. There are perilous situations and moments fraught with danger that one has to accept.

*Díaz Ordaz went so far as to say he had made a mistake. . . .*
Yes, he did, because he didn't like my campaign, he didn't like my foreign policy plans, and he was not pleased with our opening Los Pinos to the entire world. It's true. That's what he said. Well, he was within his rights.

*You didn't think you made a mistake with López Portillo?*
Not I. Díaz Ordaz very frankly admitted he had erred. He repeatedly told his friends how every day in front of the mirror while he was shaving, using a stronger word, he said to himself, fool, fool, fool. "Why, Gustavo? Because I got it wrong."

*Finally, your participation in the 1994 succession: What was the tenor of your conversation with President Salinas in March 1994—the day PRI candidate Luis Donaldo Colosio was assassinated—which Salinas has referred to publicly, but of which you have not given your version?*
We learned in the evening of March 23 that there had been an attempt on Colosio's life, and at around eight in the evening we heard on the radio and on television that he had died. Then I said, "I'm going to offer my condolences."

I had had little contact and no problems with President Salinas. I went to Los Pinos. A lot of people were arriving and Salinas was in a downstairs room with members of his cabinet and other people who had come. Then I went to speak with them and expressed my regrets.

The next day I went to PRI headquarters. López Portillo had been there already and then Miguel de la Madrid and some other people arrived at the

Plutarco Elias Calles Room, and I kept vigil there with other party figures. The entire cabinet was there, and I said some very emotional words about the candidate and the Mexican Revolution and onward and upward. They applauded. I greeted Salinas and withdrew. The other former presidents said nothing, but I saw the people and there was some applause coming from the gallery. And time passed, and Salinas declared that a few days later I had gone to recommend Emilio Gamboa [who got his start with Echeverría in the IMSS, and later was Miguel de la Madrid's secretary and a cabinet member under Salinas] for the candidacy. I've learned since, from Emilio himself and others, that they had already had considerable difficulty when he had been minister of communications, and Salinas had been on the verge of asking for his resignation. Therefore the purpose of saying I had gone to recommend him for the candidacy was to harm him. That was all.

*You never spoke with Salinas during those days except to offer your condolences.*
No.

*You neither spoke with him nor proposed a candidate?*
No. Gamboa was one of his aides. I didn't know they were at odds.

*You proposed neither Gamboa nor anyone else?*
No.

*And you had no substantial conversation with Salinas, that is, the rumor about Gamboa is simply untrue?*
I would not have been so naive as to recommend a candidate. I do know something about how all this works.

# JOSÉ LÓPEZ PORTILLO

José López Portillo y Pacheco was born in Mexico City on June 16, 1920. He studied at the UNAM School of Law and Social Sciences, and graduated with a law degree. He entered Luis Echeverría's cabinet on June 1, 1973—at the age of fifty-three—as minister of finance and he was nominated PRI presidential candidate on September 22, 1975. He was elected president of Mexico on July 4, 1976, and inaugurated on December 1, 1976. He passed the presidential sash to Miguel de la Madrid six years later.

In 1976 Mexico was a country of approximately 70 million inhabitants. During López Portillo's term of office, the Mexican economy grew at an average rate of 6.2 percent per annum. Average annual inflation was 32.7 percent, and reached 98.9 percent in the last year of his presidency. Per capita GNP was US$2,840 in 1982.

López Portillo faced three strong contenders in the race to obtain the PRI presidential nomination in 1976. Minister of Labor Porfirio Muñoz Ledo and Minister of the Interior Mario Moya Palencia were considered early favorites. Minister of Agriculture Augusto Gómez Villanueva, Social Security (IMSS) Director Carlos Gálvez Betancourt, and Minister of the Presidency Hugo Cervantes del Río were also considered contenders for the PRI presidential nomination for the 1976 elections.

Moya Palencia apparently fell out of Echeverría's grace toward the second half of the term and his candidacy began to decline from then on. In the 1980s and 1990s, Moya Palencia has served as Mexican ambassador to the United Nations (1985–1989), Japan (1989–1990), and Cuba (1990–1993). At the time the Spanish-language edition of this book was published, Moya Palencia was the Mexican ambassador to Italy.

López Portillo's most serious rival in late 1975 was Porfirio Muñoz Ledo.

Undersecretary of the presidency from 1970 to 1972 and minister of labor from 1972 to 1975, Muñoz Ledo was considered the candidate of the left and one of Echverría's favorites. When López Portillo was chosen as PRI candidate, Muñoz Ledo was appointed president of the PRI to coordinate the presidential campaign. He served as minister of education in the first López Portillo cabinet, but had to leave over conflicts between López Portillo and former president Echeverría. After serving as Mexico's ambassador to the United Nations from 1979 to 1985, Muñoz Ledo broke with the PRI together with Cuauhtémoc Cárdenas for the 1988 presidential elections. He was elected senator in 1988, running against the PRI. In 1989, Muñoz Ledo helped found the Partido de la Revolución Democrática (PRD) and was PRD's president for the 1994 presidential elections. In 1997, he was elected to the Chamber of Deputies and became the first non-PRI president of the Chamber in modern times.

José López Portillo was president during both Mexico's greatest economic boom since the early sixties and its most resounding economic crash, in 1982. New oil fields were rapidly brought onstream to take advantage of high oil prices. Heavy foreign indebtedness, thanks to abundant recycled petrodollars and low real interest rates through 1980, fueled stunning economic expansion, but also led to a maxi-devaluation of the currency in 1982 and a dramatic end-of-administration crisis. While López Portillo rebuilt Mexico's oil industry, reduced poverty and inequality to levels unparalleled before or since, carried out the first important political and electoral opening, and inaugurated Mexico's activist foreign policy in Central America and the Caribbean, he left the economy in a shambles and dramatically damaged relations with the private sector by nationalizing the banking industry in 1982. He left office as Mexico's most reviled ex-president, amidst widespread though unproved charges of corruption.

The contest for his succession involved Budget Minister Miguel de la Madrid, PRI president Javier García Paniagua (the son of former defense minister Marcelino García Barragán and thus someone with close army contacts), oil chief (PEMEX) Jorge Díaz Serrano, Finance Minister David Ibarra, and Labor Minister Pedro Ojeda. López Portillo's succession in 1982 was the last "uneventful" and "classical" succession.

❦

*Miguel de la Madrid has claimed that he never thought PRI president Javier García Paniagua was his most dangerous rival in 1981, and that his two real rivals were Jorge de la Vega, minister of industry and mines, and Pedro Ojeda Paullada, minister of labor. What do you think?*

I'm sorry to refute de la Madrid's assertion. In fact, in the presidential succession I presided over, in the final analysis only two individuals, two prospective candidates remained: García Paniagua and Miguel de la Madrid. I still maintain that the function of the "presidentialist" president* is to be as I was, someone who feels the balance. That is to say, the different specific political factors are entered like weights in a sort of balance, and the balance tilts until it definitively shows who the candidate should be. At times the weight that shifts the balance is minimal, and then our reaction is to say, "The balance was tilted by the weight of a hair." It is indeed the weight of a hair, but added to the enormous weight that lies beneath, the hair moves earth and sky.

*How was the list of presidential candidates created in 1981?*
Well, it's somewhat conventional to say that there were exactly six names, because they may have been more or fewer. One starts thinking of the succession as soon as one takes office.

*From the first moment?*
Because one has to form a cabinet, and one is aware that the next president will come from that cabinet. We knew that in designating government ministers, one of them, or someone from the cabinet, from the lower echelons (because one has to anticipate everything; the selection of cabinet members is very complicated), will be president. One has to think in the first ones, who are ministers, the deputy ministers who will eventually take their places, and so on. The rite of appointing the cabinet is something very special in the presidentialist regime, and in this case, the first possible candidates I had thought of were soon eliminated.

*Who were they?*
I had appointed Carlos Tello to head Planning and Budget and given Finance to Julio Rodolfo Moctezuma, and when Tello unexpectedly resigned, the need for balance in the Cabinet and in the country's economic policy imposed the painful necessity of requesting Moctezuma's resignation with no other specific reason than current policies. Then the entire political horizon was clouded for me, and with it the groups from which I could have thought of choosing my successor.

*Did you ever think of amending Article 82 of the Constitution to make your first*

---

*The noun *presidencialismo* and the adjective *presidencialista* are terms coined in specific reference to the Mexican political system, and reflect the absolute and unchallenged authority exercised by the president over all other government functionaries and agencies. We will use the English-language equivalents "presidentialism" and "presidentialist" herein.

*minister of the interior, Jesús Reyes Heroles, eligible for the candidacy? [He was constitutionally impeded because of his Spanish-born father.]*

No, because I thought such a move would have had an implicit dedication to two strong personalities in my cabinet: Carlos Hank González in the Mexico City government and Jesús Reyes Heroles, both sons of foreigners limited by the same constitutional impediment. If I had amended the Constitution, in the event that the Congress passed the amendment, it would be an amendment with an obvious beneficiary.

*Then there were very few players in your game at the beginning: Tello, Mocte-zuma. . . .*

Pedro Ojeda, Fernando Solana, and to some degree PEMEX Director Jorge Díaz Serrano.

*Serrano was a possible candidate from the start?*

Jorge was a possibility because he knew a great deal about oil.

*Why did you decide against him?*

Jorge had been an intimate friend of mine since childhood, and I thought very highly of him, but he collided head-on with the economic cabinet when we were making some fundamental decisions, and in 1981, months before the succession, I was obliged to make one of the most painful political decisions of my life and ask for his resignation.

*And your Minister of Finance David Ibarra?*

Well, David Ibarra was not an option, partly because one of his aides got out of hand during the campaign for the nomination. This distorted the competition for me. He started attacking Miguel de la Madrid. I still wanted to keep the country under control, and they were getting out of line. To prevent this from making my presidential power ineffective, I had to maintain a certain degree of discipline, and I did so with the faith of a true believer.

*Had you already thought of Miguel de la Madrid when you included him in the cabinet as minister of planning and budget in May 1979?*

Of course I had. Until then my main concern had been the problem of the budget, because my experience in all the areas I had managed, National Patrimony, and the Federal Power Commission had shown me that the Ministry of Finance suffered from a series of conditions that congested it and complicated many decisions.

*Did you put him to the test?*

Naturally. The basic test, as he very accurately says, was the National Development Plan. I had placed my highest hopes in this plan's being the main instrument of the country's development.

*How did you sound people out? Did you ask point-blank questions?*
One finds ways of asking, sometimes directly, others with generalities like "How are things going?" "What do you think?" or "Where are things pointing?" During the entire time people are working, one gathers information about the results they achieve from the individuals responsible, the parties affected, and mere witnesses. Then impressions are, or rather were, collected. The people one goes to (or at least I went to) were mainly *don* Fidel Velázquez and the labor sector. It was the most important sector to me because it is the most stable faction in the party, and usually the strongest when the time comes to make decisions and stand behind them. I was constantly calling on Fidel, although I consulted with other leaders as well, not just him. I think that this was one of his functions in all the administrations that came and went during his lifetime. I'm not going to say he was the great elector, but he was a great shaper of criteria for selecting candidates.

*Did he ever go so far as to express his opinions of the prospective candidates?*
Naturally, fully-formed opinions.

*Did he object to any of them?*
I can't recall. I would be lying if I told you that he strongly objected to any of them. But he thought particularly highly of Miguel de la Madrid.

*How about the business community?*
The same applies. I consulted them less frequently and their opinions were less reliable because they always reflect very specific interests, which was not the case with Fidel, for example, because the man thought, more than in class interests, in the interests of the nation.

*Some scholars maintain that the consultation process included the Catholic Church, the army, the former presidents, and the United States. Is this true?*
No, at least not in my case. The importance of the consultation is precisely that it is apparently unimportant. An explicit inquiry would produce a skewed result, expressing the special interest of the person asked, giving him the importance of an elector, and the essence of presidentialism is that there are no electors. There is a tongue of the balance, but no electors.

*In this informal consultation, did you, for example, sound out the Church?*
I can assure you that I never sounded out the Church's opinion in any way. My contact with the Church was not only rare, it was practically nonexistent,

and when I did consult with the Church, it was on very concrete issues that did not allow for the kind of generalized discussion that an inquiry of the type I practiced requires. The Church no. The army, however, most certainly.

*And what response did you receive? Did they have any preference other than García Paniagua?*

Nothing ever materialized in García Paniagua. That was the importance of what I did. I simply saw things very spontaneously, without asking specific questions or conducting concrete inquiries. García Paniagua's function within the army was to act as my liaison with the armed forces, below the institution.

*Did you ask the U.S. government about the possibility of García Paniagua? Did you receive any indication of their opinion of him?*

Never. I allowed myself no conversation with the North Americans about any aspect of Mexico's internal affairs. I wouldn't have dared. It would have shamed me.

*If you had understood, with all the nuances of the case, that the Americans thought poorly of someone, what would have happened?*

Well, naturally I would have looked for another candidate who satisfied an indispensable requisite for a Mexican politician at the level we were dealing with in this case, which was that he absolutely had to enjoy the favor of the United States. Express and underlined antipathy would have been fatal. One of the issues one is concerned with is whether the North or South Americans have any particular preference or dislike for the prospect. Obviously, the United States is more important and has to be considered. But I certainly didn't ask them. How embarrassing!

*Was the situation similar in regard to the Catholic Church? If you had known that a given candidate had very bad relations with the Church, would you have given the matter the same importance as in the case of the United States?*

I hadn't thought of comparing political forces and opinions on this particular subject. Thinking about it now, as a former president and citizen who contemplates the political process, the opinion of the Church was naturally less important.

*When did you first have the idea that you could or wanted to become president? When you were appointed minister, or before?*

Well, I certainly entertained the idea of reaching the presidency when I was promoted from director of the Federal Electricity Commission to minister of finance. I said to myself, "I'm a possible candidate now."

*When this occurred, what were your internal reflections?*

It was my tactic to have none, and since I am a man who believes deeply in loyalty, I thought only of being loyal to the president and working, that's all: "And if it serves my interests, very well, and if not, very well. The president is a friend of mine, and I am working for him. He has given me a chance to contribute, so I will work, nothing more than work and only work."

*Why do you think Echeverría chose you?*

I could get transcendental and think of important things, but I think primarily because of our close friendship from childhood, which meant confidence in my knowledge and passions, qualities, and defects. He was familiar with my abilities and possibilities, and of course my capacity. He knew my deep love for Mexico, and from his intimate knowledge of me, he knew of my patriotism, my unwavering loyalty to my country, and therefore to him. I would never betray him. Also there was my work, serious, dedicated work, my opinions expressed in meetings, the numerous meetings held at Los Pinos, the responsibilities I assumed. I never got him into problems with my decisions. I always took responsibility for what I did. I always made my own decisions, and never passed responsibility on to him.

*You didn't feel that Echeverría wanted to cling to part of his power?*

Well, to a certain degree when he designated the president, secretary, and Mexico City president of [the PRI]. As a potential candidate, I already had a structure that I had neither evaluated nor wanted to evaluate. I knew that the institutions would prevail at some point, as had occurred in the days of Plutarco Elias Calles, who had forgotten about the institutions and established the *maximato* to preserve power through pulling strings after leaving office. But I always thought that Luis was fundamentally a politician who throughout his entire life, since we were children, had dreamed about politics, and, knowing politics well as a grown man, had acted politically. In his politics, he received advice in a certain way, and I accepted this, and I would in due course see my opportunity and establish my own style. We were such close friends that he accepted my political style as I had accepted his. It was that simple.

*Don't you think that one of the factors that influenced Luis Echeverría's decision was that you would protect his interests because of your bonds of friendship from childhood and early adulthood?*

Yes, of course. He knew I would be loyal and there would be no betrayal.

*Neither political nor personal.*

No, although as time passed I realized that presidentialism had an unwritten rule: break to stabilize; and because of the very roughness of presidentialism, when a president leaves office, there is inertia from the people who used to work with him. They want, in some way, to preserve their power, and begin to try to act independently of their boss, in this case Luis. As time goes on, especially in the first few months, my minister of the interior, Jesús Reyes Heroles, began to inform me that there was an endless line of cars and politicians congregating at Echeverría's house in San Jerónimo. I realize now that he informed me of this out of malice, because he had harbored animosity for Luis since our school days.

*Since you were boys?*
Yes, and largely because of rivalries involving girlfriends that I didn't know about and that Luis may have mentioned to you. But he informed me in very negative terms of what went on at Echeverría's compound. The accumulated information about the goings-on there created an adverse situation for me at a time when I needed national unity based on confidence. Luis's possible actions or participation in politics alarmed certain sectors that he had affected, and did not contribute to a climate of confidence, which was indispensable for me to implement the policies I had proposed for my term of office. I had to call him and say, "My friend, for such and such reasons, I'm going to ask that you leave the country and go anywhere else you want. Help me, because your presence creates a problem of governability that I need you to help me overcome. Your charisma, the behavior of your people are making the country ungovernable for me." He then said something to me about Reyes Heroles that made a light go on in my head, but I didn't give it any importance because I trusted Chucho [Reyes Heroles] implicitly.

*Echeverría did say something about him?*
He made some small remark to me about Chucho, but it was neither profound, nor well founded, nor explicit. My point of view was that, however it may have been—because of Chucho's meddling or not—his presence was preventing me from gaining the full confidence of my people, and there were certain sectors that were still uncertain. I told him: "You're going to have to help me, and you're going to have to leave the country. You can have, for example, the embassy in France, or I'll even offer you the one in Spain," which immediately thereafter I offered to Díaz Ordaz, and for the same reason, so people wouldn't think there was a dispute between one and the other, and so forth. There are so many things that have to be handled subtly in Mexican politics. I told Luis, "Luis, now." Then he replied, "Look, I don't want Paris; let me think about where to go. I'll tell you in a couple of days." And then, with the frankness

we shared: "You and I have been president, you and I are politicians, you and I understand this. I obviously neither think nor hope that this will harm our friendship. I owe you a lot, I like you a lot, we have been friends all our lives, and for that very reason, I hope no harm is done." And he admitted it with great self-discipline, and days later said to me, "Look, the Paris embassy definitely not. What I want is UNESCO."

"Then to UNESCO you'll go, immediately." Things calmed down, but the implicit affirmations—I was about to say intrigues—affirmations made by [Minister of the Interior] Reyes Heroles continued, and not only against Luis, but against other cabinet members, mostly against Minister of Education Porfirio Muñoz Ledo. There was a strong rivalry between the two of them. This also explains why I felt obliged to ask Muñoz Ledo to resign, because I could no longer stand the antipathy between them and their disputes with the teachers' union, that Chucho encouraged, and Porfirio tried to quell, and the country couldn't take anymore of it either.

*Did you discuss all this with Echeverría after you left office?*
We never talked about it again. It's like a grain of sand in our friendship. We haven't talked about anything disagreeable. No, it's hard to talk about that kind of thing. Neither of us is president anymore.

*In the final analysis, you're not so convinced that Echeverría was pulling the strings?*
Oh no! I'm sure he wasn't. He received people the same way I do.

*How did your opinion of Reyes Heroles evolve?*
Chucho was one of my most brilliant aides, if not the most brilliant, to the degree that when it came to appointing my cabinet, he was the only one I let chose his own job. He immediately chose the Ministry of the Interior, which pleased me very much because I needed a strong man there to help me handle the political situation, since I was going to concentrate mainly on the economy. I needed an operator. What happened was not as evident to me at the time as it was after I thought about it. Since Jesús was the son of a Spaniard, he failed to satisfy a constitutional requisite for the presidency, and when he had the chance, since he had no political constituency to cultivate, he was a somewhat extremist, violent, and even inconsiderate minister of the interior. I began to receive complaints about his manner of treating the governors, that he received them standing up and pressured them to tell him what had brought them to the Ministry of the Interior. I realized that this was going to be a problem, because this trait was manifesting itself more and more.

*Because he had no chance to be president?*
Indeed. He had no political constituency to cultivate. That was one of the reasons. The other was that Chucho's merits warranted his inclusion in the economic cabinet. I called him and he joined the economic cabinet, and from then on, things began to happen in the press, as I discovered afterward. I gradually learned that there were confrontations in the cabinet, with people such as Roel in foreign affairs or Muñoz Ledo in education, that issues had begun to surface that were seriously disrupting our relations with the press.

*Especially in the economic cabinet?*
Certain information began to leak from the economic cabinet that I considered it necessary to keep confidential. I conducted my inquiries and it turned out they were coming from the Ministry of the Interior, and I began to feel that he wasn't running it the same way he had been at the beginning. I had to know who was responsible for what was going on. This led me to investigate the matter, and I found that the line led straight to Jesús, and then it seemed appropriate, for several reasons to say, "Well, it's over."

*Was Pope John Paul II's first visit to Mexico in January 1979 a factor?*
No, the theory about the Pope is one of the myths that someone, I don't know who—possibly Reyes himself—leaked to make himself appear more liberal.

*When he left for the UNESCO, did Luis Echeverría mention anything to you from the distant past about Reyes Heroles?*
In detail, although I don't remember precisely what he said. But, it concerned the rift Chucho—who had problems in his relationship with Luis from our law school days—was provoking between us.

*Why?*
You won't believe this, but I think it was for Luis's reputation in his youth for being a ladies' man.

*He had such a reputation?*
Yes. Luis was very attractive to women—his voice and his hands, his style, his conversation, even his figure. He had a very strong presence. Why else do rivalries between young men emerge? There was no political rivalry.

*Could you, with a convention, have convinced Javier Paniagua to accept defeat in 1981, in light of the resentment he came to feel toward you when you passed him over?*
Naturally, I was the tip of the pyramid, and all its sides and angles culminated in me. It would have been utterly impossible for a convention, for which our

bylaws made no provision whatsoever, to resolve a problem that was intended for the president to resolve, by means of an extremely delicate, totally extralegal, and extraconstitutional function. The idea of Javier handling a convention would have been unthinkable, even if he had wanted to.

*Was the unquestionable nature of the decision an essential part of the mechanism?*
Of course, that was what made it complete, and was precisely where its merit lay, in its indisputable finality. It was a tacit agreement of the operative forces, which agreed that the tongue of the balance would point the way and the problems would be resolved.

*What was Javier Paniagua's complaint in 1981?*
He didn't complain to me. There was no complaint.

*But you did talk with him after Miguel de la Madrid's nomination?*
No, I don't recall. Party discipline, military discipline, and my personal friendship with García Paniagua were upheld by feelings of mutual respect that made him discipline himself. I never felt hostility; the one who felt his hostility was the candidate, de la Madrid, who did in fact ask me directly to "get him off my back." But Miguel did it for other reasons.

*You mentioned that friendship was obviously one of Echeverría's possible reasons for choosing you, as were his familiarity with you, and your health, among others. Is health a factor?*
Of course, health is fundamental to the country's institutional life. A president who starts having health problems is a president who will begin to suffer absences, and absences require substitutions.

*In Echeverría's case, he knew that you enjoyed good health because you were lifelong friends. But, for example, how did you know that the same was true of de la Madrid?*
From working with him.

*You didn't investigate?*
No, as a matter of fact I did not. I didn't prepare a health profile of the candidates.

*If you had seeded the candidates in May 1981, where would you have put oil chief Jorge Díaz Serrano?*
In a strong position. I had to ponder the issue. If the problem I was going to leave for the next administration had been fundamentally one of income, I

would have chosen someone who knew how to handle oil. If it had been financial, well, the man I did in fact choose. If it had been a question of order, it would have been García Paniagua, for what he represented as a link with the armed forces and for his character and strong hand.

*When did you make up your mind?*
Shortly after this situation arose. I wanted to make the decision after the North-South Summit in Cancún scheduled for October of 1981.

*You would have liked to decide later. Can you remember when you finally opted for de la Madrid? When did you tell him; when did you decide in your own mind?*
The decision-making process is very subtle. The choice was taking shape in my mind so subtly that I have no precise recollections of the sequence. I can only tell you that by the time I told Miguel about it, a week or two beforehand, the decision was already fully formed.

*Did you hesitate with announcing the decision because of the process or because you doubted?*
More than doubt, because the moment one announces the chosen successor, there is a qualitative change in the process of running the country. One sun is about to set, and another is being born, and the political movements begin with the flight toward the sun that is being born. One delays it as long as possible, to maintain control of the country, until . . .

*Did you discuss your decision with your son (and de la Madrid's aide) José Ramón?*
No, with him less than anyone, because he worked for Miguel. It's a solitary decision of the tongue of the balance.

*With Rosa Luz Alegría [President Echeverria's former daughter-in-law and later President López Portillo's mistress]?*
Not with her either.

*How did you inform de la Madrid?*
Very simply. There are so many myths surrounding this moment. It transpires absolutely naturally, because that is precisely where its importance lies, in the way the decision is made, and the fact that, once it is taken, everything becomes very simple, because that's the way things work. I summoned him to a meeting, and just like in my case, when it was over I told him that the party had decided that he would be its presidential candidate. With all simplicity, in my office at Los Pinos, with the party sectors on hand, I said, "Here are the leaders of the party sectors. Let's legitimate your investiture."

*Did you talk with the losers?*
No, because they didn't know they had been considered. Not at all. It would have been an absurd formality. I had no commitment to any of them.

*Was family life a consideration?*
Naturally, it is an important factor. In Miguel's case, it was guaranteed because of my personal knowledge of him and his wife, who deserves all my respect and who took a great interest in Miguel's career. I had every guarantee that he was irreproachable in this aspect.

*Financial scruples?*
I had information from my own experience and from my inquiries. There were no rumors about Miguel's honor.

*You did investigate?*
It's what is done.

*Everyone, or only the chosen one?*
I investigated the people I felt it was necessary to; Miguel, of course. Practically my entire cabinet was under scrutiny, and I had no doubts regarding the scruples of my main cabinet members. Because, in spite of what has been said since, I think it was one of the most honest cabinets Mexico has had, above all the functionaries who managed significant sums of money.

*In the case of de la Madrid and two or three others, did you investigate?*
Yes, I'll be frank with you, we investigated, or at least I did.

*For example, did the fact that your son José Ramón worked for de la Madrid give you any guarantee that he would be treated well?*
No, quite the contrary.

*Muñoz Ledo says that he sought you out at a given moment and asked, "Why didn't you consider me?"*
So he did.

*How was it?*
It was a show or expression of Porfirio's audacity, a manifestation of his political vocation. Naturally, I felt it was impossible to take it seriously because of his position as a man who had left my cabinet, who was no longer a part of the political traditions in place since the days of Ruíz Cortines.

*It has been said that your inner circle was divided on the subject of the candidates, that your two sisters preferred García Paniagua. . . .*

I never heard about it, because they were never so bold as to propose anything to me or even raise the subject. Never. I learned afterward that they preferred García Paniagua, especially Margarita, and probably Alicia as well, but they never dared say anything about it to me.

*When did you meet Javier García Paniagua [PRI president in 1980 and son of General García Barragán]?*
I met him during my campaign in 1975 or 1976, if I remember correctly, in Coyoacán, in Mexico City.

*Why did you trust him so quickly?*
Because I saw that he was very solid, a man who knew what he wanted. He was a man imbued with popular wisdom, with very simple political ideas, devoid of intellectual complexity. He also had ties to a certain sector of the army that I planned to utilize and that I was going to need.

*On one occasion, shortly after Miguel de la Madrid was appointed minister of planning, he went to a meeting with you, and you said, "Listen, Javier García Paniagua from the Federal Security Directorate came to see me to tell me that he needed extrabudgetary funds for various items, and I wanted to ask you about it." You answered, "No questions are needed, go ahead. Treat what Javier says as though I had said it myself."*
I don't remember precisely, but it has an element of truth, because Javier was authorized to use funds for certain things that it would be indiscreet for me to disclose.

*Twenty years have passed. . . .*
Twenty years, but I am loyal to the system.

*Did you authorize de la Madrid to hand over the money without consulting you each time?*
Yes, that's correct. If it answers your question, that's how it was.

*How did Javier García Paniagua establish a relationship with your sister [and virtual Minister of Culture] Margarita, and for what purpose?*
I think they came to appreciate one another. I can't say for sure if his interest was to protect her from Reyes Heroles. Perhaps he simply supported her.

*And Margarita mentioned this close collaboration to you?*
Well no, she didn't mention it. I didn't talk much with my sister Margarita; I didn't have the time. When we met, we talked about what we had to, but nothing more.

*She didn't mention the portraits she had commissioned of Javier García Paniagua and Miguel de la Madrid?*
Which portraits?

*Some paintings. . . .*
I know nothing about them.

*I've seen the one she had done of de la Madrid, and I know the one of García Paniagua to exist. She gave them the portraits as gifts. . . .*
Margarita? My sister? Well that's a surprise. What you say surprises me, I didn't know. I'm going to ask her.

*The matter comes up because it's evident that Javier García Paniagua was angry when he wasn't chosen for the candidacy, and he evidently felt cheated.*
Well, possibly. I didn't register it as such. I just tried to find an explanation for his disenchantment. Why did he think he had a chance? No doubt he assumed that his relationship with my sister would influence me, which never happened in any way.

*You chose de la Madrid because of the financial question and because the other prospects had fallen by the wayside?*
I chose him basically because I knew I was going to leave the country with financial problems, with the threat of falling prices and monetary instability, and I had to leave a political situation stabilized by the expropriation of the banking system, but that came later. My decision, I repeat, as the tongue of the balance, was basically influenced by considerations of this kind.

*And your negative reflections regarding the others?*
Well, they didn't go so far as to be negative. De la Madrid's excellence was what stood out, not necessarily in contrast, but in terms of his suitability, let's say.

*In the end, could you have decided otherwise, or were things really already moving in that direction.*
Well, yes they were, but I still could have decided otherwise. Nothing prevented me.

*Did doubts emerge later? Did you say to yourself, "I made a mistake, I hope I didn't make a mistake?"*
Well, Miguel wasn't my candidate anymore when I expropriated the banks. I would have chosen another candidate. That was when I naturally had doubts that arose when I informed him of the decision, at the last moment, before

giving my annual state of the union address. I sent my son, and he told me
that Miguel said, "Now what am I going to say to so-and-so?" Then I said to
myself, "Good heavens! He's not behind me on this measure. I'm going to
have to reinforce it constitutionally." That was when I decided to amend the
Constitution.

*Who were your strongest, most serious rivals in 1976?*
Of my most serious rivals, Porfirio was the most intelligent. He was the only
one who understood the situation. Porfirio was the most serious, followed by
Gálvez Betancourt, because of his close ties to Luis Echeverría. It was basically
these two.

*When did you realize that Moya Palencia had fallen?*
When Luis began to hint to me that I was going to be the one. Until then I
had stayed behind Moya.

*Moya Palencia has said that when you were president and he was director of tourism
[Fonatur], on one occasion at the Fonatur house in Ixtapa you told him that you
felt great affection for the house, because it was where Luis Echeverría had informed
you of his decision in your favor. Is this true?*
No, not at all. It all took place at Los Pinos, from the first hint, which, I
understand now, was consistent with my friend's style. It was a sign that he
was somehow leaning toward me. There was nothing anywhere else. It took
place at Los Pinos.

*I asked Echeverría the same question. He told me with a smile, "Well, the truth is
that I had been insinuating to López Portillo for a long time that things were going
his way."*
I understand that now. They were incidents that elucidate the chain of events
for me. I did not interpret them at the time as anything more than clues to a
mystery that was gradually becoming clearer.

*What conflicts arose during your campaign in 1975–76? What about General Cuenca
Díaz's nomination for governor of Baja California in 1976?*
The question of General Cuenca was a decision very close to the president.
Echeverría started promoting the general's candidacy well in advance, basically
because of the pressure that General Cuenca placed on him. He was someone
to whom the president clearly owed something.

*Don't you think it had something to do with the events of 1968 and the friction with
General Barragán?*

No, I don't think so. To the best of my knowledge, Cuenca didn't participate much in 1968.

*No, but General García Barragán did, and he had been an adversary of Echeverría's.*
Well, yes, but it would be within the structure of the army. That's the only way it would make sense. If you assume that's possible, I'll admit it was a possibility. It made me aware of Echeverría's debt to Cuenca for some commitment, some special circumstance. The fact is, it happened. Luis knew that I had another candidate for Baja California. General Cuenca also knew, he had made part of his career, the most important part, in Baja California and he was very interested in becoming governor to make a political career for himself there. He no doubt called the president, and the president granted his request.

*How did Echeverría bring it to your attention?*
He didn't, the decision just came out through the PRI.

*But appointing the governor for Baja California usually fell to the new president. . . .*
Well, Luis didn't offer me an explanation, and I didn't ask for one, nor did Porfirio give me one or I ask for one. I just accepted it as a natural thing for the president to do for a friend.

*I've been told that one of the reasons you gave de la Madrid complete freedom in forming the Congress in 1982 is because you still remembered that Echeverría had put a lot of people in the Chamber of Deputies and in the Senate in 1976.*
The facts are correct, but the reasons are not. The real reason was that it was my way of doing things. I thought the party needed to start working differently—more spontaneously, more from the bottom up—and that I didn't really need a Congress full of people owing me gratitude for their positions.

*But you did feel in 1976 that Echeverría had appointed a lot of people?*
Well, Luis is passionate about politics, and it seemed natural to me for him to perpetuate the line of his regime. That's what it was.

*Having seen the succession mechanism through several cycles, do you think the president consciously or unconsciously has a candidate almost from the start whom he tries to impose, and that he sometimes succeeds and other times fails?*
Well, I don't know of any case that coincides with such a description. In my case, I had other prospects early on, including Moctezuma, Carlos Tello, and others. Circumstances were what made me change and replace my cabinet members to avoid being left with no cards to play.

*Is the formation of the cabinet the most difficult, solitary moment?*
Definitely, because one is thinking that one of the cabinet members will be the next president.

*That isn't discussed with anyone either?*
Absolutely not.

*Among the cabinet members you appointed at the beginning, there were three prospective successors?*
Among those I appointed at the start? Well, I had Moctezuma, Tello, and someone else.

*In* Mis Tiempos [My Times], *you end up accepting that the Ministry of Finance and David Ibarra were right about the magnitude of the 1981 fiscal deficit, and not Miguel de la Madrid.*
In the Ministry of Planning, yes.

*At the time, didn't you think that the optimistic figures Minister of Planning and Budget de la Madrid was presenting might be related to the succession?*
No, I didn't think of it. It may have been naive of me, but I didn't.

*None of your advisers mentioned it to you?*
None.

*Didn't you feel you had been misled?*
Yes, I did feel misled. I tried to get them to give me congruent and consistent information. I insisted on it with my economic cabinet. Otherwise the cabinet's decisions would have been reduced to a coin toss. I wanted to make well-grounded decisions.

*You had to decide on the basis of false data?*
It is assumed now that the data was false.

*You don't relate it to the problem of the succession?*
No, I can't say I do. Perhaps my naiveté and my belief in public service make it impossible for me to think that way. But I couldn't say it or admit it.

*José Ramón says that if you had accepted Ibarra's figures showing that the deficit was going to be bigger, there would have had to be larger budget cuts and de la Madrid, not Ibarra, would have had to make the cuts. Were you aware of this?*
No, it only occurs to me now.

*Didn't you realize that this would have been the equivalent of acknowledging that Ibarra was in the right?*

No, because I didn't know the data was faulty at the time. I only found out about it later.

*When did you begin to understand the problem with the data?*
Later, but not right away, of course. So much so that I used it as the basis for my decision. It was later. I don't remember the date.

*While you were still president, or after leaving office?*
Perhaps after leaving office.

*You mention in your book* Umbrales *a conversation in late 1982 between José Ramón and Carlos Salinas at a dinner party during which Salinas told him, "We're going to have to hit your father hard," and José Ramón obviously told you about it immediately. Didn't you see the relationship with the disguised figures of 1981?*
Can you believe it? No, not at all. I couldn't imagine that such long-term relationships could be established for such a devious political purpose.

*Do you think de la Madrid deliberately disguised the figures? Or did de la Madrid's team deceive him for him to in turn deceive you?*
I have no idea what happened. All I know is that it happened.

*You felt that de la Madrid was taking out insurance by keeping José Ramón and Rosa Luz Alegría so close to him.*
Well, I was not so naive as not to think it. But it struck me as a natural political maneuver, part of ambition, with no negative overtones, because it harmed no one.

*No, but it gave de la Madrid an advantage over the others. . . .*
Well, yes, it gave him an advantage. The same thing happened as when someone told me, "Miguel goes to see his psychiatrist before going to his meetings with the president." He's a man who takes care of himself, and is smart and capable enough to do it. It's one of his traits. And it may have been one that helped bring him to power.

*Why did you advance the designation of the candidate in 1981?*
Because of the North-South Summit in Cancún. I wanted to address the matter calmly, since the succession decision was already resolved, and because there was a lot of intrigue, a lot of unrest, and I wanted to be calm for a summit that was of the utmost importance to me.

*And you received no indication that Javier García Paniagua, PRI president and son of former defense minister General García Barragán, was working from within the army?*
No.

*That he wanted to speed things up and pressure you?*
No, on the contrary. It was my impression that he was completely loyal, and therefore a possible [presidential] prospect.

*You had said the opposite: that you wanted to designate the candidate after Cancún so as to arrive in Cancún with the power of your presidency intact.*
Yes, but at the last minute I thought it was better to arrive with the matter resolved than have it remain pending during the summit.

*And in general you think that the attitude of de la Madrid's administration in regard to you and your administration in general went beyond the idea of "breaking to stabilize"?*
Well, probably so; it was evidently more rigorous, more radical, more unpleasant than what had happened before. Who was responsible? I don't know.

*In* Umbrales, *you suggest that the emissary of de la Madrid's administration in this sense, if not the man directly responsible for the attitude, was Carlos Salinas.*
I don't know.

*And now, in retrospect, where do you think such a strong urge to break with your regime came from?*
I attribute it to the fact that my government destroyed the prestige of the banks, which disturbed some in the system, who then somehow conspired to take this prestige away from us (this is the hypothesis). I was accused of what I reproached the businessmen of: unlawful gain, looting the public coffers, and so on, everything that was announced to undermine my reputation.

*Your son suggests that if you had nationalized the banks sooner, let's say eight or ten months earlier, it would have been not only a more strategic decision, based less on exigencies of the moment, but also one that would have been binding on the candidate, whoever he may have been. Do you agree with this interpretation?*
Well, maybe so, because de la Madrid evidently wasn't the candidate for the bank nationalization.

*José Ramón suggests that you may have made a mistake in not wanting to put anyone in the Chamber of Deputies or Senate and in the cabinet, that you tied your own hands with de la Madrid in the succession. He claims that this was a mistake because you were left unprotected. . . .*
A lot of politicians have told me the same thing, adducing that an outgoing president covers his back with the Congress, which works at least for the first congressional term. But I wanted the PRI to work better, and for the same

reasons that I stayed out of this problem with Echeverría, I didn't get involved in it with de la Madrid.

*But although your aides and friends weren't prosecuted legally, but politically, they were left unemployed, excluded. . . .*
One of the features of presidentialism is precisely that power is exercised for six years, after which a new power takes over, and this new power is the renewal that gives the country hope and respite. The logical thing is for the personnel to be renewed. I wasn't obliged to guarantee jobs for my aides. I felt a stronger obligation to the country than to my aides.

*You didn't think, "I'm going to be left alone"?*
Never. The possibility of a total renewal is a characteristic of the system. That's how presidentialism works.

*Did you talk with Salinas in the days after Colosio died in 1994?*
No, not at all. I read about it in the papers, and that was all.

*He didn't ask you what to do?*
Never.

*He didn't invite you to breakfast?*
No. That's not the style of Mexican presidentialism.

*And you didn't approach him?*
I didn't try to. I didn't meddle, and I was not called upon.

*And you didn't send any messages one way or the other?*
I deeply regretted the situation. I had an intuition about what was to come, but that's all.

*You had no contact of any kind with Los Pinos during those days?*
None at all.

# MIGUEL DE LA MADRID

Miguel de la Madrid Hurtado was born in the Western city of Colima on December 12, 1934. He studied law at UNAM, and received a master's degree in public administration from Harvard University. De la Madrid joined José López Portillo's cabinet on May 19, 1979, as minister of planning and budget. He was nominated PRI presidential candidate on September 25, 1981, and elected president on July 4, 1982. He was inaugurated on December 1, 1982, and handed power over to Carlos Salinas de Gortari on December 1, 1988.

In 1982 Mexico was a nation of approximately 73 million inhabitants. During Miguel de la Madrid's term of office, the Mexican economy grew at an average rate of 0.2 percent. Average annual inflation was 86.7 percent, but soared to 159.2 percent in 1987. Per capita GNP fell to US$1,990 in 1988, lower than in 1982.

De la Madrid was not a candidate from the start of López Portillo's term. Minister of Finance Julio Moctezuma and Minister of Planning and Budget Carlos Tello were seen as early contenders, as were, later on, oil company czar Jorge Díaz Serrano, Labor Minister Pedro Ojeda Paullada, and Finance Minister David Ibarra, and perhaps most importantly, PRI president Javier García Paniagua. Trade Minister Jorge de la Vega Domínguez was also in the race.

When de la Madrid was appointed minister of planning and programming in 1979 he became a leading contender. When the decision was made in late 1981, both Ibarra and Díaz Serrano were out of the running for different reasons. López Portillo was left with Pedro Ojeda, Javier García Paniagua, and de la Madrid.

The former would have been the candidate, according to López Portillo, if the primary concern was economic; the latter would have been chosen had the key concern been political stability.

García Paniagua (1935–1998) was the son of former Minister of Defense (1964–1970) Marcelino García Barragán. He served in the Ministry of the Interior as director of the infamous Directorate of Federal Security (1976–1978), the government's intelligence police. García Paniagua was often criticized for resorting to repression against political enemies during his time as chief of the intelligence police. He was also reported to have resented de la Madrid's nomination and to have vowed to take revenge against López Portillo. During de la Madrid's term, García Paniagua did not occupy government posts. Carlos Salinas made him police chief of Mexico City (1988–1991) and director general of the national lottery from 1991 to 1994. García Paniagua died as this book was being written.

De la Madrid's term in office was in most respects a tragic one for Mexico, not totally as a result of the president's actions. López Portillo passed on a disastrous economic and financial situation, compounding the effects of sky-rocketing world interest rates, plunging oil prices, and an enormous foreign debt. For the first time in nearly half a century, per capita growth was negative for an entire sexennium; psychologically, the impact of the brutal 1985 earthquake was equally devastating. When de la Madrid's term neared its conclusion at the end of 1987, the stock market collapsed, capital flight began anew, and the currency was drastically devalued. De la Madrid closed off his administration amid domestic and international scandal resulting from the elections of 1988, widely viewed as having been stolen by official candidate Carlos Salinas from dissident candidate Cuauhtémoc Cárdenas, the son of Mexico's most important and admired twentieth-century president, Lázaro Cárdenas. In addition to Salinas, other contenders for the PRI nomination were Finance Minister Jesús Silva Herzog, Interior Minister Manuel Bartlett, and Energy Minister Alfredo del Mazo.

Despite these travails, de la Madrid undertook important changes in Mexico's economy. The country became a member of the General Agreement on Tariffs and Trade (GATT) in 1985, and began a dramatic process of trade liberalization in late 1987. Closer ties with the United States were also established, though for a time Mexico maintained its independent foreign policy, particularly through the Contadora initiative in Central America. Miguel de la Madrid is largely viewed as a transitional president.

*At least since Echeverría in 1975, there has been a formal list of presidential hopefuls before the nomination. In your case, you openly acknowledged it. With López Portillo, it was evident. How is the list prepared? How were you included in the list, and how did you decide?*

I don't think there is a preconceived list from the time an administration takes office. It takes shape gradually in accordance with public opinion regarding the performance of government ministers, who, thus far, have been the ones entitled to aspire to the candidacy. I think that all government ministers, in principle, are given a chance. The only exceptions to date have been the ministers of defense and the navy. As the administration advances, public opinion makes its preferences known, and lists of prospective candidates emerge, not because they are drawn up in the president's office or at PRI headquarters, but as a natural process. When I was president, in 1987, we tested the procedure called *la pasarela*\* with the president officially announcing the names of the six party members we were considering. The six names were already on everyone's lips.

*The list of the "six distinguished PRI members" included at least two who would hardly have been considered authentic contenders: Mexico City mayor Ramón Aguirre and Minister of Education Miguel González Avelar. Therefore, there were two groups: one with the four real contenders, and another with two who were being given a chance. There's more to it than just public opinion. I doubt Ramón Aguirre or González Avelar would have been included in the list if you had relied purely on public opinion polls.*

The fact of the matter is that they were ranked lower, but they did have some support. The strategy the party used in those days was to draw up a list of six, because it has always been considered desirable to have five or six prospects to distribute the conflict that normally arises when one of the members of the group is going to be favored. The procedure we followed then was that, beginning in March of 1987, PRI president Jorge de la Vega traveled to different parts of the country, visiting local PRI leadership and public opinion leaders, and gathered information regarding their feelings about the PRI's prospective presidential candidates. We met after completing these inquiries. Naturally I had my own sources of information through my contact with the other party organizations and opinion leaders, as well as political, business, labor, and peasant leaders, so it wasn't hard for us to reach the conclusion that these six would make up the list. Finally, the six of them handled themselves decorously in

---

\*As in a runway parade at a fashion show.

their presentation to the PRI National Executive Committee and before the public. Their appearances were broadcast on television and radio and received full press coverage. This stage of the process was over by August. The party and I agreed to take a two-week recess to allow the effects of the annual State of the Union address and the national patriotic holidays to pass, and to resume the exercise afterward. I'll explain how we did it. Jorge de la Vega repeated his inquiries, not going to all the states, but summoning the party leaders here [to Mexico City], talking with them and seeing which of the six were in the lead. Meanwhile, I kept my eyes on the press, and what people who visited me and opinion leaders had to say. Finally, we decided the time was right to designate the candidate. The date was set for October 4. I instructed Jorge de la Vega to have the [PRI] Political Council inform me of the results of its session, and privately I invited the Political Council members, who were approximately twelve in number, to breakfast with me and give me their assessment of the situation. I didn't share my thoughts with Jorge before October 4.

*You didn't tell Salinas either?*
On Friday, October 2, I told Salinas that I thought that he had a strong chance, and that he should remain calm and discreet, but that we still couldn't give him anything definite.

*You didn't say the same to anyone else?*
No, no one.

*Only Salinas. . . .*
Only Salinas. Then, on Sunday, October 4, at breakfast with the PRI National Executive Committee, Jorge de la Vega announced that, after exchanging points of view with the party leaders and within the committee, they had concluded that there were three finalists: Minister of the Interior Manuel Bartlett, Minister of Energy Alfredo del Mazo, and Minister of Planning and Budget Carlos Salinas, but that they felt it was necessary for me to give my opinion. Then I said that, in my opinion, these were indeed the final three, and that since they had asked for my opinion, I chose Carlos Salinas, but that I invited all the members of the National Executive Committee to express their opinions.

*And what were their opinions?*
They all expressed a preference for Carlos Salinas. There was no doubt, no hesitation, nothing. Then they went to the PRI headquarters and the official announcement was made to the PRI's Central Committee. After the meeting, I phoned Carlos Salinas and informed him.

*Many people with reason to know are of the opinion that until 1964 there was real consultation with various sectors—with government ministers, union leaders, and former presidents, especially Lázaro Cárdenas (1934–1940) and Miguel Alemán (1946–1952) and perhaps also with the Church, the armed forces, etc.,—regarding the presidential succession, but that this was no longer the case from 1970 on. Díaz Ordaz (1964–1970) imposed Echeverría (1970–1976) without discussion or consultation, making Echeverría a nonconsensus candidate. The process of consultation either disappeared or became so subtle and elliptical that it gave way to a mechanism that, while not implying direct imposition, was certainly much more individualized than before. Do you agree with this division into two periods?*

I'm not entirely clear on the matter. I don't know whether or not this supposed consultation with former presidents, the army, the Church, and even with the North Americans ever actually occurred. I'm inclined to think it did not. As president I realized that López Portillo had not conducted explicit, express consultations. He had been testing the waters, investigating, asking questions. But making explicit inquiries? I think not. I conducted no such inquiries. I handled the entire process of the presidential succession from within the party, and we made our collective decision on October 4. There was no explicit consultation with anyone else in my case, and I doubt there had been in the past.

*Would the idea about PRI presidential nominations attributed to Fidel Velázquez [leader of the sole workers' union of Mexico] that "if you move you don't appear in the photograph" be false in this case?*

No. Naturally, I discussed the issue of the succession with Fidel Velázquez. I was invited to breakfast one day before my nomination by the labor leaders, including *don* Fidel. They said, "We know that you are one of the party's prospective candidates. All we want to tell you is that we can't make our support for you public yet; we have to wait for it to be decided, but we want you to know that we have a personal preference for you." That's as far as it went.

*As president, how did you treat the issue with* don *Fidel? Did he oppose Salinas?*

No, not at all. Salinas constructed his candidacy very artfully. As part of his job, he was in frequent contact with the other government ministers, governors, and the social sectors, above all because we had to be persuasive and open to dialogue in order to apply our economic program. He was in constant contact with Fidel Velázquez, with other labor leaders, business leaders, and with society in general.

*Do you recall anyone expressing opposition to any of the prospects?*

Well, of course there were Cuauhtémoc Cárdenas and Porfirio Muñoz Ledo.

From the outset the Democratic Current* was founded in response, among other things, to fear of Salinas becoming the presidential candidate, because they thought Salinas represented a school of economic thought contrary to their own. There was also a measure of personal antipathy. In Cuauhtémoc's case, I'm not sure what it was due to, but Porfirio felt that he lacked a personal relationship with Salinas.

*Porfirio told you this himself?*
Yes, of course, he told me so directly. He said: "With Salinas I don't have a platform to make myself understood, he's the only one I don't know, the only one who hasn't sought me out." They were very open about their opposition to Salinas's candidacy.

*When did you first feel that José López Portillo was clearly testing the waters with you?*
I think the turning point came in 1981—one year after I was appointed to the Ministry of Planning and Budget—when we presented the National Development Plan.

*Did López Portillo send you around to convince, seduce, or calm people and constituencies?*
Yes, I was exposed to many quarters of the political system. That was how it worked, but I did not take the opportunity to insinuate that I was already a prospective candidate. I thought, "I'm the Minister, that's my function. But I also have a chance at being a candidate, depending on how well I do my job." I told them, "No, there are other, very good possibilities," and I sincerely thought this was true. I thought that the really strong contenders were Minister of Labor Pedro Ojeda and former Chiapas governor and minister of trade Jorge de la Vega, in that order. It never occurred to me, as López Portillo claimed afterward, that Javier García Paniagua was my real rival.

*It never occurred to you?*
I didn't get the feeling. Javier García Paniagua once said to me frankly, "Miguel, it's going to be you or me," and I answered, "It can't be, Javier. There are others, not just we two." López Portillo has suggested that this was so, that in the end he had two alternatives: Javier if the problem on the horizon were political or myself if it was economic. I have a hard time believing it.

*And why do you think García Paniagua was not chosen?*
Well, because García Paniagua was the prototype of the old-school Mexican

politician: very wily, very knowledgeable about the vicissitudes of the country's political life, especially in regard to party matters and political issues.

*When did you meet José López Portillo?*
I met him at law school. He taught a course on theory of the state. I took his class in 1953, and got a 10 [the highest possible grade]. That is, I made a good impression, didn't I? Later there were chance meetings in the courts, which I frequented in the course of my legal practice, but without our relationship growing particularly close. Later, when he was appointed legal director of the Ministry of the Presidency, I was assistant director of credit, and I had to coordinate a lot of my work with the ministry and as a result I came into more frequent contact with him.

*You were never friends?*
If you mean friends in the sense of spending time together in a personal or family context, no.

*Did you consult with anyone else concerning the succession during your two and a half years in the cabinet?*
With my staff, that is, with my deputy ministers: Carlos Salinas, who directed economic and social policy; Manuel Bartlett, my political adviser; Bernardo Sepúlveda, in foreign affairs. We tracked the course of events and occasionally discussed how the situation was evolving. I gave them my guidelines: "Gentlemen, our work is what will make or break us. I want discretion. I don't want attacks on my competitors, because I don't think that's how things should be done. Help me create a positive atmosphere." And they really all did a very good job of it.

*Carlos Salinas has said that one of his strong points in the 1987 succession was that he came with a team. Did you offer López Portillo the same advantage in 1981?*
I tried to create a first-rate team to fulfill the responsibilities López Portillo had entrusted to me in the Ministry of Planning and Budget. The challenge was to make the ministry work, something that for various reasons neither of my two predecessors in the post had achieved. I made every effort to choose a strong team. Naturally, I chose my deputy ministers and directors from among people I knew and trusted, but I made sure they were all well qualified. I appointed Francisco Labastida [afterward governor of Sonora, Zedillo's minister of the interior, and PRI presidential candidate in 1999], also a fully formed career politician, whom I had known as a top analyst in the Ministry of the Presidency

and later in the Ministry of Finance as tax promotion director in the planning division. He was more mature than Carlos Salinas at the time. I made Carlos Salinas economic policy director, and he achieved splendid results. I kept Rosa Luz Alegría [Echeverría's ex–daughter-in-law, López Portillo's companion, and minister of tourism] because I knew that she was very efficient and close to President López Portillo, and I didn't want to start out with problems. I think the idea that technocrats lack political skill or sensitivity is wrong. I think that in any government job, I would say from general director up, one either has political sensitivity or fails. It was a strong team made up of outstanding individuals. History has proven so. Many of them are still active, and their careers speak for themselves. I think that this gave López Portillo the impression that there was a strong team at the Ministry of the Interior, and that this also influenced his thinking.

*And was Salinas's team a factor for you in 1987?*
Yes, it was. Salinas showed me that he was a good leader, and that his ministry worked very smoothly.

*Was Salinas's team better than del Mazo's or Bartlett's?*
Yes, it was more coherent, with a stronger team spirit.

*Why do you think López Portillo chose you?*
I think he thought that my experience as the man responsible for Mexico's economic policy was an important asset for the future. I also think my candidacy was sure to be well received by the real sources of power. None of the sources of power opposed me, nor was I seriously distrusted by any given sector. I think these were the main factors. These and a personal liking that we developed. Finally, when he told me that things were going my way, it was somewhat more expected than when I told Salinas, for example. I had a meeting on Monday, and my nomination was on a Friday. He told me, "I think there are strong currents in the party leaning toward you; I think you're well prepared, basically because of your experience in economic policy and your ideas for planning, which reflect my own convictions. So get ready." That was all the explanation he offered me.

*You understood perfectly that you could not lose?*
He also said, as I also said to Salinas, "Listen Miguel, I'm telling you this in advance, but you know that in these matters you can't count your chickens before they're hatched, so be very reserved and try not to make any public demonstrations, and we'll wait a few days to make the final decision."

*What happened with García Paniagua?*
Well, I think Javier García Paniagua felt encouraged by López Portillo, but I don't know whether or not he had any grounds to do so.

*Gabriel García Márquez has claimed that López Portillo's sister Margarita commissioned portraits of you and of Javier García Paniagua*

As far as I know she commissioned portraits of three of the prospective candidates. I have mine hanging in my living room. She had one done of Javier and one of another contender. Margarita definitely preferred Javier.

*López Portillo didn't say no to anyone, he just said yes to the chosen one. He offered García Paniagua no explanation, but García Paniagua complained all the same.*

García Paniagua lodged a complaint, but it was more implicit than direct. Naturally, as soon as López Portillo informed him of the decision, García Paniagua resigned from his post as PRI president. When I arrived at the final meeting, López Portillo said, "Javier says it would be inappropriate for him to continue, that a new party president should be appointed. What do you think?" I answered, "Well, I think Javier should stay. We're friends. He can help me. He knows things that I don't. I'd like him to stay on." Javier insisted, "No Miguel, use all your own people, your team. I'm no use to you in this." I answered, "But you can help me Javier." He stayed on unwillingly, but began speaking poorly of López Portillo, and reports reached López Portillo, including the rumor that García Paniagua was issuing threats against José Ramón López Portillo, and then he said, "No, I can't let him do this." López Portillo had had the highest opinion of Javier. He had said, "Listen, Miguel, I recommend that you use Javier; he would make a good minister of the interior."

Javier felt betrayed. I realized this and was very concerned, because Javier was totally absent from my campaign for the nomination, from the moment I became a prospective candidate until the Assembly, which was to be held on October 10, but he was slinging mud at López Portillo.

*In what terms?*

He felt betrayed by López Portillo.

*López Portillo deceived him?*

Javier felt he had deceived him, given him false hope—"this is betrayal, you'll pay for this" and the like. I told the person who reported this to me, "Look, I shouldn't know who reports this kind of situation. You have access to the media—you make it public." López Portillo learned of it and mentioned it to me: "I hear Javier is very angry with me, and with you as well, that he's not supporting your campaign. He's very angry and I don't think he should remain at the head of the party." I answered: "Sir, it's for you to say when." [Afterward, when] I was leaving for a campaign trip, as I was arriving at the airport, I got a call from López Portillo. "Miguel, I just wanted to let you know that

I've decided to castle [as in chess]. Javier is going to the Ministry of Labor, and Pedro Ojeda from the Labor Ministry to the PRI. I think you and Pedro Ojeda get along well."

"Yes, that's so, Mister President."

"I'm doing it to help your campaign."

*Was García Paniagua upset, or, if you'll pardon the words, "pissed off"?*
Very, very pissed off, but I didn't see him as likely to take action. I never perceived any threats of this type.

*Then there's the ever-delicate problem of covering your back. Do you think López Portillo considered, or could have considered among his reasons for choosing you, the fact that you would cover his back?*
I never felt, in his relations with me, that López Portillo expected me to cover his back. Rather, he thought I would represent the continuation of certain fundamental endeavors of his.

*Might your closeness with José Ramón López Portillo have been a factor in this sense? The idea that he would think, "He'll look after Pepe, they're already friends."*
I think it was important to him.

*Didn't López Portillo think you would look after Rosa Luz Alegría better than the others?*
He knew I got along well with her.

*What was your impression of PEMEX director Jorge Díaz Serrano? Did he have a chance?*
Look, I never got the impression that López Portillo was inclined to favor Jorge Díaz Serrano for the presidency. He had great affection for Díaz Serrano and had cause to be grateful to him. He thought he was a good director for PEMEX, which was important to López Portillo as part of Mexico's economic recovery. From that point of view, Díaz Serrano did a good job for him. But I don't think López Portillo promoted Díaz Serrano's candidacy.

*When I asked José López Portillo whether personal factors counted, he said yes: health, family life, and financial integrity. He told me: "That's something we do investigate." Did you know anything of this?*
I didn't know they had investigated me, but I did know it was a factor. I don't know how far the investigations went. I had led a financially honest life, and I knew it was a factor. It didn't bother me.

*When do you think López Portillo made up his mind?*
I think it was a process. It's hard to say now.

*I quote José Ramón López Portillo's Oxford doctoral thesis: "de la Madrid was considered by many to be adept in orthodox economics, although he espoused relatively heterodox points of view in his climb up the bureaucratic ladder to the presidency. He proved himself to be flexible enough to take part in, support, and even promote López Portillo's expansionist economic policies, dissimulating his own economic position to avoid endangering hipolitical future. De la Madrid said: 'No cabinet member would have deliberately thwarted the president and his basic philosophy, because it would have been suicide to do so, and political survival is what matters most in the cabinet.' According to de la Madrid, there were limits to what a minister could say to the president, especially in the context of a heterogeneous cabinet, plagued with ideological and political conflicts, and the government's dogmatic focus on economic growth and creating jobs." Is he correct?*
I've always been orthodox and conservative when it comes to economics in the traditional sense of the word. But I thought I didn't have to go to extremes to be effective, that I had to try to use my ideas to temper the expansionist policy the president adopted, so much so that I got us to lower the target figure of 10 percent put forth by Minister of the National Patrimony Oteyza to 8 percent in the National Development Plan, bringing us closer to the 6.5 percent proposed by Minister of Finance David Ibarra, which I felt was a prudent figure. But when I started at Planning and Budget, the plan was already launched. We were going to achieve 8 percent growth, especially in view of the forecasts for oil prices at the time. Also, I think that no member of any governmental cabinet can uphold a position that totally contradicts that of the head of state, because they either resign or are asked to resign.

*Does a technical minister, with no presidential aspirations, have a wider margin to argue with or oppose the president?*
Well, yes, but I was in the economic cabinet. I had to face the issue of the economy, and my problem was to moderate policy without causing a split. So I moderated our target from 10.5 percent to 8 percent growth to establish a fundamental goal. Moreover, also in my capacity as minister of planning and budget, I struggled to prevent excessive spending that was concentrated in three areas, PEMEX mainly, the Department of Agriculture, and the Mexico City government. I never could control these three entities, because they had a bilateral agreement with the president giving them carte blanche. When I came along, the decision was already made.

*In his dissertation, José Ramón López Portillo explains that, when oil prices dropped in 1981, a debate in the cabinet ensued concerning the size of the fiscal deficit that would appear for the year, and what measures to take. He links this to the succession, and mentions considerable evolution in the Ministry of Planning and Budget (SPP) figures. The first estimate sent by SPP in July 1981 was for a deficit of 490 billion pesos. By September the figure had risen to 866 billion, nearly a twofold increase in three months. Was this play of figures part of the succession?*

As I recall, there were no further economic cabinet meetings to deal with significant issues after the session where we discussed the problem of oil prices. We were on the threshold of the succession, which took place in late September, and I lost the thread of the economic policy debate after that last meeting in June 1981. The rest is history. We had the problem of keeping oil prices high while we were losing markets. The government maintained that the slump in prices was temporary, that we had to get past this period of low prices, and meanwhile compensate our losses with short-term foreign debt. The significant increase in short-term debt occurred at the end of the year, after the price of oil fell. I didn't get involved, because there was no opportunity for me to do so. There was no economic cabinet meeting held for the purpose.

*But you and SPP dressed up fiscal deficit statistics presented to López Portillo?*
That's not how I remember it. López Portillo had the impression that we manipulated the figures, in contrast to David Ibarra's more realistic estimate. I don't remember that we did so deliberately. As I say, after the meeting in June, we never discussed the matter again.

*And your aides, didn't they get a little carried away with the numbers?*
If they did, I didn't notice, because I was chosen for the candidacy in late September, and I almost immediately took Salinas, who was the economist at SPP, with me. We didn't have time to review the problem.

*But this evolution of statistics took place from July to September, that is, before the unveiling. . . .*
The issue did not arise again, nor did I see it. There was no climate for it.

*You saw no budget figures?*
No.

*You sent them directly to the Ministry of the Presidency?*
Yes.

*The numbers are surprising, reflecting a marked change from at first a very prudent, obviously very optimistic, calculation to one that devastates the economy two months later. Is it not so?*

Indeed. But look, I think this new estimate of the deficit, with the implication that my area, Planning and Budget, dressed up the statistics, was not known before I was designated candidate. If President López Portillo had thought SPP had deceived him, I might not have been the candidate, so I think it must have been afterward.

*López Portillo has suggested that he postponed the decision almost until he had no choice, because of the irreversible and momentous nature of the final step. What do you think about this?*

He had made it his goal to make the decision after the Cancún summit, in late October, but something made him move it forward.

*He says he did not doubt his decision, but that when he nationalized the banks, he would not have chosen you. . . .*

Probably not. He says in his memoirs that I was not the right candidate to handle the nationalization process.

*Echeverría says that the moment of greatest solitude and the most difficult time for a president is when he chooses his cabinet, because he knows that among those he is including will be his potential successor. Who were you thinking of in these terms when you appointed your cabinet in 1982?*

I began thinking of the cabinet in October. I had two months left. I had to take steps, conduct inquiries, do research, and I was inclined to bring most of the people who had worked with me during the campaign and in the previous administration. This was how I chose Manuel Bartlett—a political adviser of mine when I was minister of planning and budget, who had been general party secretary and a fundamental figure in my campaign—for minister of the interior, and how I chose Carlos Salinas, who had worked for me since my days in Finance, and later in Planning and Budget, to head that ministry.

*Which of the cabinet members you chose were in your mind from the start as possible candidates to succeed you?*

At first I didn't have a clear idea of who might make good candidates. I knew in principle that the traditional figures would be eligible: minister of the interior [Bartlett], minister of finance [Silva Herzog]—but not because of the individuals in question. Rather, I thought, "For the time being, we'll get to work and the best prospects will stand out for their performance and be recognized by public opinion."

*How important was Jesús Silva Herzog's forced resignation in 1986?*
It was a turning point. It was a very unpleasant episode for me because Silva Herzog had been a friend of mine since the beginning of our careers in public life, since the Banco de México. We were very close, personal friends: our families were close, and I considered him an important prospect.

*You always saw him that way?*
As a prospect. The problem is that Silva Herzog and Salinas didn't see one another as teammates. I think Silva Herzog always felt, let's say, that he was more entitled to manage economic policy, and he reacted negatively when he saw Salinas gaining ground. The two of them began to rub one another the wrong way, and Salinas behaved more astutely than "Chucho" [Silva Herzog] who began vociferously to criticize our economic policy. He threatened to resign and no longer functioned for me as minister. He didn't present his reports, didn't offer me options, but only vague, very general criticism. Then, in 1986, I had to make the decision to fire him. He was also interested in leaving by then.

*At the time of your separation, in the context of the 1986 crisis, and the visit to Mexico by Paul Volcker, chairman of the U.S. Federal Reserve, what were the positions of Silva Herzog [in Finance] on the one hand and Salinas [in Planning and Budget] on the other?*
They were never entirely different. It was a question of nuance. Silva Herzog felt that we had to cut public spending. "OK," I replied, "tell me where and how." He never followed through on it. It was a very generalized criticism, but mostly, he didn't want to work as a team. I ordered the two departments to meet to present me with options, and Chucho stopped attending the meetings, sending a deputy minister in his place. I said, "He can't just ignore my instructions to meet and try to reach, if not a reconciliation, at least some clearly defined options." And that's what Chucho failed to do.

*When Silva Herzog left, you could have appointed a strong minister to replace him, one perhaps without ties to any of the prospective candidates. You decided to appoint Gustavo Petriccioli, who got along well with Salinas. You handed economic policy over to Salinas. . . .*
I did so consciously. I felt that if I repeated the mistake of appointing someone who would reproduce the strife between SPP and Finance, it would make life very hard for me. I preferred Petriccioli, whom I knew to be a consummate

negotiator, and who had good relations with Salinas. I consciously ratified Salinas as my economic policy director, with no further discussion.

*Did Salinas really win the theoretical debate over the operational deficit and the primary surplus? Was it an idea that he proposed and in turn convinced you, and then Washington, to agree with?*
Conceptually, it came from SPP and Salinas, obviously, but with strong support from Pedro Aspe, who later became Salinas's minister of finance. The concept of the operational deficit had not been put forth previously. The concept of the operational deficit as something different from the total financial deficit arose as part of the arguments we presented to the IMF [International Monetary Fund]. We were able to demonstrate that we had in fact corrected the imbalance in public finances, and that the deficit was caused by the financial burden of our debt.

*Didn't it seem odd to you that when the idea of the operational deficit suddenly appeared, Silva Herzog left the Ministry of Finance, and the North Americans, who had been unyielding up to then, said, "What a good idea you've just had. We're going to lend you more money." . . .?*
I think the IMF and the U.S. Treasury recognized the need to yield in their positions. When the problem of a new oil-price crisis appeared in January and February 1986, I gave a strong speech here in Mexico City, saying that it was more than we could stand, that we had to react, and reiterating the thesis that, in order to be able to pay [its debt], Mexico had to grow. I hardened my position, taking advantage of my new minister of finance, and Gustavo Petriccioli was able to go before the IMF and negotiate with much greater firmness.

*What was your opinion of Manuel Bartlett?*
I saw Bartlett as a serious contender, very able and very professional. He was one of the finalists. The three finalists were Minister of the Interior Bartlett, Minister of Energy, Mines, and Parastatal Industry del Mazo, and Minister of Planning and Budget Salinas.

*Did you include Alfredo del Mazo in your cabinet with the intention that he run?*
Yes.

*For that specific reason, to see if he could?*
Yes, and to have another option.

*When did you make the decision?*
I think it was in the second half of September of 1987.

*Did the governors ever openly voice their opinions?*
Yes. Some spoke out in favor of Bartlett, and others in favor of Salinas.

*And Salinas was chosen as the PRI presidential candidate?*
Salinas was the one who in the end I felt had the strongest degree of "approval" among the real sources of power both inside and outside the party.

*How so?*
Because they thought he had been a good minister. Because he had worked well with them, because they felt that he would continue my economic policies. There were no reservations about his candidacy.

*And on a personal level as well, although he wasn't a personal friend of yours?*
No, because the age difference between us is nearly fifteen years. Carlos had always been a subordinate of mine, and we formed no personal friendship. We were friends at work, not in our private lives. The one I had the strongest personal friendship with was Alfredo del Mazo. He's my *compadre*.

*Carlos Salinas vividly remembers an occasion, probably in early 1987, when you and your wife invited him and his wife to lunch in Cuautla, alone, with no other aides present. Was this to test him one last time, or to give him a sign of special favor?*
It was the first time I invited the Salinas family to my house in Cuautla. But I had invited other people, also cabinet members, both to Los Pinos and to Cuautla, for the sole purpose of socializing, and with no ulterior political motives. In general, I had a very limited social life, since I was so rushed and bombarded with work when I was president. But now and then I invited some of my aides to watch movies in the projection room at Los Pinos on Sunday afternoons. I remember Manuel Bartlett, Francisco Rojas, and Alfredo del Mazo coming, and I also invited many of my aides to Cuautla. It was neither an isolated case nor a sign.

*Why not del Mazo or Bartlett?*
I thought Salinas enjoyed the greatest degree of consensus, and had the clearest platform. I'll tell you how it was. For personal and family ties: del Mazo; for friendship and camaraderie: Bartlett; for cooperation and results, loyalty, and the defense of my ideas: Salinas.

*How much did you investigate the three of them?*
As a matter of fact, I conducted no personal investigations.

*Two of them, Salinas and del Mazo, were from wealthy families, and Manuel Bartlett somewhat so.*

Bartlett inherited certain wealth from his father. None of them was extraordinarily rich. They were upper-middle-class bureaucrats. They didn't live ostentatiously.

*You didn't think it might be worthwhile to investigate?*
No, nor did I want to investigate their personal lives. I knew more or less what their family lives were like. I knew that some were a bit naughty. But their pranks didn't go so far as to endanger the stability of their families, as far as I could see. It may be necessary to be more careful about the matter in the future, although it's shameful to mix public and private life. As things change, not just in Mexico but around the world, we will soon see hyper-scrutiny of the private lives of our candidates and presidents, and we'll have to know at least what ground we are walking on, and what weaknesses exist. But there was no significant attack whatsoever on Salinas's private life or his financial dealings during his campaign.

*There is no proof, but the Salinas family's fortune at the time could only be explained by* Don *Raúl Salinas's career, no?*
Yes. I knew that *Don* Raúl, who was minister of industry and trade under López Mateos, had money. I thought *Don* Raúl was already far away, and Carlos appeared to be quite independent of his father.

*You didn't see the Salinas family as a very close-knit group, as a clan with a certain thirst for revenge?*
It didn't appear so to me.

*How about Salinas's top aides?*
José Córdoba, Salinas's chief of staff, was a technician, an adviser who, as far as I know, had no significant business relations with anyone. He was very close to Salinas, but I knew that Pepe Córdoba had earned Salinas's confidence. What happened was that Córdoba assumed an exaggerated role in the Salinas government in the Ministry of the Presidency. He overstepped the bounds that a minister or presidential adviser should respect, and became a participant in top-level decision making. I had not noticed this when Córdoba was Salinas's adviser at Planning or when he worked with him on his campaign.

*Didn't you know about what has been dubbed Salinas's "dark side"? Didn't anybody tell you about it? Not even his enemies? Bartlett?*
I think Bartlett and Salinas had a nonaggression agreement. Bartlett, who was supposedly responsible for political intelligence, never brought me information about Salinas, perhaps because as a competitor he didn't want to seem to be

playing unfairly against Salinas. It appears that Salinas appointed Bartlett minister of education, even though he may not have managed the electoral process with the necessary efficiency. Salinas kept Bartlett in Education for two years, and then helped him go to Puebla as governor.

*Don't you get the impression that from 1986 to 1987, the figures of the Promotion and Growth Program were exaggerated? Were the statistics dressed up for you? Did SPP and Salinas present you with an overly optimistic picture?*
Well, optimistic, yes, because we had got through 1986 and the country needed to catch its breath after the brutal squeeze.

*Was the devaluation of 1987 an act of carelessness?*
No. There was significant capital flight after the stock market crash in November 1987. The devaluation was provoked by circumstances. It was not a preventive or planned action on the part of the government. There was no other remedy. I think the Mexican stock exchange collapsed, and the economic community was suddenly faced with problems it had preferred to ignore, such as the fact that we still had very high inflation and the Mexican stock exchange was overinflated. There I do think that we were careless in managing our securities market policy. The market was allowed to grow too much, and I think it failed us.

*When you decided to make Salinas the candidate, did you know that this might produce internal strife in the PRI?*
Well, it certainly did with the Democratic Current, with Cuauhtémoc Cárdenas and Porfirio Muñoz Ledo and the group that followed them. But I didn't think Cuauhtémoc and Porfirio would be able to make anything of the movement. Frankly, I underestimated them. I thought theirs were merely personal positions, ambition for personal power and opposition to the economic policy. I never thought that they would be capable of generating the opposition that they have.

*Do you think this occurred spontaneously, or did the system, and perhaps Bartlett himself, allow them to act?*
Perhaps, because Bartlett underestimated Cuauhtémoc and Porfirio.

*Did Bartlett play rough with you and Salinas after losing the race for the candidacy? Was he hurt?*
No. But he was hurt. Losers are always hurt. It shows in their attitude, their personal relations. Their morale suffers. Alfredo del Mazo was the hardest hit.

*You offered no explanation to anyone?*
It's not done.

*Not even to del Mazo, because of how close you were? Did you seek him out to explain what had happened?*
No. "It wasn't you," and that's all, nothing further. I think it was a procedural error on my part not to expressly inform the runners-up that they had been eliminated. I relied on messages sent through the party president. I told Jorge de la Vega, "Talk to all of them, and tell them not to move until there are clear signals." But I didn't do it. I think I lacked foresight there.

*When you decided to go with Carlos Salinas, did you mention it to anyone?*
No. Not even my wife and children, or my chief of staff Emilio Gamboa. I told absolutely no one. I hadn't even told Jorge de la Vega about Salinas.

*Did you have any doubts during the campaign?*
I had observations, doubts about how the campaign was being handled, but I no longer felt that I was in a position to intervene directly. Having had the experience of López Portillo giving me a free hand in everything, I gave Salinas the same treatment. I didn't intervene at all in Salinas's campaign, nor did I participate in the process of selecting candidates for Congress and Senate, nothing.

*Did you ever think you might have been wrong?*
No. I honestly think I made no mistake, given the prevailing circumstances at the time. If Salinas made mistakes, if things went badly for him at the end, well, that was his problem. But I remember that the first three years of his administration were glorious in all respects, with growing prestige, economic policy triumphs, and victories in the midterm elections. I think the problems began in the second half of his term. That he reacted badly to power; that he seemed, later on, to let the problem of his brother go too far, and committed other types of political errors. That in 1994 he fell apart with the rebellion in Chiapas is another matter. That he was wrong in his exchange-rate policy is also another matter.

*Do you think Porfirio and Cuauhtémoc were with Bartlett, and ultimately broke with the PRI because they realized Bartlett wasn't going to be the candidate?*
It was my understanding, rather, that they said, "Anyone but Salinas."

*Manuel Camacho, who worked with Salinas at the time, has a theory concerning Cárdenas and his break with the PRI. In his memoirs, which were, in fact, as Manuel Camacho himself told me, documents stolen from his home in 1994, he says: "Cuauhtémoc Cárdenas began to be an obstacle to the type of unveiling President de la Madrid wanted. At the time, any change in the rules for selecting the PRI presidential candidate would be seen as an attempt to weaken the president's will, and therefore to support other candidates who would undermine the progress toward financial reform that had been de la Madrid's main objective. As a result of this perception, from then on pressuring de la Madrid was equivalent to attacking Salinas, and attacking Cárdenas was equivalent to supporting de la Madrid by increasing Salinas's chances of attaining the candidacy. Although there were no prior personal differences between Cárdenas and Salinas, their political interests diverged from then on." What comment does this warrant?*

Evidently, the ideology of the Democratic Current that Cuauhtémoc and Porfirio led revolved around protesting against the economic policy in place and opposing Carlos Salinas. As a result, they wanted the president to leave the decision to free competition within the party, thinking that this type of arrangement would give them a better chance of getting something out of it for themselves, or negotiating the candidacy. Faced with this situation, I refused to back down, and we went ahead with what we might call the traditional approach of leaving the direction of the process and the final judgment in the hands of the president.

*In your first talk with candidate Carlos Salinas, the very night of October 4, did he ask you to replace Jorge de la Vega with Manuel Camacho as PRI president?*
He did, and I refused. I felt a certain lack of confidence in Camacho's political maturity.

*Was Manuel Bartlett appointed PRI secretary general in 1981 at your request?*
Yes. I asked the president to do it. When López Portillo told me, "I'm going to castle. Javier García Paniagua is going to Labor and Pedro Ojeda is going to the party," I replied, "I have ideas of my own about the other members of the Executive Committee."

*You have no doubt that it was wise to leave Bartlett in the Ministry of the Interior for the final year?*
None whatsoever. I think, for institutional reasons, that it was good for him to remain. I didn't want to replace any of the losers. If I replaced Alfredo del Mazo, it's because he told me he no longer wanted to remain in the cabinet.

*You didn't fear that Bartlett, having lost, would react resentfully?*
No, I always felt that Bartlett was very institutional.

*Did Salinas ever propose replacing Bartlett?*
No, never. It was, and still is, my opinion that Bartlett acted very institutionally. I had no reason to replace him. Also, I had heard that Salinas and Bartlett had close ties of friendship, and perhaps even an agreement.

*Salinas would have us believe that Bartlett was to some extent responsible for having allowed Cárdenas's candidacy.*

He never did so explicitly. Not only Salinas, but other people in politics as well, thought it odd that traditional splinter parties and PRI allies should go with Cárdenas. Some people still suspected that the Ministry of the Interior had failed to act in a timely fashion to prevent this situation. I think one splinter party, the PARM [Authentic Party of the Mexican Revolution], was an opportunistic and divided party that tended to bet on the highest bidder and had been losing ground drastically. Another splinter party, the PPS [Popular Socialist Party], had criticized the government's economic policy harshly, and blamed Salinas. The move by the PPS struck me as very logical, ideologically speaking, while with the PARM it was a case of pure and simple opportunism. I think the great strategist of all this was Porfirio Muñoz Ledo. He put together Cárdenas's entire strategy, convinced the PARM to nominate him as its candidate, convinced the PPS to join the campaign, and assembled the entire political front that supported Cuauhtémoc.

*Might the question of whether or not Bartlett let it get by him have been a factor?*
It's on his conscience.

*Did de la Vega tell you in 1987 and 1988 that the Salinas campaign didn't look good to him, that the voting wasn't going to come out the way it had always done in the past? Or did you have other information in addition to what de la Vega provided?*
Well, yes, I heard that there were internal problems between Carlos's group and Jorge de la Vega on the one hand, and other party officers, the party sectors, and the governors on the other. In Mexico City, proper coordination between the Mexico City mayor, the Federal District PRI leader, and Salinas's team was not achieved. I warned Salinas to take action, but I couldn't get involved in organizing his campaign.

*When did it dawn on you that the election was going to be complicated?*
About two months before Election Day. Support for Cárdenas grew toward the end, in the last two months.

*At what time on July 6 did you begin to learn that things were getting very complicated?*
In the afternoon.

*How were you informed?*
By the Ministry of the Interior.

*By Manuel Bartlett directly?*
Bartlett came right out and told me that things were going very poorly, that it was going to be rough. I said, "Well, how bad is it? Are we going to lose?" But he answered that it was not that bad. Around 7 PM he informed me that Mexico City was very bad, as were the states of Mexico and Michoacán. Then he said, "I can't release these results because they are very biased, and although the results from states where I think we'll recover lost ground will come in later, if we announce a trend in favor of Cárdenas from the outset, no one will believe us later." That was when he failed to release the results as he had promised, until 11 PM, because they really hadn't come in. He overestimated the computer system and the information didn't arrive. But he knew numbers would soon be arriving that would most probably help Salinas. Bartlett said, "It's when the votes from the strong PRI states, like Puebla, Chiapas, and others, come in that we'll even the score." And so it was.

*But was it his decision to defer releasing the results?*
No. He asked me about it, and I agreed with him.

*Did you go see him that night or did you talk by telephone?*
By telephone.

*Jorge de la Vega says he went to see Salinas several times that night, to ask him to give his victory speech. He recalls that Salinas didn't want to. De la Vega called you and informed you of this. How did this occur?*
Salinas was at PRI headquarters, holed up in an office with his advisers Manuel Camacho and José Córdoba. In another office was Jorge de la Vega. I was at Los Pinos, and Bartlett at the Ministry of the Interior. The three centers were in contact by telephone. I called Salinas twice at one point. "Haven't you thought of declaring your victory?" I asked. He answered, "The problem is I have no grounds to do so." I insisted, "Listen, Carlos, this is going to give people cause for suspicion, because the PRI candidate traditionally appears around 11 PM or midnight to proclaim his victory. If you don't, there will be problems." He replied, "Well, yes, but I don't feel that I have sufficient grounds." According to Jorge de la Vega, this was the posture Camacho had advised him to adopt. Finally Jorge said to me, "Look, Mr. President, if we don't go out and declare victory, it's going to sully our image, so if you'll authorize it, I'll make the announcement." I answered, "Go ahead, do it."

*Why do you think Salinas was reluctant?*
He was also receiving reports that Cárdenas was ahead, that there were doubts

regarding the handling of information. He wanted to be more delicate, mainly on the advice of Camacho, who thought that if the publication of results was handled more gradually, it would be easier to negotiate with the opposition.

*You don't think that, in Guerrero for example, the numbers were "corrected" after the fact?*
It wasn't so much that they were corrected a posteriori, but rather along the way, using traditional PRI methods of getting voters to the polls, of inflating voting at polling stations with no representation from other parties—the kinds of things that were possible in the past. I don't doubt that the procedure was used in what we might call the least developed states like Guerrero.

*A statement of yours concerning the rebellion in Chiapas coincides with an idea of Jorge de la Vega's. You told me: ". . . and then Salinas fell apart when the rebellion broke out in Chiapas." De la Vega says, "I saw Salinas in a difficult situation on three occasions: the incidents at La Laguna during his campaign, when people rejected him; July 6, 1988; and the Chiapas rebellion. He seemed stunned, although at other times he's a man who stands up and fights back." Could you elaborate on this idea?*
I would elaborate on it as follows. As de la Vega says, Salinas was always very keen, fast to react, always with a solution at his fingertips. That was my impression. He had five splendid years of government, with an excellent domestic and international public image. Everything seemed to be going well for him. Then came January 1, 1994, and I say he fell apart not because I saw it—he didn't call me for the entire month of January—but from reports I received from sources close to him that he was very depressed and stunned. That's why I say he fell apart.

*Did you notice, in retrospect, a similar reaction on July 6, 1988?*
On the telephone, yes.

*When did you see him again?*
A few days later, and he had already recovered. I noted that he was in very poor spirits that evening, but I didn't see him. De la Vega did find him very down.

*Did you talk with Salinas in March 1994, when Colosio was assassinated?*
Colosio was assassinated on March 23, 1994, and Salinas invited me to breakfast on Saturday, March 26. We went to Los Pinos, and my first comment was that he was under stress and sad. His eyes filled with tears during the conversation. We talked about the tragedy and he asked my opinion of his options. I said,

"There are two alternatives. One is to amend the Constitution to allow the current cabinet members to compete, and the other is no amendment. In my opinion, a constitutional amendment is unfeasible, because the opposition parties, and even people in the PRI itself, will reject it resoundingly. I don't think you can pull it off. Let's talk about the idea of no constitutional amendment instead. It reduces the field. I'm simply going to tell you what I think the options are, without recommending anyone, because I no longer have the responsibility or the criteria for the decision. You're the one to know, but from the outside I see the following alternatives."

The options were PRI president Fernando Ortiz Arana, Fernando Gutiérrez Barrios—who was not in the administration—Colosio campaign chief Ernesto Zedillo, and Francisco Rojas at PEMEX. These were the cards I said I thought were feasible for him to play. I gave him pros and cons for each one. I tried to be very skeptical, not to load the dice to the point where he would say, "He came to recommend so-and-so to me." In the case of Ortiz Arana, he said, "No, I'm not sure he's completely viable." Of Gutiérrez Barrios, "No, we can't go backwards." He defended Zedillo because I told him, "Zedillo's assets are that he is a good economist, and a competent official. As to his liabilities, he lacks political experience and I don't know how his relations with the army are as a result of the matter of the official textbooks he put out [when he was minister of education]." I stopped there. He said to me: "There's no problem with the army and he's a fast learner." We moved on to Rojas and he made no comment, and I didn't have much to say either: "I don't have to go into the pros and cons of Francisco Rojas because he's a close friend of yours; you know him better than I." I said, "He's a good functionary. He's loyal. He's a man of ideas; some say he has no political experience, but I think no PEMEX director would survive without political experience." The only one he defended with conviction was Zedillo. As I left, I said to myself, "It's [going to be] Zedillo."

*He had already resolved the matter?*
I think so. Look, a movement favoring Ortiz Arana began as of Thursday or Friday, and this seems to have made Salinas very angry. He disciplined Ortiz Arana in a very heavy-handed and clumsy way. I think he had already chosen Zedillo by the time we spoke, and to my knowledge Pepe Córdoba's opinion carried considerable weight with Salinas in his decision to make Zedillo the replacement candidate.

*Salinas has said the following: "Córdoba came in with the most precise, convincing arguments at the right time." Is this true?*
Indeed. I think Pepe Córdoba had felt a strong liking for Zedillo from early

on, since the third year of the Salinas administration, when Zedillo was minister of education, mainly because of the incident with the textbooks. Then Córdoba and Jaime Serra [minister of trade], who worked as a team, realized that Zedillo had missed opportunities, and swung over to Colosio.

*Were they with Colosio?*
Yes, because Zedillo had been weakened.

*It has been said that when Colosio's widow, Diana Laura, went to see Salinas a few days after Ernesto Zedillo was designated, she inquired "Why Zedillo?" Salinas answered, "It's what Luis Donaldo wanted." To which she replied: "That's not true. Luis Donaldo had already informed you of his intention to replace him [as his campaign manager]." And Salinas said: "But that message never reached me. . . ."*
Yes, there was a lot of talk that Colosio was going to replace Zedillo.

*The version has been published that Pepe Córdoba was the messenger. This would explain why the message never arrived, wouldn't it?*
But Salinas knew that Colosio wasn't working well as a candidate. I told him so at the beginning of February: "Colosio isn't getting off the ground. In the first place because, faced with Chiapas, and the leading role Camacho is taking, Colosio hasn't known how to say 'Here I am,' and second because I have observed a lack of integration in the PRI campaign team," [which was divided between] the formal leadership of Ortiz Arana and the group of Colosio supporters. He replied, "How about you? Have you talked to Colosio? Or tried to contact him?" "No." "And he hasn't contacted you?" "Not at all." He said, "You're going to see Colosio soon." Colosio called me the next day. I hadn't seen him in person since the day he was nominated. He called to tell me that he was there, and that he hoped we'd be in touch, and that's all. But I didn't try to contact him, because it's not in the rules of the game. I saw Colosio around the middle of February. He came to see me here. He asked me, "How do things look to you?" I repeated what I had said to Salinas: "Look, Luis Donaldo, I don't see that your campaign has taken off, and from the outside I see no cohesion in the party."

*Was that before or after his speech on March 6?*
Before. I said to him, "Look, Luis Donaldo, there's nothing else to do but for you to take hold of your campaign. Furthermore, it's easy. Call the PRI leaders and say to them, 'Gentlemen, I'm running this campaign and you're responsible for this and you for that. Cooperate and I'm going to check up on you every week.' It's that simple." He answered, "Yes, the time has come. I'm going to

do it, and I do think I'm going to have to introduce new methods and make changes in my team."

*He didn't say anything about whether he felt he had to distance himself from Salinas?*
No, nothing. I asked him, "How are you getting along with Salinas?" "Very well," he replied. "Look," I said, "during the campaign the risk of rifts and misunderstandings between president and candidate is very high. Don't let yourself fall into the trap, because it won't help your campaign." He reacted vehemently: "Under no circumstances."

*According to Salinas, by this point he had told Colosio that he had to start to take a certain distance. . . .*
Well, yes, it's normal. When I was the candidate, López Portillo also told me, "Listen, Miguel, you know my theory of rupture for stability, so criticize me."

*López Portillo said this to you?*
He did. I answered, "Look, Mr. President, I know I have to take my distance, but I will decide when and how. That is, I don't feel that I have to start criticizing you. I'll decide how I do it."

*You didn't say the same to Salinas when he was the candidate?*
No.

*When did you learn how to achieve a successful succession?*
Well, I knew how it had been done before.

*From your own experience?*
From the experience of the system.

*There's no collective memory?*
Formally? No, but the system was basically that the president conducted the process and was the final judge or decision-maker. I said, "I'm going to control the process in regard to time and method, and I'm going to place an innovative stamp on it by handling the succession from within the party, relying heavily on the party, on Jorge de la Vega, without the side deals that have been made in the past." When Jorge and I came to evaluate the suitability of announcing the six prospective candidates, we agreed on the issue, and I thought, "It's much better that the party president make the announcement, instead of an officious spokesperson as has been the case in the past." I was convinced that it had to be done from within the party. That's why I handled the process the way I've described to you, with Jorge de la Vega making the announcement,

inviting the six to the *pasarela*, and with the final breakfast where the entire Executive Committee made the decision with me. It was not like previous occasions, when the president had just picked up the telephone or announced his decision.

*But your knowledge came above all from your experience?*
From historical experience. We all have observed how things were done. I had very fresh personal memories of the transfer of power from Díaz Ordaz to Echeverría, from Echeverría to López Portillo, and from López Portillo to me. That was my personal school.

# CARLOS SALINAS

Carlos Salinas de Gortari was born in Mexico City on April 3, 1948. He studied economics at the National Autonomous University of Mexico (class of 1969) and obtained a doctorate in political economy and government at Harvard University in 1978.

He entered Miguel de la Madrid's cabinet on December 1, 1982, as minister of planning and budget, was nominated as PRI presidential candidate on October 4, 1987, elected president on July 6, 1988, and inaugurated on December 1, 1988. He transferred power to Ernesto Zedillo on December 1, 1994.

In 1994 Mexico had over 80 million inhabitants. During Carlos Salinas's presidency, the Mexican economy averaged 3.7 percent annual growth and 15.9 percent annual inflation. Per capita GNP was US$4,180 when Salinas left office in late 1994.

In late 1987, Salinas faced two strong contenders for the PRI presidential nomination, Minister of Interior Manuel Bartlett and Minister of Energy, Mines, and Parastatal Industry Alfredo del Mazo. Del Mazo was perceived as de la Madrid's closest friend among the three. De la Madrid appointed him minister in 1986 to make him a presidential contender. Del Mazo went on to serve as ambassador to Belgium and the European Community (1988–1990) and was the PRI candidate for the first democratic election of the Mexico City mayor in 1997. He lost to Cuauhtémoc Cárdenas, the man who broke with the PRI in 1987 as a result of Salinas's nomination.

Manuel Bartlett served as minister of the interior from 1982 to 1988. He had previously served as de la Madrid's personal adviser from 1979 to 1982. Bartlett had also worked with 1976 presidential contender and Minister of the Interior Mario Moya Palencia. After Salinas's election, Bartlett went on to serve as minister of education (1988–1992) and governor of Puebla (1992–1998). The son of a former governor of Tabasco, Bartlett competed as a candidate in the historic PRI presidential primaries in 1999. He came in third with less than 5 percent of the PRI vote.

Early on during de la Madrid's term, Jesús Silva Herzog, the minister of finance (1982–1986), was seen as a serious contender for the presidency. When he was forced to resign in 1986, his presidential aspirations ended and Salinas's increased. Silva Herzog served as ambassador to Spain (1991–1993) and in 1994 President Zedillo appointed him minister of tourism. Most recently, Silva Herzog won the PRI primary for the 2000 elections for mayor of Mexico City, the same primaries that designated Fernando Labastida as the PRI presidential candidate.

Carlos Salinas probably left a greater mark on Mexico than any of his predecessors since Miguel Alemán (1946–1952) and perhaps since Lázaro Cárdenas (1934–1940). For better or for worse, he transformed Mexico in more ways than the other presidents in this book. He achieved notable levels of popularity domestically and adulation abroad only to become the most reviled ex-president in modern Mexican history. While he did little or nothing to democratize the old political system, he dramatically changed the structure and logic of the Mexican economy and aligned Mexico with the United States in unprecedented ways. His support of the North American Free Trade Agreement (NAFTA), overnight trade liberalization, widespread privatizations, and unabashed courtship of foreign investment all flew in the face of Mexican tradition. They have had an enormous impact on Mexico's economy and society, even if they have not yet fulfilled their promise of growth and prosperity. After five years of apparent success, everything fell apart for Salinas in 1994. The Chiapas uprising that January, the assassinations of his successor in March and his former brother-in-law in September, the collapse of the currency in December just after he left office, and the arrest of his brother Raúl in February of 1995 on charges of murder and later of wanton corruption, all transformed him into Mexico's favorite villain. Today he is a tragic figure, living in exile in Ireland, waiting for his day in the court of Mexican public opinion.

❧

*In May 1979, when Miguel de la Madrid appointed you minister of planning and budget, did you immediately perceive that you had become a possible candidate since you had worked with him at the Ministry of Finance?*
That's right. I had to choose between staying on at Finance with my former economics professor David Ibarra, or going with de la Madrid, with whom I had worked directly for only a few months, but who I had known in a pro-

fessional context for several years. It was during this last year that he asked me to work for him in the Ministry of Planning and Budget, in a job similar to that which I had been doing at Finance. I decided to accept his offer because I had always admired his talent and personal style, and recognized the opportunity to learn from his knowledge and experience.

*It has been said that, from very early on, you had a sort of student group with long-term plans to reach the presidency. A statement is ascribed to your father, Raúl Salinas, on learning of your nomination: "It took twenty years, but we made it."*
In the first place, he didn't say it. I did. It was a kindly way of telling him that one way or another he had been a contender to succeed López Mateos. And he wasn't successful. My father never encouraged us, or at least me, to harbor presidential aspirations, nor did he foment ambition for power or government posts in me. What he always did instill in us was a dedication to public service.

*Is Fidel Velázquez's declaration that "If you move, you don't appear in the photograph" true?*
I think you have to understand its significance. If someone who has been asked to hold a position to solve problems and uses it to serve himself and his own political interests, then he's not useful for the job he was asked to do. It was not only an option, but an obligation, of my job that I cultivate communication, dialogue, and ties with legislators and relations with other ministers and with the various interest groups. I did it every day for the five years I was minister, and as president I saw my secretaries and aides do it daily. It seemed indispensable. Why? Because they had to do this kind of work to get their jobs done as well. I always maintained that cabinet ministers should not become the ambassadors or representatives of interest groups and lobby the president on their behalf, but the other way around. There, it was necessary to move. If you didn't, you didn't appear.

*When did you begin to feel that you were one of the prospective candidates? Was it when Finance Minister Jesús Silva Herzog left the cabinet, or before?*
Well, when the National Development Plan I had been entrusted with drafting had worked well and we had achieved consensus on the budget within the government, I began to think so. Also, there had been no serious disputes with the governors, and we had managed to maintain a dialogue with the labor and business sectors.

*How was your debate with Jesús Silva Herzog, in regard to both economic policy and your obvious dispute over the succession?*

I don't think the succession was in dispute in 1986. We had had a terrible time a few months earlier, with the September 1985 earthquake, followed by yet another abrupt fall in oil prices. The situation in Mexico was very tense, and there was really no cohesion around the president.

*You don't recall occasions when anyone disguised an issue, concealed a problem from you, or tried to prevent you from learning about something?*
No, I neither heard of nor detected any deliberate attempt to conceal significant problems or bad news from me. There may have been—and in fact there were—cases of insufficient or deficient information, but that's very different from a deliberate intent to cover up bad news.

*You didn't start working with Miguel de la Madrid until May 1979. Did you ever develop a personal friendship with him?*
I think the use of the term friendship requires that we specify what we mean. We weren't friends from childhood, due to our age difference, nor did we develop what might be called personal ties, but we did share convictions, actions, decisions. In that sense, I would say that we were friends in what I consider to be a valid sense of the word.

*When do you think the three finalists in the 1988 succession were clearly defined?*
I've heard this theory of the three finalists, and I've always come back to the idea that Manuel Bartlett was a formidable competitor, while Alfredo del Mazo had certain traits that I thought would prevent him from being considered seriously for a responsibility like the presidency. The man I always felt might have a chance was Attorney General Sergio García Ramírez.

*Miguel de la Madrid has mentioned that he got the impression that you and Manuel Bartlett had reached a nonaggression agreement, a sort of understanding to compete without trying to harm one another.*
I would not go so far as to say we had an explicit agreement. However, I knew that conflicts with my fellow cabinet members would create problems for the president, and that in those days, a minister who made problems was a candidate, but only for a trip home.

*Did Minister of Finance Jesús Silva Herzog want to be president?*
You'd have to ask him. He acted as though he really did want to. It seemed to me that he did, but he didn't know how to handle himself. He may deny it now, but it was my impression that he wanted quite badly to be president.

*When do you think de la Madrid decided that you were the best man to succeed him?*

That I don't know. He told me on Friday, October 2, that there were strong currents in the party favoring my candidacy. My reaction was to immediately go and prepare a speech, to be ready if the occasion should arise, and to remain calm. I remember that at the end of our meeting that day he said, "Carlos, you've competed with the six prospective candidates, and I want to tell you there's a very strong current of opinion in favor of your candidacy. Nothing is for certain here until the party announces its preference. Be discreet and be ready, because the party has said that it will announce its choice on Sunday."

*Before that, did you get any feeling that you were the one?*
No, because I had heard and known of many who had assumed they were. And history doesn't remember them as presidents, but as also-rans.

*Was there no point at which you felt that de la Madrid had made up his mind?*
There was nothing more than a very cordial personal gesture. A few months before [the nomination] he was kind enough to invite my family to his house in Cuautla, to an entirely informal dinner party. It could have been a signal, but I don't know whether he did the same with anyone else. He occasionally invited us to his birthday parties, but there was no bond of friendship from youth.

*Was the dinner in Cuautla different?*
I think so, because of the dates. I did the same thing, six years later, with Luis Donaldo Colosio.

*Why do you think de la Madrid chose you?*
That's a question he would have to answer. He evaluated the qualities I mentioned. I worked institutionally to serve my fellow citizens, and with absolute and unfeigned loyalty to the president. I built consensus and alliances. I always spoke my mind. But also, I made sure to present my working team for him to see with whom I was going to work. When I was president, I treated him with great respect and courtesy, and in the very courteous, respectful, friendly relationship we maintained while I was president, he never gave me the feeling that he had any doubts.

*He seems to be the only person who has no regrets.*
I hope there are two of us. But I think there are more.

*It has been said that when Cuauhtémoc Cárdenas and Porfirio Muñoz Ledo left the PRI in early 1987, they did so because they thought you were going to be the candidate. Some say they split because they were backing another candidate, in particular Bartlett. How was it that Cuauhtémoc became candidate for the PARM in*

*October 1987, which was surprising to say the least considering the control that the Ministry of the Interior was supposed to wield over the so-called state-controlled or splinter parties?*

All the parties in the world use different methods to choose their candidates. There's no definitive formula. It seems to me that the great flaw of the method tested in 1987, whatever virtues it may have had, was that it provoked disunion. I don't mean to say by this that the previous processes were better, but that the method used in the succession had to guarantee party unity and cohesion, and it failed to satisfy this requisite. So great was its failure that it became the last straw in producing one of the most significant splits in the party's history, represented by the Critical Current, later called the Democratic Current. It was a miscalculation in all respects.

It's true that the dissidents were opposed to the PRI's traditional method of selecting its candidates, but the method we ultimately used didn't manage to convince them that the party was becoming more democratic. Nor did it succeed in neutralizing them as promoters of open debate concerning the party's options for the candidacy. Instead it produced splits between the factions favoring the various prospective candidates, and even last-minute confusion encouraged by the immaturity of some and the unchecked ambitions of others.

There was yet another miscalculation in the method chosen in 1987. At the start, we thought that only a few people were involved in the Democratic Current, but it turned out to have the support of five million voters. The decision taken by Cárdenas and Muñoz Ledo—and others after them—to break with the party was partly a result of this phenomenon, which did little for the party's internal cohesion. It also corresponded, of course, to their own political project and personal ambitions. They had practically announced their intention to leave the PRI at a party event at the National Auditorium in early 1987, intended to be a show of unity, with the presence of all the surviving former presidents. At the end, after party president de la Vega's speech, Porfirio Muñoz Ledo practically announced his departure from the PRI.

I had cordial relations with Cuauhtémoc Cárdenas. My father had known Lázaro Cárdenas, and I had the opportunity of meeting him occasionally at my parents' house. But it was mostly in my capacity as minister of planning and budget that I had got to know Cuauhtémoc Cárdenas during his term as governor of Michoacán. I had gone to his last annual address as governor on President de la Madrid's behalf, and had been on several official trips with him. When I visited him, he always treated me courteously. I have several gifts he gave me during these visits, and others that he brought when he came to see me at Planning and Budget to try to find solutions to the problems he was facing as governor. I would say ours was a courteous, respectful relationship, with good communication. The theory that they left the PRI because of my candidacy was elaborated after the fact.

*Former Minister of the Interior Manuel Bartlett claims that there was no way to stop Cárdenas from being nominated by the PARM, and that in any event it was your responsibility as candidate to handle the situation. What do you think?*
Well, to the degree that as Minister of the Interior Bartlett had coordinated the 1986–1987 electoral reforms, which had given the smaller parties a boost, he was the one with influence over the various parties. This influence was not managed from the PRI or Planning and Budget. It is my impression that it was made easy for Cuauhtémoc to be nominated for the PARM because the Ministry of the Interior lost all or at least part of its influence when Bartlett failed to be nominated by the PRI.

*Did you also ask Miguel de la Madrid to replace party president Jorge de la Vega just as you asked him to replace Manuel Bartlett as interior minister after your nomination?*
De la Vega had behaved splendidly with me. He was a career politician, with excellent manners, and he had acted with deference in the process of selecting the candidate. I thought he had done a good job as party president, so I spoke highly of him. I recalled that, when he was nominated six years before, de la Madrid had not spoken well of party president Javier García Paniagua to President López Portillo, so I openly declared my appreciation of Jorge de la Vega.

*When did you begin to feel that Cuauhtémoc was going to get a lot of votes? When did you begin to realize that things were getting complicated in the 1988 election?*
When the population began to feel the effects of the devaluation of November 1987, mainly in the first quarter of 1988.

*Did you contemplate the possibility of losing the 1988 election?*
No. I never saw any poll that suggested the possibility. All the polls published by organizations such as Gallup or newspapers such as *El Norte* and *La Jornada* showed that my candidacy was in the lead nationwide. Also, our own internal polls showed, from the first quarter of 1988, that the PRI was going to win with around 50 percent, followed by Cárdenas with 30 percent and PAN candidate Manuel Clouthier with the remaining of 20 percent.

*Did you have contact with the opposition during the 1988 campaign?*
I had a long, positive, respectful dialogue at Luis Donaldo Colosio's house with Heberto Castillo [the late leader and candidate of the Mexican Unified Socialist

Party (PSUM)] several months before the election. I asked Colosio as my campaign coordinator to invite Castillo, and he accepted the invitation. We had a very respectful conversation, on excellent terms. I always had great respect for him, and I met with him when he had not yet withdrawn his candidacy in favor of Cárdenas.

*On the election night, July 6, 1988, you had assembled your staff at PRI headquarters, in the upstairs office, with a packed hall downstairs. The hours passed and you didn't give your victory speech. Time and again Jorge de la Vega asked, almost begged, you to give your victory speech. You didn't give it until the next day. Why not?*

Because the speech was going to be a defining moment, and one thing I could not do was to fail to acknowledge the new realities. President de la Madrid told me that Mexico City mayor Ramón Aguirre had predicted a few days before the election that we would win all the districts in Mexico City. In fact, we lost all forty. The opposition didn't sweep us because it hadn't joined forces behind common candidates. Cárdenas had about 47 percent in 1988, the same percentage of the vote as in 1997 [when he won the Mexico City mayoral election]. The result came as a great shock to the traditional structure of the PRI, which was used to winning elections with 80 percent or 90 percent of the vote. I was not willing to give a speech that failed to recognize this new reality. The first thing I had to do was to talk with the party structure, get more reliable figures, and talk to the president to share my view of the matter with him. Once I had gone through all this complex political maneuvering, the time came to give the speech, and I publicly affirmed that the days of having a virtual single-party system in Mexico were at an end.

*How were the results obtained?*

The information from several regions was slow in coming, but a significant part already confirmed what the polls had predicted. We saw, once again, that the opposition vote was divided, with an evident preference for Cárdenas, followed by PAN candidate Clouthier, with a regional imbalance. If the opposition had formed a coalition, with Cárdenas's National Democratic Front (FDN) and the PAN behind a single candidate, the election result would have been PRI 50.7 percent, opposition coalition 49.3 percent, but since the vote structure was, or rather is, divided in three, my PRI candidacy won not by one percentage point, but rather with 50.7 percent as against 31 percent for the second-place candidate. We won by a margin of nearly 20 percentage points, with approximately four million votes more than Cárdenas.

*It has been said there were three channels of information: the Ministry of the Interior and the Federal Electoral Commission, the old* PRI *system run by Jorge de la Vega, and, according to de la Vega, you had your own system. Is this correct?*

We also had a system that attempted to resemble a rapid count or exit polling, but at a very rudimentary level. It became evident in this election that it was crucial to ensure timely information to give election results credibility. This was a fundamental consideration for the political reform measures that my government would later promote.

*Why did the system crash?*

Well, you'd have to ask the people who were responsible for it, because it was the third factor that complicated the first days of my presidency. After the other two I've mentioned—the dismemberment of the PRI and the devaluation—came this third problem, presenting the election results. I understand that it was very complex, because methods for obtaining timely information were not in use as they were in other countries, where results are available immediately through quick counts and exit polls. In other words, the 1988 electoral system was not designed to process truly competitive elections, as was the system for which we reached a consensus for 1994. Also in 1988, the opposition parties didn't want the information to come from the center, but rather they wanted it to be relayed from each polling station to the 300 electoral districts, and then from the districts to the center. What this produced in practice was a traffic jam. It seems to me, however, that the most regrettable aspect of the election and the hours that followed was that no sufficiently clear explanation was offered to dispel the suspicion stirred up by the lack of timely information. Moreover, the opposition, as a political tactic, said, "Faced with the lack of information from the authorities, we'll use our own information, and it shows us as the winners."

It has also been proven since that the information Cárdenas had did not show him to be the winner. It was taken from a very biased sample of the districts and precincts where he evidently controlled a majority of the vote, from which they had projected nationwide results that obviously proved to be wrong. We also know now that there was nothing in his information system to support his claim to victory. In fact he declared himself the winner as part of a political strategy.

*You said that you wanted to talk with de la Madrid before giving your speech. Why?*

To exchange opinions.

*What was the tenor of the conversation?*
My talk with the president was fluid, and later I discussed it with de la Vega. I made it clear that I was going to give the end-of-the-virtual-single-party-system speech, but they made the observation that it was best not to acknowledge this, since it was still a question of trends.

*De la Vega says that you insisted that Minister of the Interior Manuel Bartlett and the Federal Electoral Commission had to announce your victory, and that he insisted that it was impossible, that Bartlett couldn't do it that night. Manuel Camacho and José Córdoba were with you in the upstairs office, and Camacho in particular didn't want you to give a victory speech.*
Well, the rules initially stipulated that the Federal Electoral Commission would announce the election results. Something similar had occurred six years earlier, and there was friction between the party and the Ministry of the Interior, because in 1982 the party told the Ministry of the Interior, "You go or I go." Then, in 1988, I decided to adhere to the established election rules, and respect the Electoral Commission's responsibility for announcing the results, but it issued no statement. Then the party president appeared to make his announcement based on the information we had. In fact he insisted on doing so. I said, "Go ahead," and after he made the announcement, I gave my definitive speech about the end of the virtual single-party system in Mexico.

*In his so-called* Memoirs, *Manuel Camacho claims that he proposed a meeting with Cárdenas two days after the 1988 elections. Is this true?*
Yes.

*Camacho writes: "I proposed to Salinas that we meet with Cárdenas, and to Cárdenas that we meet with Salinas. The meeting was a show of good faith by both Cárdenas and Salinas."*
It's true, and I have kept the meeting confidential until now. I'll confirm it because Camacho's text mentions it.

*Camacho goes on to say, "I proposed that, within the law, there be a technical team to check the data. Salinas asked me to specify the proposal without ruling out the possibility of a revision. Cárdenas reiterated his position. At the end, Salinas proposed that he and Cárdenas remain in contact." Is this true?*
Yes, but there was something very important. At one point, when Manuel Camacho said to Cuauhtémoc Cárdenas, "This was a clean election because the votes were counted," I thought Cuauhtémoc was going to get up and leave, and all he did was to look him in the eye and say, "I disagree." That was all. And I know why Camacho said what he did. Because he knew that nine out

of ten of the 55,000 vote-count certificates were signed by a representative of either Cuauhtémoc Cárdenas or Manuel Clouthier.

*How was the tone of the meeting?*
I would say it was tense for a few minutes at the beginning, and then the conversation flowed, touching on topics related to the way he had run his campaign, how I had run mine, how he felt after the intense campaign schedule. Then we discussed ways to ensure clear and convincing election results.

*There was no room for understanding or negotiation? Or was it the beginning of an aborted negotiation?*
The question is, what was there to negotiate? All there was to discuss, from my point of view, was precisely the idea of analyzing the numbers, strictly within the law, and if any doubts remained, proceeding to investigate them, which is what has ultimately been done with the 55,000 certificates, one by one. That was my proposal, but in the end [the opposition] didn't want to do it.

*Is it true that, in early September, you suggested to Manuel Camacho that he offer Cárdenas the position of Mexico City mayor, but that there was no time to transmit the offer?*
Yes. I discussed with Camacho possible options for incorporating the currents and opinions Cárdenas represented in my administration. It seemed to me that, having won the election in Mexico City, a good option for Cárdenas was that he be the city's mayor. It seemed appropriate to me, and I authorized Camacho to propose it to him.

*When did you begin to visualize your cabinet? All [the former presidents] say, "The cabinet is the key," and choosing it is a president's most solitary, difficult, and, in a certain sense, most definitive moment.*
Well, in the first place, since the cabinet can be modified during the presidential term, it's hard to consider it definitive. Second, there are different ways of structuring it. In my case I had to focus on bringing together all the different currents in the PRI, and therefore my cabinet represented a very wide spectrum.

*How did the competition between the cabinet members who later became prospective candidates emerge?*
Their profiles took shape as their objective circumstances evolved. I'll give you some examples. As party president, Colosio immediately undertook a process of approaching the PRI constituency in each state of the republic, and mending relations that had been strained by the conditions in which many legislators had lost in the 1988 elections. He worked intensely to support the candidates who

had lost their respective elections, and attend to those who, even having won, lacked the overwhelming majorities they had enjoyed in the past. It was necessary to bring them together and begin the internal restructuring of the party for the upcoming National Assembly. Simultaneously, within the government, in the financial area, Minister of Finance Pedro Aspe immediately started to review Mexico's stance with regard to our foreign debt, with a radically innovative approach, since we were insisting for the first time on reducing the debt rather than just renegotiating the payment schedule. In Mexico City, there was a climate of tremendous tension, because it was where Cárdenas had emerged victorious. Mayor Manuel Camacho would have to conduct his business with great sensitivity to govern the city without resorting to the use of force. In Foreign Affairs, Fernando Solana, with great talent, had taken initiatives to demonstrate Mexico's ability to assimilate the changes brought about by the end of the Cold War. Fernando Gutiérrez Barrios, at the Ministry of the Interior, was dialoguing with the parties. I took office on December 1, 1988. The next afternoon, I was in the National Palace with the leaders of the PAN discussing the terms of the political reform.

*And by the third and fourth years, above all with Colosio in the cabinet, how did the struggle evolve?*
I would say that the 1991 federal election was the most significant event in Colosio's becoming eligible for the candidacy. He showed a great ability to unify the party, and knew how to use the work of the government in the party's favor, thereby facilitating the important election results that we achieved.

*There was a dinner at the Presidential Palace in Los Pinos on September 2, 1993, a month and a half before Colosio's nomination with several of the prospective candidates and Mexican Workers' Federation (*CTM*) leader Fidel Velázquez.*
Who told you about it?

*A long dinner, where first they spoke, and then you spoke about each of the prospective candidates, and then you left with* don *Fidel.*
Maybe to accompany him to his car.

*What did* don *Fidel say at the dinner?*
I asked him, "What do you suggest they do?" and he replied, "That they stay united, that there be camaraderie, that they work for the president and fulfill their responsibilities."

*He didn't express any opinion when he was alone with you?*
No, of course not. *Don* Fidel was extremely discreet.

*He never went so far as to express an opinion about any one of the candidates?*
No, only certain reservations regarding Camacho.

*In what sense?*
That he saw him as very unrestrained.

*What might he have meant by "unrestrained"?*
He said, "He nearly went so far as to propose an alliance to me." He said, "What's going on with this kid?"

*Camacho acted too much on his own initiative?*
Occasionally.

*Camacho claims that his weak point was that he made friends with the president's enemies, and that, while this did not disqualify him, it was a formidable obstacle to his presidential aspirations. What do you think?*
Camacho was an excellent mayor, and was able to handle the job of governing Mexico City the way I asked him to and the way he was convinced it should be done, through dialogue, without confrontation or repression. Also, he made significant progress in solving the basic problems that afflict the nation's capital. I have only praise for his work as mayor. Although Camacho significantly strengthened the PRI in Mexico City and was an active participant in promoting PRI candidates for elected office, and supported the party in various other ways, his political style made him the object of hostility within the party at the national level. Manuel Camacho was a very difficult prospect from the party standpoint because the way he got results in Mexico City made the national party organization feel that he took too complacent an attitude toward the party's most aggressive adversaries.

*Why Colosio?*
Well, in the first place, he had managed to bring the party together, introduced important reforms, and had shown an ability for leadership among the different PRI constituency groups. He had proven that he had the capacity to reform the system from within. Colosio was going to really inspire the modernizing factions in the party. Also, with his talent for negotiation he had known how to build bridges with the party's earlier generations. He had shown strong political skills in the government. In the Ministry of Social Development, which he was the first to head, he gave the program *Solidaridad* a fundamental dimension, achieving very encouraging results in terms of equality and justice in Mexico.

Colosio was the best option for reforming the system from within, precisely for his convictions and his political and professional qualities. And his personal qualities were also remarkable. No one can contradict those of us fortunate enough to know him well, to talk at length with him, to share illusions, hopes, struggles, and frustrations, when we say that Luis Donaldo was outstanding in his generosity, his high ideals. Naturally he was strong of character, but Colosio was never bitter or resentful. And when he gave his word, he kept it. His were exceptional human qualities. How we've had need of them in these times that have been so bleak for us all. How we've missed him.

*When you told me about the dinner party President de la Madrid invited you to in Cuautla in 1987, when you were minister of planning and budget, you said, "I would do the same thing six years later." What were you referring to?*
To the fact that I invited Luis Donaldo Colosio to my home in Ticumán, Morelos. I think it was in October or early November 1993. My family and I had him over with his wife, Diana Laura.

*You did this with the same intention as de la Madrid did with you?*
My informal family visit at de la Madrid's invitation in 1987 was very pleasant, and was a show of good will on his part. Since it had been such a thrill to me, I wanted to share a similar moment with Colosio six years later. It was one of our pleasantest times together. The night sky was very clear in Ticumán, and we went and sat in a small gazebo to have a glass of wine and chat with the warmth and fraternity that came from our years of close friendship and the delightful moment. I knew that his legitimate desire to be the presidential candidate was in full effervescence, but I could also perceive in this intimate moment that his ambition did not outweigh his modesty.

*You didn't have a similar relationship with Pedro Aspe?*
I also had a close, personal relationship with him, and we visited one another frequently. I had, and still have, a very special fondness for him.

*But not the kind of even more filial relationship that you had with Colosio, even though the age difference between you did not justify it?*
It wasn't filial. It was a question of affinity, tremendous affinity.

*When did you feel that you had decided?*
Well, Colosio's candidacy emerged after all the positive signs in November 1993. The situation was ideal in late November. Normally the candidate is nominated in September or October of the year before the election, but we must bear in mind that, in contrast with all the prior presidential elections, as a result of the reforms introduced during de la Madrid's term of office, the 1994 elections were to be held in late August, and not in early July. So No-

vember was a good month for the nomination, and it coincided with the ratification of the North American Free Trade Agreement in Washington, which took place a few days before. Public opinion was very favorable, the national mood was very positive. Colosio's nomination was announced on Sunday, November 28, 1993. I had talked with him the day before.

*One day before?*
Yes, on Saturday, November 27.

*How did the meeting go?*
I invited him to talk that morning at Los Pinos. I told him I'd become aware of very strong currents within the party in favor of his candidacy. I told him I knew one gets excited upon hearing those words. I told him that the PRI was practically at the end of its process of reflection. I had had intense discussions with Fernando Ortiz Arana, who had shown extraordinary loyalty and ability as party president. We felt that the time was right, in regard to both the time remaining before the elections and the country's mood. Colosio and I were from the same generation and had a very intense personal relationship, and it was a moment of great responsibility, of great emotion. I said: "But it's not for real until it happens, because of political conditions that you know as well as anyone, so discretion is of the essence." The next day, I met with the PRI National Executive Committee. I had already talked with several of its members, and the conclusion was that the time was right, and that Colosio was the natural candidate. Then I asked him in. He was waiting in the library.

*This was on Sunday, November 28?*
That's right. Then they went with Colosio to party headquarters. Fidel Velázquez, who was extremely fond of him, was radiant, and said: "Listen, Mr. President, we'll go to party headquarters in just a minute; I just have to go see some comrades who are assembled for a rally." In response to his clear intention to announce his nomination in advance, and with evident joy, I said: "Wait, *don* Fidel, I think the party wants you to all go together." He accepted good-humoredly, and they boarded a bus together, and went and announced Colosio's nomination in a very warm, emotional event. The next day, I held my customary Monday morning meeting with the *Solidaridad* committees, but Colosio did not attend. We celebrated his new responsibility together.

*What happened with Manuel Camacho? Start with the dinner party at the home of the minister of the interior a few days before Colosio's designation, where Camacho and the other prospective candidates arrived first, and you arrived later. Who proposed it?*

I don't remember whether I proposed it or not. I'm sure that the minister of the interior organized it, having discussed it with me beforehand.

*You had already decided by then?*
The party was leaning heavily toward Colosio.

*Then came the dinner party, and what happened?*
They were conversing among themselves, and what I remember about the dinner party, to which I gave little importance, is that it had a precedent that provides the context in which to understand its significance. At the end of the November 20 Revolution Day parade by the National Palace, I had assembled my cabinet members to tell them, "Gentlemen, a few days ago we achieved the ratification of the North American Free Trade Agreement. We have an exciting stage ahead, and I think we should recognize the extraordinary job Minister of Trade Jaime Serra has done negotiating the Agreement." There was a very warm demonstration of support for Jaime, and I told them, "Jaime has informed me that José Córdoba helped him greatly in his work." I remember that Camacho mentioned that he didn't think it was appropriate for the president to recognize José in this way for something like NAFTA. But all I did was to recognize the reality of the situation.

*You don't remember expressing special praise for Camacho at the dinner?*
I remember having praised all of them, every one.

*When this dinner party took place, was it already clear what was going to happen?*
By the time of the dinner party, the trend was very strongly in favor of Colosio, but the party had not reached an internal consensus on the matter.

*It has been said that the purpose of the dinner party was to deceive Camacho. According to Camacho himself, after the November 20 parade and the cabinet meeting at the National Palace, he felt a certain reserve on your part toward him, and he decided to have a very decisive, detailed, and explicit talk with you. Is this true?*
He spoke with me at some point around then. The fact is that Camacho, who always was brilliant, can sometimes be somewhat vague, and I don't think he was as clear and precise about matters as he has claimed years later to have been. It seems to me that he has tried to present a stereotyped image of two factions that he thought existed within the government to strengthen his position, and that in reality he misconstrued the way political events were unfolding.

*According to the deceit theory, you were frightened after your talk with him and organized the dinner party to soothe and "deceive" Camacho. Is this true?*
It's lucubration, and like in so much hearsay, these interpretations are only put

forth to further personal political ends. We've seen their maximum expression and greatest abuse in recent years, which explains why they're so overworked, although we have to recognize that they leave a trail of confusion and injury. There was no more praise for the dinner guests than when we all lunched with Fidel Velázquez. The message I wanted to share with them was, "I wish all of you could be [my successor], because with this good a team, each one, on his own terms, deserves to be, but only one can."

*You weren't afraid Manuel Camacho might break with you during those days?*
No.

*Or attempt a coup?*
No, because I relied on Manuel's institutional conduct. He rewarded my trust in him, except in his failure to go congratulate Luis Donaldo Colosio when he was nominated on November 28, 1993.

*In January, after the uprising in Chiapas, you had a conversation with Camacho, from which emerged the idea of sending him as peace commissioner to negotiate a cease-fire. He insisted on discussing the issue of the succession, to which you responded, "What are we going to gain from this discussion, what's the use? It's already decided and there's nothing to be done about it." He said, "My only question is not why Colosio, but why not me." And he claims that you answered: "Manuel, I think you made some mistakes in your interaction with the team and errors in your political position. You're sincere and I know what you think. You're intelligent and well-informed, and from time to time your questions and answers, in cabinet meetings, for example, have evoked adverse reactions that have accumulated over time. This attitude of yours has gradually isolated you from the rest of the cabinet. Believe me, that's how it is, Camacho. You made the mistake of forming alliances with my worst enemies and this undermined people's trust in you."*
It wasn't incumbent on me to give him an explanation, and faced with his insistence, I pointed out that he had indeed isolated himself from the rest of the team, and that in the political context his affinity with the party's adversaries eliminated him as a potential PRI nominee. Now, with the prevailing climate of hostility toward me, he wants to make a personal issue of it. This may be because he wants to create a political edge for himself, to respond to the people who question him for having worked for me until the end saying, more or less: "Look, [Salinas] didn't choose me for personal reasons." And that's not how it was.

*What happened with Manuel Camacho the day Colosio was nominated? You didn't tell him beforehand?*

The party has never told anyone anything before the nomination. All the participants knew that the party didn't tell in advance. We also knew that, win or lose, we had a responsibility to the party to stay together behind whichever candidate was nominated. We all participated under these rules, and I'm sure that that's how they all understood it, as in the case of Pedro Aspe, for example, who immediately went to congratulate Colosio.

*But Manuel did not. What happened with Manuel?*
Manuel called me on the telephone moments before the party announced the nomination. I couldn't take his call. I was following things very closely, and once the party nominated Colosio, Camacho called me and said, "I know Colosio is going to be nominated." I said, "He already has been." Then he said, "Why wasn't I told about this before?" I answered, "Manuel, because the PRI never tells," and I continued, "but Manuel, I think it's very important that you stop by and see Colosio." He replied, "Well, I'm not going to until I can talk with the president." Faced with this attitude, I replied, "Then come tomorrow morning and we'll talk." I even called him again the same afternoon, with one of Colosio's top aides on hand, to tell him that it was important that he go and visit candidate Colosio, but he refused, saying he wanted to talk to me first.

The next day, which was Monday, November 29, we talked frankly and with respect. I made it clear to him that the party had made its decision, and since it was obvious that he was showing absolutely no enthusiasm for Colosio, I felt that he would have to leave the Mexico City government. Then I invited him to continue working for me, as part of the natural reordering of responsibilities that went with the formation of the new campaign team. I offered him the Ministry of Education, which I knew had always interested him, or Foreign Affairs, which had been his academic specialization. He agreed to stay on as minister of foreign affairs. In reality, his attitude by no means represented an internal crisis in the party, which was in fact consolidating its forces behind Colosio, but was rather a personal demonstration on his part, which was handled with no great difficulty. Thus, Colosio's nomination went off without desertion by party militants or organizations.

*You have wondered in reference to Zapatista leader Subcomandante Marcos and* NAFTA, *"Couldn't the question be posed the other way around, that is, what if the plans of the government's critics, claiming that the government refrained from acting against the guerrillas to avoid affecting the* NAFTA *negotiations or the succession, included the appearance of the guerrillas and ensuing massive repression to derail the* NAFTA *negotiations and block a promising presidential candidacy?" What does this mean?*

I think it's very clear, because the people who complain that we didn't finish off the guerrillas in 1993—something experience in other countries has proven would not have been possible in only a few months—were in fact demanding that we apply a repressive solution to a problem that has shown itself to be eminently social, with all the consequences this would have entailed. I think massive repression of indigenous groups in 1993 would have derailed NAFTA. This would have been insignificant, however, in comparison with the unrest it would have provoked in Mexico in the year that marked the twenty-fifth anniversary of the 1968 student movement, with a much more engaged, critical, and open society.

*At the time, you didn't know who Marcos and the Zapatistas were?*
I had received some reports from the Ministry of Defense in mid-1993 indicating the existence of a training camp, and reports had been published in Mexican magazines. But information regarding a guerrilla force of the size that materialized in January 1994, no. As to its name, you should bear in mind that there are over two thousand organizations in Mexico that bear Emiliano Zapata's name.

*Why was Ernesto Zedillo appointed Colosio's campaign manager in December 1993?*
That Saturday, November 27, 1993, after experiencing the intense emotion I mentioned, Colosio discussed various aspects of how he wanted to structure his campaign, which was a sign that he was mentally prepared should the opportunity arise. He mentioned that he needed to have someone in charge of coordinating the campaign and proposed Carlos Rojas, who had coordinated the *Solidaridad* program from its beginnings, and was deputy minister under Colosio.

*He didn't suggest that you replace the PRI president, and you didn't offer to do so?*
No, Ortiz Arana was doing a fine job.

*Then he proposed SEDESOL deputy minister Carlos Rojas, and what happened?*
It seemed to be an excellent choice. The problem was that Carlos Rojas was Colosio's natural replacement in the Ministry of Social Development (SEDESOL), and also was responsible for consolidating the entire *Solidaridad* program. We shared these reflections, and he grasped the strategic importance of having Carlos Rojas at SEDESOL. He said he understood, then he lapsed into thought and said, "Well then, Ernesto Zedillo." It also was hard for me since Zedillo was doing an excellent job as minister of education, and it was necessary to consolidate the educational reform process already under way. But I couldn't refuse him twice, so I granted his request.

*There is the rumor that Colosio had reached an understanding, either with you or someone in your inner circle, that Zedillo would be relieved of his duties as campaign manager?*
When?

*Before the assassination. You never discussed the matter with Colosio?*
With him, no. Neither of us proposed it in our conversations.

*Did Colosio ever complain to you that Manuel Camacho's designation and activities [as Chiapas peace commissioner] were causing problems?*
Yes, of course we discussed it. He felt that since January 1994 there had been more media coverage of the commissioner than of his presidential campaign. I said I understood what he was saying, but that it depended neither on the campaign nor on the campaigns of the other candidates, because the media were not covering any campaigns. The problem in Chiapas was so overwhelming that media attention focused on the topic and on the possibility of uprisings in the rest of Chiapas and other parts of the country. In this context, the commissioner's position got heavy media coverage precisely because he was the peace commissioner for Chiapas. Establishing dialogue and negotiation ended the risk of an armed conflict with little chance of success from a military standpoint, but which from a political and social perspective demanded negotiation. We had simultaneously reached an agreement between the presidential candidates to ensure clearly democratic conditions for the elections, and also transformed the entire electoral apparatus in favor of civil society.

*When did you exchange points of view with Colosio about Camacho in Chiapas, the media, and the arguments you gave him? Was it in late January or early February?*
No, I discussed the crisis in Chiapas with Colosio in early January. I would say that during the early hours of the uprising, and until January 5 or 6, the changes in the cabinet were already being planned, and we were planning our response to the uprising. I discussed it with him, because it meant changing my minister of the interior and designating a peace commissioner. Colosio, who always had the refinement to understand matters of state, understood the government initiatives. However, he did point out at the time that if we had to call on Manuel Camacho's negotiating skills, it should not be from the Ministry of the Interior.

*How was Camacho appointed commissioner?*
Well, the Chiapas uprising produced an upheaval in the political climate in which we were carrying out our government project and promoting the electoral

campaigns. Although the Zapatista offensive was immediately contained, and achieved no military success, it shook the country and had unprecedented worldwide impact. As the first hours and days of January 1994 passed, a chain of events unfolded that began to complicate and seriously endanger the very possibility of holding the elections. This is why I decided to channel the conflict in Chiapas politically, knowing that the priority as far as the campaign was concerned was the PRI candidate. Colosio and I discussed it; I told him my idea of designating Camacho peace commissioner, because he had distinguished himself in the Mexico City government precisely for his negotiating skills.

*And what did he think of the idea?*
He said, "Mr. President, just don't make him minister of the interior." And I replied, "Very well, he'll be commissioner."

*Why do you think he said that?*
Because he didn't want Manuel in the Ministry of the Interior.

*Where did the initiative to involve him in Chiapas come from?*
Well, the decision concerning Chiapas wasn't made on the first or the second or the third day, but as the whole domestic and international situation grew more complex, and in response to the evident urgency of finding a way to contain the conflict. By January 7 or 8, Camacho had visited me, but Colosio and all my cabinet members had as well.

*Did Camacho propose that you send him to Chiapas?*
Yes.

*He said, "I want to be the commissioner."*
Yes, of course.

*As if to threaten you with leaving if you didn't consent?*
No. That's another story I've read somewhere. But that's not how it was, because if there had been any threats, I wouldn't have appointed him commissioner.

*Is it true that Colosio wanted to start his campaign in Chiapas, and that you told him not to go?*
Indeed. He expressed an interest in going to Chiapas from the outset, but I explained that as the PRI candidate, and given that the armed group had rebelled against the government and also the PRI, his presence there would be very complicated.

*You have said that it was important to place a certain distance between the* PRI *candidate and the outgoing president, as always happens. Did Colosio also perceive this, or was he more reluctant to accept it? How did you discuss the matter?*

As my campaign manager, Colosio had been with me in Tlaxcala in January 1988 when I relaunched my presidential campaign in the wake of the November devaluation, after we introduced a series of harsh economic measures that had been greeted with generalized popular rejection. I relaunched my campaign in Tlaxcala with a speech affirming that I had no commitment to continuity. It was a very difficult and important moment, because it represented a shift away from the government in my capacity as candidate, without withdrawing support from the economic measures already announced.

*Did you speak with Bartlett, for example?*

With Bartlett, with García Ramírez [attorney general under de la Madrid and former PRI president]. It was a period when I was listening to opinions.

*With Fidel Velázquez as well?*

Yes. I had to find out who satisfied every requirement. I decided to conduct these inquiries to guarantee that I had considered every option.

*Is it true that you still ask yourself why you didn't opt for Francisco Rojas, the head of* PEMEX, *and that when you were first asked this question, you had no definitive and complete answer?*

It's true, but I have an answer now that I think will still have to wait for the right circumstances to be revealed.

*How long did you think you had to resolve the matter?*

I thought we would be able to hold Colosio's funeral with full respect for his memory, in light of the abominable tragedy that had occurred. In fact, what I found was that while we were en route to his burial in Sonora, factions were already taking shape, and there were currents in the PRI trying to impose a replacement candidate.

*When did the screening process begin? Did you begin seeing people even before Colosio's funeral?*

No, not until afterward. As to Colosio's speech in March 1994, we didn't discuss it even though he took the trouble of sending it to me beforehand. It wouldn't have been appropriate. But I had sent him a note pointing out that one of the options for relaunching his campaign was, precisely, that he distance himself from the government. Members of his campaign committee informed me personally that they did not share my idea of separation or distance between the campaign and the government.

*Do you remember when?*
It must have been in late February or early March. But I got an answer on behalf of the campaign informing me that under no circumstances could this be an option.

*Did Zedillo disagree with the idea of the separation or distance between the campaign and the government?*
Yes, he did disagree.

*You conducted a sort of accelerated inquiry in the days following Colosio's assassination in March of 1994 regarding the choice of Colosio's substitute. Whom did you speak with and what did they say?*
I spoke with all the former PRI presidents, and naturally with the acting [PRI] president, several aides, former [Mexican] president de la Madrid, and several of my rivals from 1988.

*Did you see the former presidents?*
I saw de la Madrid and Echeverría.

*At your request?*
Luis Echeverría burst into my office on the very night of Colosio's death. I came down from my study to receive him. I had asked that he be shown into the Morelos room. He expressed his regrets to me, and immediately suggested that the candidate be someone who had had nothing to do with Colosio, and proposed Emilio Gamboa [Miguel de la Madrid's former secretary and Mexican Social Security Institute (IMSS) director]. This surprised me, because I didn't know at the time that Gamboa and Echeverría had a particularly close relationship.

*And he took his leave of you?*
Well, actually I saw him off and got back to what I had to do. But at the same time, Augusto Gómez Villanueva, a very close aide of Echeverría's, had already started collecting signatures and organizing groups to support PRI president Ortiz Arana, without his knowledge.

*What was the tone of your conversation with Miguel de la Madrid?*
I asked him to breakfast on Saturday, March 26, to exchange opinions about what had happened and to hear his opinion.

*Did he propose a candidate?*
His opinion and his advice, as always, were of a most serious and institutional nature.

*Did you decide without talking to the prospects?*
It was a unique process that required intense discussion and negotiation with the principal PRI members and currents.

*But you did speak with Zedillo.*
Yes, on several occasions.

*About whether he might be the one?*
Only once.

*With whom did you test the waters about the idea of amending the Constitution to allow other cabinet members to assume the candidacy, and what were their reactions?*
We have to remember that Article 82 of the Mexican Constitution stipulates that no government minister or deputy minister, administrative department director, attorney general, or state governor can be elected president unless he or she resigns from his or her position six months before the corresponding election. The tragedy occurred almost five months before the election. None of the officials disqualified under the aforementioned article was eligible for the candidacy.

Faced with this situation, and as I have said, in the midst of our pain over losing Colosio, I had to consider all the options. The possible constitutional amendment required, above all, the votes of all the PRI legislators in the Congress, and then in the local legislatures. The opinion prevalent among the PRI legislators was that they would not support the constitutional amendment, and several governors also expressed the opinion that the local legislatures would be reluctant to pass such an amendment.

*First the PRI didn't want to do it, and then the PAN?*
The PAN also made it clear that it was impossible for them to participate in an ad hominem constitutional amendment. I asked the PAN for its opinion after hearing the PRI's opinion.

*You didn't speak with Muñoz Ledo or Cárdenas?*
No.

*What about the option of postponing the elections?*
I also analyzed it with Minister of the Interior Jorge Carpizo. He told me it was impossible to change the date to get around the constitutional limitation,

since it would prevent us from complying with the legal requisites for the election.

*Is it true that the most convincing and opportune arguments in favor of Ernesto Zedillo came from Minister of the Presidency José Córdoba? What were these arguments?*
They were convincing and opportune. They were close friends, more so than I imagined at the time. I do not know why Zedillo has treated Córdoba the way he has.

*Was Camacho discussed as a possibility?*
No, none of the PRI members at any time suggested that Camacho replace Colosio as candidate.

*In previous cases, the outgoing presidents chose a second prospective candidate as a backup. Porfirio Muñoz Ledo in 1975, Pedro Ojeda Paullada in 1981. . . .*
And it seems that's how it was in 1987 with Jorge de la Vega, but in this case, when Colosio picked his campaign team, he personally requested that Zedillo be his campaign manager.

*But why did you close the doors knowing that, by definition, there could be an accident?*
Because it never entered my mind that anything as tragic as [Colosio's assassination] could befall us.

*Did you propose that Aspe remain as finance minister? Did you ask Zedillo to leave any of your close aides in their posts?*
I transmitted a proposal regarding one of my aides.

*What about deputies and senators?*
The party selected its candidates for both chambers of Congress during the campaign. This is why, as of November 1, 1994, when the Congress formally convened, it answered to the new administration.

*Do you think that the negotiations with the Zapatista National Liberation Army were well handled?*
I think Manuel Camacho negotiated very well. As to the negotiations themselves, he handled the process seriously, with a sense of responsibility. Above all, we were able to start the dialogue quickly, because we presented the commissioner as a representative of the president, not a salaried government official, who was in direct communication with the president and therefore able to respond promptly. All this contributed to his indispensable credibility with the

rebel group. We can't forget what someone who has participated in guerrilla movements since the 1970s has written recently, that when these kinds of groups go to war, it is because they have thought about it for a long time, and therefore it is very difficult to convince them to negotiate. However, this is exactly what we did in the first three months of 1994. It was a truly remarkable achievement to get the guerrillas to the negotiating table less than two months after they had declared war on the government. The pressure civil society placed on the EZLN [Zapatista National Liberation Army] was crucial.

*Did you do well to preserve the Mexican presidential succession mechanism?*
I mentioned earlier that when Colosio was PRI president, we had a long conversation about the party's internal reform process, its system for selecting candidates, amendments to its declaration of principles and bylaws, and a new plan of action. Much of what we discussed was reflected in the Fourteenth Party Assembly, and also in the Fifteenth, when Colosio was in the government. After promoting reforms in the PRI and encouraging its transformation from the presidency as a party member, I was convinced that my work had to consist, above all, of helping to reform the system from within, guaranteeing party unity. This would in turn ensure that the candidate who ultimately emerged would be capable of facing this great challenge, and Colosio certainly was. Therefore, I am convinced that the procedure used was appropriate, at the time and under the circumstances, to accomplish this fundamental objective within the party.

*You have no doubt that you did well to preserve it, or do you think you should have considered abandoning it?*
I think that under the circumstances, and above all given that Colosio was fully committed to implementing profound reform from within the system, it was the most suitable procedure for nominating him.

# EPILOGUE: JULY 6, 1988

Here is not the time or place to analyze the infinite number of interpretations given to the chain of events that began on July 6, 1988. The purpose of the following note is simply to add some further observations to what is already known. Carlos Salinas was announced as the winner of the elections with 50.7 percent of the vote. Cuauhtémoc Cárdenas, the former PRI governor of Michoacán and the son of PRI founder and Mexican president Lázaro Cárdenas, obtained 32.5 percent of the official count, and PAN candidate Manuel Clouthier came in third with 16.8 percent.

A first premise in explaining the subsequent events is the overwhelming astonishment caused by the initial results as night fell on July 6. The argument Salinas outlines in his interview, which is presented in detail in a book published in late 1994 (*Elecciones a Debate: Las actas electorales perdidas*, Diana, 1994)— a kind of unofficial but authoritative Salinista version of the 1988 elections— that the PRI candidate and his campaign team had opinion polls prepared by Ulises Beltrán and the PRI Electoral Action Department that predicted an outcome similar to what was ultimately officially recognized as the election result is technically correct. However, the polls in question—copies of which were made available to the author by José Córdoba two days after the election, and which Carlos Salinas failed to provide the author even though he mentions them in his interview—could be interpreted in different ways. The last, taken between June 27 and July 3, gave the following nationwide figures: 20 percent for the PAN, 46 percent for the PRI, and 28 percent for the FDN (Cárdenas's National Democratic Front, the predecessor of the PRD), similar to the official July 6 results. However, the data for Cárdenas strongholds such the Federal District and the state of Mexico from the beginning of the aforementioned period—much more reliable than data for the rest of the country—deviated considerably more from the final results, underestimating the FDN vote by more than 10 percent in these two areas, 15 percent in Cárdenas's home state of Michoacán, and 23 percent in Morelos. In contrast, the poll significantly "over-estimated" the PRI vote in the party's strategic states: Oaxaca (+16 percent), Veracruz (+14 percent), Puebla (+25 percent), and Chiapas (+37 percent). It sufficed for the Salinas team to "deny" the nationwide results at the polls and acknowledge those for the Mexico City metropolitan area—a logical tempta-tion—to guarantee an ample margin of victory, with over 55 percent of the vote nationwide. The evidence available then and now tends to suggest that Salinas's people were confident their candidate would win with well over 50 percent of the vote, possibly losing to Cárdenas in the capital and the state of Mexico, but not two to one.

This conclusion must be qualified with one further consideration. Salinas's pollsters have confided that trends showed a rising curve for Cárdenas and a downward curve for Salinas. They knew that in a matter of days or weeks after July 6, Cárdenas would overtake Salinas.

That said, the magnitude of the retrospective "rectification" of the election results was the subject of a bitter debate among the Salinas inner circle, since each available alternative had different potential political repercussions. If we admit the premise of an ex post facto modification of the final totals—which has by now gained nearly universal acceptance—we can understand the dia-bolical dilemma Salinas and his team faced. Several alternative hypotheses must be reviewed.

First is the hypothesis most damaging to the PRI's interests—that Cárdenas won and the election results were altered to give Salinas an illegitimate victory. The fraudulent threshold for victory could be set below or above fifty percent. In the first case, the PRI would be obliged to negotiate with the opposition, and in the second it could impose Salinas with only the PRI's votes in the electoral college. The second hypothesis is more favorable to Salinas—it sup-poses that Salinas won anyway, but by a margin considerably below the official figure of 50 percent. In this case, the PRI would avoid undesirable negotiations with the opposition.

The 50 percent threshold was decisive because with less than half the votes in its favor, the only way the PRI could obtain a majority in the electoral college and ratify the presidential election was by applying the governability clause of the federal electoral code. Thanks to the provisions of this clause, if the PRI failed to obtain an absolute majority of the first-past-the-post congressional seats at stake, the majority party in the Congress would be favored by complementary proportional representation seats, thereby obtaining a majority of half plus one, or 251. For example, if the PRI obtained 42 percent of the vote and two hundred of the three hundred first-past-the-post seats, it would automatically receive an additional 51 proportional representation seats, raising its total to the 251 votes necessary to ensure an absolute majority in the lower house, which acted as an electoral college to ratify the presidential election. However, it would be a frighteningly precarious majority, vulnerable to blackmail on all fronts. This may have been the strongest objection to settling for less than 50 percent. In contrast, with over 50 percent of the vote, and subtracting annulled votes and blank ballots from the total, the PRI would be assured 260 or 261 deputies, an uncomfortable cushion, but a cushion nonetheless. With less than 50 percent of the vote, the PRI would have to negotiate with at least one of the opposition parties, and the demonstrations, accusations, discredit, etc., would not necessarily be avoided. This was probably the strongest argument put forth by the partisans of the 50 percent option. The cost of both strategies was likely to be the same, but the advantages of passing the 50 percent mark greatly outweighed those of staying below.

There is abundant proof of electoral tampering—sacks of uncounted ballots appearing in the rivers of Guerrero, unrealistic voter participation rates in Chiapas, complaints of various kinds of fraudulent practices at precincts—but it has never been possible to incontrovertibly quantify its effects. What evidence is there today of the size of the adjustment and who was responsible for it? Fraud there was. But was it fraud to win or fraud to pad the margin of victory? There are estimates of "landslide" precincts, that is, those where the PRI obtained abnormally high vote percentages—80 to 100 percent—as well as opposition arguments concerning the illogical, incomprehensible, and unjustifiable distribution of the PRI vote in the country's 55,000 precincts. Others have painstakingly examined the strange calculations carried out in the first days following the election. These show that in a group of 43 districts distributed throughout Baja California, Jalisco, the Federal District, the states of Mexico, Michoacán, Morelos, and Sonora, the PRI's advantage was nearly identical to and only slightly below the (abnormally high) number of votes annulled, a first inexplicable coincidence. All these items of evidence clearly suggest a Cárdenas victory reversed by fraud. But it is also known that in nearly ten years it has not been possible to unearth evidence—documentary, verbal, mathematical, or otherwise—to conclusively demonstrate that Salinas lost and Cárdenas won. The facts cannot be ignored that neither the PAN nor the FDN had efficient and comprehensive data processing systems and, above all, that they never pooled their party data to form an overall, nationwide picture.

The "electoral packages," that is, sets of marked and unmarked ballots and tally sheets from each precinct, were the subject of a bitter dispute in 1988. The government refused to open the packages, and after being deposited in the Chamber of Deputies, they were burned thanks to (yet another) PRI-PAN joint vote in 1992. However, a copy of each tally sheet was saved, and the full set was remitted on diskette and hard copy to the National Archive in November 1994. The aforementioned unofficial version of Salinas's triumph (*Debated Elections*) undertakes to whitewash the election, based on 55,000 of these sheets.

The main essay in the cited collection discusses various ways of determining that Salinas's victory was real. This would be accomplished by the accounting for votes from precincts that were in some degree dubious: precincts marred by excess voting; absence of signatures of precinct opposition representatives; and various combinations of the two, including their impact on the results obtained by the PRI's adversaries. The reconstructed election results oscillate between 41.7 percent for Salinas and 36 percent for Cárdenas (the least favorable scenario for the PRI) and 48 percent for Salinas and 33 percent for Cárdenas (the most favorable to the official party). From this, the author concludes that under no circumstances was an opposition victory feasible. He acknowledges "tacitly" that significant fraud was indeed committed, but in this version it served only to pad the difference, not to reverse the outcome. This is the most serious, grounded, and honest attempt made by Salinas's sympathizers to prove that their candidate won in 1988, even though major tampering may have been committed (of up to 9 percentage points) ex ante or ex post, with deliberate intent, by inertia, or both.

Several challenges have been mounted to this argument, some strictly technical, others from logical and political perspectives. These latter provide the most convincing support for Cárdenas's claim to victory. In the first place, the "Salinista" theorists base their arguments on a simple but debatable premise: that fraud occurred in a quantifiable and strictly circumscribed universe of "dirty" precincts. The size of this universe may vary, depending on the limit established for defining the tainted precincts—varying from 90 percent, 80 percent, to even 75 percent for the PRI—or whether one disqualifies precinct tally sheets not signed by a representative from one or more opposition parties. The scale of the fraud in question varies depending on where this threshold is set, but is always limited to the data in the tarnished "universe." In other words, the two universes—the "clean" and the "dirty"—are considered sealed compartments. However, this procedure, on principle, excludes the possible adulteration of election results in the "clean" universe, that is, where the PRI obtained, for example, 50 percent of the vote, and where the tally sheet on file in the National Archive bears the signatures of representatives from both opposition parties. It dispenses with two essential elements that are perfectly plausible scenarios even in the "clean" universe. One of these is a possible fraudulent 10 percent increase, that is, from 40 percent to 50 percent, in "nonlandslide" precincts, for example, and the other consists of the use of fraudulent opposition signatures, either forged when the votes were counted or days later, or purchased with bribes on election day. This kind of tampering would not be accounted for in the "cleansing" process, since a precinct where the PRI went from 40 percent to 50 percent is not a "landslide" precinct, and a tally sheet formally bearing opposition signatures, even when they have been forged or bought, does not belong to the "dirty" universe. However both these types of "corrections" did contribute a considerable number of fraudulent additional votes to the PRI's total. In all, approximately 20 million Mexican voters cast their ballots at 55,000 precincts, that is, an average of 363 per precinct. In reality, however, the distribution was very uneven. As many as 1,000 real or fictional "citizens" voted at some precincts, while at others barely 200 cast their votes. Therefore, an average of 50 spurious votes per manipulated precinct within the "clean" universe would be a conservative estimate. If this adjustment had been applied during the days after the election in a sufficiently large number of precincts, let's say 20,000, the PRI would have added another million votes to its tally in the "clean" universe, in addition to the estimated "help" in the "dirty" universe.

A million votes represented between four and five percentage points, depending on the estimated total number of voters. If we accept the middle-ground hypothesis of *Elecciones a Debate*, that is, 44 percent for Salinas and 35 percent for Cárdenas in the "clean" universe, and subtract 5 percent from Salinas's total and add it to Cárdenas's to account for the type of fraud, the ensuing result is 40 percent for Cárdenas and 39 percent for Salinas. The arithmetic of the official history, added to a rough but conservative estimate of the tampering within the "clean" universe, gives Cárdenas a minimal advantage, but an advantage nonetheless. None of this in any way proves that it was so, but it undeniably suggests that, beyond the fraud in the "dirty" universe, it would have been possible to reverse the election result through such a bold and ambitious—and nevertheless entirely feasible—adjustment of the "clean" universe. This represents the first strong, consistent argument in favor of the theory of "fraud to win."

The only unchallengeable way to detect this fraud after the fact would have been to compare the ballots with the sums on the tally sheets package by package. Since the packages, and in particular the ballots, were incinerated, this approach was precluded. Therefore, the second argument to support the "fraud to win" theory is based precisely on the impossibility of such a verification process. The mere act of burning the packages for purely bureaucratic reasons casts doubts on the conceptual underpinnings of the arguments on which Salinas's apologists base their position.

An alternative—imperfect and inconclusive, perhaps—would be to meticulously examine the tally sheets in the "clean" universe in search of anomalies: forged signatures recognizable as such due to their recurrence, uniform and repeated handwriting, typeset statistical aberrations, and so forth. This exercise *is* possible, using the tally sheets on file in the National Archive, but apparently no one has undertaken to carry it out. The Archive keeps records of the documents researchers consult and, according to its director, no request to review them has been made since the papers were received in late 1994. It would appear that no handwriting, x-ray, or statistical analysis of the "clean" documents has been practiced. No institution or private individual has to date mustered the necessary funding, will, and expertise to organize such a project.

Nevertheless, summary examination of 100 tally sheets carried out by the author suggests several possible conclusions that, while tentative and incomplete, are nonetheless interesting. With no great diligence, tally sheets were found that fit the description of the "clean" fraud. For example, on the tally sheets for precincts 37, 41, 41A, and 41C in the seventh district in Guanajuato, the opposition party signatures are identical, and the margins in favor of the PRI candidate are small (e.g., 123 to 60 and 77 to 53). Also, on the tally sheets for precincts 3, 9, 10, and 11 in the first district in Coahuila, the signatures of the representatives of several opposition parties are all identical, and once again, the PRI's advantage is significant, but not overwhelming. (As a matter of fact, total votes for Cárdenas at precincts 10 and 11 exceed PRI votes, although at precinct 11 the numbers are clearly altered.) Thus, these tally sheets qualify as "clean," yet fail to stand up under even superficial scrutiny, without going into handwriting and x-ray analysis of the originals. An investigation of this kind applied to the 30,000 tally sheets from the "clean" universe, endowed with sufficient funding and the appropriate human and technical resources, could perhaps unravel the truth regarding the confusion and manipulation of 1988.

The final item of evidence of PRI "fraud to win" that should be considered along with the others discussed here is a version—shaky, blurry, and for the time being impossible to corroborate, yet fascinating nonetheless—of the actions taken by part of Salinas's team during the days immediately following the elections. The problem confronting Salinas's aides, assuming their willingness to alter the election results and regardless of whether such alteration was intended to pad the victory or reverse the outcome, was mathematical and technical in nature. From a technical standpoint, it was a question of time and data-processing capacity: running the program necessary to solve the problem, on the only computer available for the job—the Ministry of the Interior's UNYSIS—and in a reasonable time, required software the creation of which represented a formidable challenge. In mathematical terms, the algorithm was easy to construct, but the matrix was overwhelmingly large. The mathematical dilemma had been resolved, years earlier, by economists dedicated to solving typical national accounting problems. Ever since the invention of the input-output matrix by Wassily Leontieff, government statistical offices around the world had faced the challenge of how to construct a matrix between census periods, or how to elaborate a nationwide input-output matrix without taking a full census. The technical problem was how to invert a matrix, or fill some empty cells, making use of some full and immovable cells: input data from the previous census, new midterm data, and the result of the matrix in the lower right-hand corner.

In electoral terms, the problem was identical. The matrix consisted of 550,000 cells (ten for election results on one side, 55,000 on the other for the number of precincts, assuming that only the presidential election was altered), and the figures in some cells were immobile. There were four restrictions of a political nature that so defined them: not to touch the "perfect" precincts—that is, those with a strong, unchallenged PRI vote—to leave the numbers already announced by the PRI intact, not to disrupt a full state election, and, finally, not to move figures for precincts where all the parties were fact represented. The result (the lower right-hand cell) was given—the 50 percent and a fraction that Córdoba, Chirinos, and the PRI old guard had insisted on. The task at hand was to change the results in the remaining precincts/cells, to complete the equation without overstepping the bounds imposed by documented reality (number of registered voters per precinct, etc.).

There is a story according to which one or two members of Carlos Salinas's polling team, and of his personal inner circle, traveled to England during the days immediately following July 6, 1988, for interviews with the British authors of the RAS method for calculating biproportional matrices. The purpose of their journey was to solicit help in designing a program that would perform the operations required in the available time. There was one further condition. It had to be possible to run the program several times, because it would be necessary to apply political criteria in the light of the numbers that appeared in certain cells. The PRI could not win 300 votes at precinct 3A in the fourth district in Veracruz, for example, because it was in a neighborhood with a history of voting loyally for the PAN. The travelers returned to Mexico and formed a team of three or four operators for the Ministry of the Interior computers—present the night of the election, with a command of the technical operation—with an equal number of PRI political experts, all leading authorities in Mexican electoral geography.

The political and technical problems were resolved very quickly. By the third week in July, a complete matrix had been drawn up, and the number of votes the PRI should have obtained in every precinct to assure the PRI over 50 percent of the total without violating the above-mentioned restrictions were calculated. The covert team proceeded to arrange the tally sheets and electoral packages accordingly, and to operate in the Chamber of Deputies. The implications for the tally sheets are similar to those we have already inferred. If after running the program the PRI needed 50 votes more in precinct 11 in the first district in Coahuila, the tally sheet was recreated with blank forms printed by the National Printing Office, adding the fifty missing votes and altering the total, but without altering the other figures, even to the point of conceding victory to the opposition for the precinct in question when necessary. Also, forged signatures of opposition representatives were included to fully validate the new tally sheets. Once the numerical problem was resolved, the issue was reduced to a political proceeding—formidable, no doubt—of persuasion, pressure, and outright vote buying in the electoral college. There were splendidly ordered packages. Tlaxcala governor Beatriz Paredes told José Newman: "If you have to open packages, open mine. They're OK." In these cases, ballots and tally sheets coincided, since it had been possible to arrange everything. There were surprise packages, such as those of the supposed PRI deputies who received opposition ratification of their numbers in their respective states, but on arriving at the electoral college found that the certificate placed over the ballots showed a higher figure than that counted by the district committee. This has been rumored to have been the case of, among others, Orlando Arvizu in the third district in the state of Hidalgo. The time frame for completing this book was insufficient for me to confirm these rumors. The evidence suggests that they contain a strong measure of truth, but does not yet offer proof.

There is one provisional, tenuous, and inevitably unsatisfactory conclusion to be drawn from these reflections. There simply is not sufficient new evidence to date to alter the idea that many embraced in 1988 regarding the magnitude and purpose of the electoral fraud of July 6 of the same year. That is, the new material tends to support, however inconclusively, the theory of "fraud to win"—that Cárdenas was the true victor. However, the evidence—which exists—has yet to be seriously examined. With the disposition and resources for the task, it would be perfectly possible to reach a definitive conclusion regarding what happened that summer. The responsibility for Mexico's ignorance on this count lies with all segments of the Mexican political spectrum and society. What is lacking is the political will to know.

# INDEX